Lecture Notes in Computer Science   11711

More information about this series at http://www.springer.com/series/7410

Stefanos Gritzalis · Edgar R. Weippl ·
Sokratis K. Katsikas · Gabriele Anderst-Kotsis ·
A Min Tjoa · Ismail Khalil (Eds.)

Trust, Privacy and Security in Digital Business

16th International Conference, TrustBus 2019
Linz, Austria, August 26–29, 2019
Proceedings

Springer

Editors
Stefanos Gritzalis
University of the Aegean
Mytilene, Greece

Sokratis K. Katsikas
Norwegian University of Science
and Technology
Trondheim, Norway

A Min Tjoa ⓘ
Software Competence Center Hagenberg
Hagenberg im Mühlkreis, Austria

Edgar R. Weippl
SBA Research
Vienna, Austria

Gabriele Anderst-Kotsis
Johannes Kepler University of Linz
Linz, Austria

Ismail Khalil
Johannes Kepler University of Linz
Linz, Austria

ISSN 0302-9743   ISSN 1611-3349 (electronic)
Lecture Notes in Computer Science
ISBN 978-3-030-27812-0   ISBN 978-3-030-27813-7 (eBook)
https://doi.org/10.1007/978-3-030-27813-7

LNCS Sublibrary: SL4 – Security and Cryptology

This Springer imprint is published by the registered company Springer Nature Switzerland AG
The registered company address is: Gewerbestrasse 11, 6330 Cham, Switzerland

Preface

This book presents the proceedings of the 16th International Conference on Trust, Privacy and Security in Digital Business (TrustBus 2019), held in Linz, Austria during August 26–29, 2019. This year's conference continued the tradition of being a forum for disseminating original research results and practical experiences.

TrustBus 2019 brought together academic researchers and industry partners to discuss the state of the art in technology for establishing trust, privacy, and security in digital business. The conference program included four technical papers sessions covering a broad range of topics, from permission models and cloud, privacy, proactive security measures to cyber-physical systems. The papers were selected by the Program Committee via a rigorous reviewing process (each paper was assigned to 4 referees for review) and 11 papers were finally selected for presentation. The main topic of the accepted papers relates to privacy; this reflects the importance of this topic, particularly in Europe. A strong focus on this topic established Europe as the leader in this domain of research.

The success of this conference was a result of the effort of many people. We would like to express our appreciation to the Program Committee members and external reviewers for their hard work, and to the members of the Organizing Committee.

We would also like to thank Ismail Khalil for his help and for promoting the conference, and for the continuous support of the TrustBus conference series. Special thanks go to the Editorial Director of Springer for including these conference proceedings in the *Lecture Notes in Computer Science* series.

Last but not least, our thanks go to all of the authors who submitted their papers, and to all of the attendees. We hope you find the proceedings stimulating and beneficial for your future research.

August 2019

Stefanos Gritzalis
Edgar R. Weippl

Organization

General Chair

Sokratis K. Katsikas   Norwegian University of Science and Technology, Norway, and Open University of Cyprus, Cyprus

Program Committee Chairs

Stefanos Gritzalis   University of the Aegean, Greece
Edgar R. Weippl   SBA Research, Austria

Steering Committee

Gabriele Anderst-Kotsis   Johannes Kepler University Linz, Austria
Ismail Khalil   Johannes Kepler University Linz, Austria
A Min Tjoa   Technical University of Vienna, Austria

Program Committee and Reviewers

George Aggelinos   University of Piraeus, Greece
Preneel Bart   Katholieke Universiteit Leuven, Belgium
Rudolph Carsten   Monash University, Australia
David Chadwick   University of Kent, UK
Nathan Clarke   Plymouth University, UK
Frederic Cuppens   ENST Bretagne, France
Josep Domingo-Ferrer   Universitat Rovira i Virgili, Spain
Prokopios Drogkaris   Laboratory of Information and Communication Systems Security, University of the Aegean, Greece
Jan Eloff   University of Pretoria, South Africa
Eduardo B. Fernandez   Florida Atlantic University, USA
Simone Fischer-Huebner   Karlstad University, Sweden
Sara Foresti   Universitá degli Studi di Milano, Italy
Steven Furnell   Plymouth University, UK
Juergen Fuss   University of Applied Science in Hagenberg, Austria
Dimitris Geneiatakis   Aristotle University of Thessaloniki, Greece
Dimitris Gritzalis   Athens University of Economics and Business, Greece
Stefanos Gritzalis   University of the Aegean, Greece
Ferrer Josep L.   University Islas Baleares, Spain
Christos Kalloniatis   University of the Aegean, Greece
Georgios Kambourakis   University of the Aegean, Greece
Maria Karyda   University of the Aegean, Greece
Vasilios Katos   Bournemouth University, UK

Spyros Kokolakis	University of the Aegean, Greece
Costas Lambrinoudakis	University of Piraeus, Greece
Martucci Leonardo	Karlstad University, Sweden
Antonio Lioy	Politecnico di Torino, Italy
David Megias	Open University of Catalonia, Spain
Chris Mitchell	Royal Holloway, University of London, UK
Markowitch Olivier	Universite Libre de Bruxelles, Belgium
Rolf Oppliger	eSECURITY Technologies, Switzerland
Maria Papadaki	University of Plymouth, UK
Andreas Pashalidis	BSI, Germany
Günther Pernul	University of Regensburg, Germany
Nikolaos Pitropakis	Edinburgh Napier University, UK
Joachim Posegga	ISL - University of Passau, Germany
Panagiotis Rizomiliotis	University of the Aegean, Greece
Rios Ruben	University of Malaga, Spain
De Capitani di Vimer Sabrina	University of Milan, Italy
Pierangela Samarati	University of Milan, Italy
Antonio Skarmeta	Universidad de Murcia, Spain
Katsikas Sokratis	University of Piraeus, Norway
Stephanie Teufel	University of Fribourg, Switzerland
Aggeliki Tsohou	Ionian University, Greece
Diamantopoulou Vasiliki	University of the Aegean, Greece
Edgar Weippl	SBA, Austria
Christos Xenakis	University of Piraeus, Greece

Organizers

Contents

Audit, Compliance and Threat Intelligence

Privacy

Do Identity and Location Data Interrelate?
New Affiliations and Privacy Concerns
in Social-Driven Sharing

Katerina Vgena[1]([⊠]), Angeliki Kitsiou[1], Christos Kalloniatis[1],
and Dimitris Kavroudakis[2]

[1] Privacy Engineering and Social Informatics Laboratory,
Department of Cultural Technology and Communication,
University of the Aegean, 81100 Lesvos, Greece
kvgena@aegean.gr
[2] Department of Geography, University of the Aegean, 81100 Lesvos, Greece

Abstract. Various researchers summarize that location-sharing applications are used extensively in users' daily practice not only for getting advantage of services but also for representing themselves in the online sphere. At the same time, users' privacy concerns are expressed in the most demanding way towards both social media applications and software designers. This incompatibility between users' every day practice and their beliefs is widely discussed in the academic community, indicating the informational privacy paradox phenomenon. Although, there is no need to focus on the notion of paradox itself for the needs of our analysis, attention should be paid regarding possible affiliations with users' personal information, i.e. location and identity attributes. Both location and identity characteristics are thought to potentially reveal users' personal information, thus lead to users' identification. What is more, users' location and identity characteristics seem to interrelate while creating new possible affiliations. These new affiliations that arise through our analysis are going to represent the contribution of our work in hand. In that way, the affiliations may enable conclusions about user's identity, thus, enable user's identification. That is because, information may be connected in ways that were not present in the first place, revealing more information than the user originally intended. Last but not least, this paper proposes further explanation for informational privacy paradox as well. Therefore, it is vital to reconsider and adopt alternative privacy strategies.

Keywords: Identity and geolocation attributes ·
Informational privacy paradox · Geolocation data · Privacy concerns

1 Introduction

Location sharing applications are widely used for plenty of reasons [1] which can be both linked to practical issues [2], such as using online services (purpose-driven location sharing) and to social oriented issues (social-driven sharing), such as feeling part of the online community [3], while at the same time being able to express oneself.

© Springer Nature Switzerland AG 2019
S. Gritzalis et al. (Eds.): TrustBus 2019, LNCS 11711, pp. 3–16, 2019.
https://doi.org/10.1007/978-3-030-27813-7_1

In that sense, users more often than not, reveal personal information to represent themselves [4, 5] while they also tend to reveal their membership to specific groups in order to gain social capital through their profiles [3].

The way that users opt for their representation may combine both identity and geolocation data. That is because both identity and geolocation data can represent their online personas. For example, users tend to utilize geolocation services in order to locate themselves in Higher Institutions not only to provide geospatial context but rather to enable reviewers of their online content to draw inferences about their academic status [6].

However valuable this information may be for a user to adequately represent his/her social sphere while online, it includes a number of potential risks as both location and identity characteristics may enable user's personal information disclosure [7]. In this regard, users may disclose more information than they think due to the affiliations created among location and identity attributes. A descriptive representation of user's identity is enabled through this combined disclosure that can potentially facilitate his/her targeting, despite his/her initial need for concealing personal information [7]. These new affiliations that derive from the combination of identity and location information are not intended by the user him/herself and frequently go unnoticed. Focusing on this type of information disclosure, our analysis is going to shed light on these new affiliations which will provide further support for deconstructing the informational privacy paradox.

In this respect, the aim of this study is to broaden understanding in the way that users' digital identities interrelate with geolocation information, providing new affiliations in identifying users' normativity and thus making predictions about past, current or future habits and choices. More precisely, the innovation of this concept is that the reciprocity among location and identity attributes may reveal more personal information than the user originally intended, therefore, this research paper will contribute in identifying users' potential concerns in different contexts (combination of social and location attributes). As both identity and location information may convey personal information, new dimensions of users' privacy concerns are introduced. In this way, our analysis intends to provide supplementary methodological tools for developers and designers to incorporate users' identity and location attributes while designing privacy requirements.

The study draws on both social identity and location privacy theories, through an interdisciplinary approach, to identify how users' social characteristics may be affected both in different contexts and around the clock, while it also provides additional explanations for the informational privacy paradox. Finally, and most importantly, this paper intends to create space for further argumentation so as alternative privacy strategies to be adopted in order to address the aforementioned unintentional information disclosure.

From that perspective, it is important to note that there is an increasing interest for designing more personalized privacy strategies which will be in accordance to users' needs. Those privacy strategies will address users' needs as they will adapt dynamically in different contexts (place and time). An example of that could be providing users with notifications about potential posts from online games while being at work in the morning. That kind of notifications will not be available during afternoon at home. In this way, users will have the opportunity to reconsider their online content and make appropriate decisions based on respective recommendations. In any case, those recommendations will be easily disregarded in case the user is willing to proceed with his/her post. Additional argumentation and research under this spectrum will provide the necessary background for designing our future work towards examining appropriate privacy strategies.

The rest of the paper is structured as follows. Section 2 presents related work on the field of users' location privacy concerns. Section 3 analyses users' location privacy concerns, focusing on the social-driven sharing aspect through deconstructing the informational privacy paradox. Section 4 discusses users' everyday online representation, based on the geolocation information they provide, indicating the interrelation of their identity and location and their common attributes. In the last section, some concluding remarks and the limitations of our work are discussed along with future directions of the study.

2 Users' Location Privacy Concerns

Privacy concerns are perceived of prior importance as "Privacy is regarded as a fundamental human right, internationally recognized in Article 12 of the UN Universal Declaration of Human Rights" (p. 3) [7]. Apart from that, research has paid attention to privacy concerns related to users' identity and location, as they are both thought to possibly reveal their personal information [7–10]. Specifically, handling users' location and identity information introduced several location privacy concerns. In that way, researchers designed possible solutions, such as LocX in order to address this issue. LocX uses an encrypting mechanism to protect users' exact geolocation data in location-based social applications (LBSAs) so as only users' friends to have access to it, in a way that secures potential information leaks regarding users' activity through tracking or predicting habitual actions [11].

Using geosocial networks and updating location information, while online, has already been investigated as it can potentially trigger users' concerns in handling personal information [8–10]. More specifically, after reviewing some previous solutions in addressing privacy issues in proximity services, such as Louis, Lester and Pierre, FriendLocator and VicinityLocator, Mascetti, Freni, Bettini, Wang and Jajodia propose a similar approach that deals with sharing one's location with friends after being mutually accepted as friends in a geo-social network [12]. The absence of a more detailed way in describing social relationships is also underlined in Marwick [13]. Absence of scaling in identifying friendships from acquaintances introduces a new issue, which is further explored in Snekkenes [14]. The type and the amount of information that users are willing to disclose with their acquaintances have been discussed in Consolvo, Smith, Matthews, LaMarca, Tabert and Powledge's work [15], exploring the same question as Snekkenes, i.e. "Who should have access to what location information under which circumstances?" (p. 1) [14]. Snekkenes underlines the necessity of defining a number of important concepts and paying special attention to language before being able to design appropriate privacy policies. Accuracy settings concerning location, user' identity, time and speed should also be adjusted by the user himself/herself in order to meet their preferences [14].

The most crucial finding of the aforementioned studies is that users' most important concern, when deciding upon revealing their location, was about the identity of the requester, the reason of the request and the granularity of the information requested [14, 15]. User's activities and mood were additional factors when deciding about a potential disclosure of information. What is more, when users opted for less descriptive location information it was not for protecting their location information but rather because they thought that a more general description of place would be more convenient for the requester in order to identify the place of his/her presence. This type of conveying meaning reminds us of Grice's Cooperative Principle, as linguistic maxims [16] enable speakers to follow specific rules for successful exchanges. The maxim of quantity is related to conveying only the necessary amount of information needed, while the maxim of manner is related to the clearest and briefest way in expressing meaning. The argument concerning users inclination in sharing of their thoughts is useful for other users to better understand their current location, is further supported in Tang et al. research [3].

Another study that deals with who and how information is accessed, is discussed in Marwick and boyd [17]. This study also focuses on the way information is interpreted and which strategies teenagers use to control their data revelation while online. As shown by their research, teenagers opt for managing their privacy settings on Facebook, to distinguish their online audience, while they also filter and delete content that judge as inappropriate, despite the difficulties they face in doing so. Another commonly used practice by teenagers, in order to control the amount of information revealed through their Facebook accounts, is encoding context by practicing social stenography [17]. That is to say, users limit the amount of information provided in each of their faces by encoding what they want to protect in each face. In that way, information about their private life, for instance a breakup with a boyfriend/girlfriend, cannot be leaked either into their student's face and get accessed by their teachers or into their child's face and, as a consequence, get accessed by their parents. Encoding posted messages enables only close friends of the user who share common knowledge to understand the true meaning of the otherwise public Facebook posts.

However, research has already tried to tackle the question about how users' privacy concerns regarding location should be addressed [3, 7–11, 13–15, 17], there is still a lot of effort to put into intertwining specific social and location attributes. Social and location attributes represent users' personal information that should remain private or shared only to the desired number of online friends during their loggings in social media [7, 8, 10, 13, 15, 17].

3 Privacy Paradox and Location Information in Social-Driven Sharing

Users' privacy concerns do not prevent them from updating their geolocation data via their online location-sharing applications [1]. In that point, it is important to keep in mind that geolocation data can potentially reveal personal information [7]. In other words, users reveal personal information which are linked both to geolocation information and information about their social identity. For example, according to Acquisti and Gross's research, users disclosed an important amount of personal information, while on Facebook [1]. Personal address or mobile number were among information that was shared publicly [1]. In other terms, Myles et al. highlight users' tendency to turn part of their intimacy into extimacy for entertainment purposes [5]. Extimacy is a term used to signify user's personal information or content which will be shared in social media aiming to amuse and engage the online community [5]. Having that in mind, it is understandable why privacy concerns are thought to be "only a weak predictor" of a user's membership on Facebook (p. 44) [1].

In addition, users, despite sharing information about their identities and their privacy concerns, also seem to disclose location information via sharing geolocation data willingly, while geotagging [4, 5]. Users' waffling between their privacy concerns and their everyday practice has already been investigated by previous research, known as the privacy paradox [4].

Kokolakis in his study sheds light upon the complex notion of informational privacy paradox by questioning its core, providing a number of possible explanations [18]. In that way, his conclusions enable researchers to understand possible explanations for users' information disclosure while online. For the purposes of our analysis, two possible explanations related to location privacy will be explored. More precisely, the first explanation can be linked to benefiting from the advantages of using social media applications. The second one is related to engaging in social encounters via disclosing information such as age, gender or other personal information [2]. In that way geographical information can also be revealed as it also carries personal information. For instance, users geotagging themselves as "interested" in local festivities or concerts for attracting the interest of their online friends and thus, eliciting a possible positive response on their part too. Another example could be stating users' actual address for spotting nearby events and, as a consequence, draw their friends' attention to take part in them.

Therefore, users engage in social media practices in order to be advantaged by social media's benefits, believing that personal information is not going to be used in suspicious ways (malware or private profit) [7, 10, 19]. Generally, users rely on optimism while disclosing personal information. Optimism refers to human neurology as people tend to generally believe that they are less likely to be exposed to a misfortune [18]. Focusing on privacy behavior, according to Kokolakis, previous studies have also concluded that users perceive themselves as less vulnerable to potential privacy risks or that they are less likely to be attacked by malicious users in comparison to other users [18].

Another equally important explanation concerns users' need to gain social capital. More precisely, users want to acquire social capital within their social media practice and therefore they reveal part of their intimacy to take advantage of being part of the online community [18]. An example of that could be geospatial landmarks, which frequently aim to add prestige to users' profiles. That is to say, Higher Institutions names which are used as landmarks, in a way that does not only describe users' place in the world, but it rather constructs them as members of the academia, thus, eligible to gaining socio-economic or educational status [6].

Drawing on the example of using location descriptions to gain social capital, it would be interesting to discuss how users handle their privacy concerns in social-driven sharing in order to provide supplementary evidence in explaining the informational privacy paradox. For the purposes of our analysis we are going to accept Tang et al. differentiation between social-driven sharing and purpose-driven location sharing [3]. Their work focuses on participants' choices when sharing their location data in social-driven sharing, indicating that "a non-trivial amount of location information is leaked in social-driven sharing" (p. 10) [3]. In this regard, it is vital to identify possible explanations on why users may share more information than they actually think.

According to Tang, it is expected that "just as general-purpose information sharing is driven by social capital, large-group location sharing will also be driven by similar motivations like social capital" (p. 3) [3]. Researchers concluded that users use place descriptions (naming devices) differently when sharing location data for social-driven location sharing. Social-driven location sharing also favored location descriptions as "as an indirect way to enhance their self-presentation so that they appear more interesting to others in their social network". Users opted for highly prestigious names of public places to add social capital to their online profiles [3]. That is also a possible explanation for users' willingness to utilize hybrid names. Hybrid names are preferred as they are thought to be "more descriptive since they provide both geographic and semantic information" (p. 7) [3].

Users also seemed to prefer sharing their activity rather that their location data in social-driven location sharing. In that way, they tended to use descriptions of places that enabled their online friends to jump into conclusions not only about their location (where they really were), but also about their activity (what they were doing). Consequently, descriptions of place (where) are endowed with additional representations of prestigious places to add characteristics that are related to users' social identity and social capital [3].

Besides users' willingness to adequately represent themselves by disclosing information in order to boost social capital, this representation often comes with a tendency to protect their privacy. As Tang underlines, users tend to "balance between maximizing their social capital while protecting their own privacy" (p. 9) [3]. Users may adopt a series of strategies in order to protect their privacy, such as opting for semantic place names. A possible explanation for using semantic names might be using information that is only available to a limited number of individuals in a way that blurred location data and thus provided the user with plausible deniability advantages. Another means for handling users' location data is by sharing their activity instead of their geographical place. In that way, they both limited the amount of information revealed, and they also enjoyed plausible deniability benefits [3].

Having discussed users' concerns and possible explanations on why they tend to disclose personal (both identity and location data) while geotagging in social media, it is important to proceed in identifying users' everyday practice through their location representation.

4　Representation of Socio-spatial Information

Geolocation may also enable to disclose user's personal information. Geolocation, according to Lahlou, is a subcategory of life-logging as it is defined as "one specific case of 'action-location': the capacity to locate the position of an object in an 'activity space' at a given time" (p. 9) [8]. In other words, disclosing user's geolocation data sheds light upon valuable information on user's activity because except for the attribute of location (where), it also defines a specific time (when) that the action (what) takes place [8, 15, 20]. As geolocation can prove to be quite descriptive for users' online activity, it is important for our study to examine possible information disclosure thought the attributes of location privacy.

According to [10] there are three attributes of location privacy which may contribute in identifying users' profile, namely, identity (who), position (where) and time (when). Each attribute can be described in a different level of granularity. More precisely, the attribute, *who*, relates to information such as user's name, gender, age, etc. The attribute, where, reveals information about user's x and y, his/her neighborhood, city, country. The attribute, *when*, unveils information about time. Time can be described in hours and minutes, or as a more general description, for example, part of the day, week, month or year. Previous research indicates that location privacy is constituted not only by a set of coordinates, i.e. GPS geographical representations of (x, y), or use of naming devices for places but also by user's activity [10]. Last but not least, the attribute, *what*, which is linked to user's activity, can reveal information on his/her actions, for example his/her occupation, recreation time, sleeping, eating, walking and other habits. Activity was introduced as an integral part of location attributes (who, when, where), after extensively reviewing the subject area in question, to describe what the action is or what the user is doing at a current moment [10].

Both geodata and identity characteristics are thought to carry personal information, since user's space of action endows user with characteristics that can be revealing for his/her social status, geographic location or future intentions [8]. Combing location attributes can trigger the identification of users' habits and thus, users' identity. This is why, location information is "treated as one type of personal information, like age, gender, or address" (p. 7) [7].

According to [11], geosocial applications are likely to represent a "primary source of information about our surroundings" (p. 1). Geolocation data is also perceived as personal information in Ruiz Vicente, Freni, Bettini and Jensen work [21]. Activity (what) is perceived as "a trajectory in this space, where behavior can be described as changes in some of these parameters" (p. 9), while activity space (where) represents "the general space of all variables that can describe a subject's state in the world: emotional state, social position, goals, geographical position, movements, belongings, etc." (p. 9) [8]. Identifying users' attribute of where and what while online may lead in inferences about their social status, geographic places or ambitions, identifying them as biographical subjects through tracking their trajectories [8, 19].

Researchers define location privacy as "the sensitivity of the association between a user's identity and the user's location, be it the user's past, current, or anticipated future locations" (p. 2) [21]. Making predictions about user's past, current or anticipated future locations, additional information can be disclosed about user's normativity and thus his/her trajectory while online. Combining location (where) and temporal information (when) may lead to user's re-identification and thus, reaching conclusions about his/her past, current or future habits [21]. Repetitively, the identification of these attributes can potentially lead in identifying users' habits while online and consequently in generating affiliations about their online normativity, potential predictions and future choices [8, 10, 19]. That is because, users will have already been identified as biographical subjects through their past records [8, 19].

Except for being able to identify user's normativity through their trajectories, additional information may be derived from combining distinct location and identity attributes. For example, reaching conclusions about user's identity (who) and place in the world (where) may create a number of potential concerns, which are linked to absence privacy and thus, vulnerability to theft or revelation of users' relationships or additional information on the frequency they meet with other users [21].

Bao et al. location recommender system [22] is an example of location-based and preference-aware recommendation system that extracts information from user's location history in order to match them with other users' social opinions according to his/her previous logs. In their example, a user who has already been identified as a "sommelier" may enjoy information about potential places of interest from other users with the same interest, i.e. wine bars.

At this point, it is important to note that each location privacy attribute may be disclosed in a different level of granularity. Descriptions can vary from rather vague descriptions to exact depictions of identity, place, time or activity. The vaguer the disclosure of information, the more difficult it gets to combine part of or all four attributes, thus, targeting user's identity.

However useful this fact can be, being able to predict user's actions and future choices through analyzing habits or affiliations, tracking his/her normativity may arise additional privacy concerns, since people tend to combine information in order to gain knowledge on a topic or a person. Based on Marwick *People are very resourceful at combining information from disparate digital sources to create a "bigger picture" of social activities. The human impulse to eavesdrop or overhear is augmented by information provided by those they survey on Twitter or Flickr"* (p. 13) [13]. The above-mentioned phenomenon, known as "social surveillance", is defined as "the process by which social technologies like Facebook, Foursquare and Twitter let users gather social information about their friends and acquaintances" (p. 13) [13]. Marwick utilizes the case study of social roles on Facebook to examine how users interact with other users through social software and power, indicating the changes provoked in social roles, disclosures and publicity due to social surveillance. In that way users choose in a very careful manner which personal information to include and which to exclude in order to initiate social relationships, while at the same time preserving social boundaries [13].

Furthermore, according to role theory, social identities and circumstances tend to provide anticipated ways of individuals' behavior [23, 24]. As Marwick notes "Different social contexts are typically socially or temporally bounded, making the expected social role quite obvious." (p. 9) [13]. In Marwick's research, roles such as employee, academic, daughter, boss and parent are rather separate from one another, while the content of each role may create tension when it is accidentally revealed or disclosed to another face (who), which should be deactivated for the needs of a specific setting (where). Despite the need of individuals to keep their faces' needs apart from one another, technological advancements make it easier for these boundaries to be violated. The tension or awkwardness that may arise due to face disclosure in an unexpected setting may draw on the incident of content collapse [13, 25]. More precisely, context collapse occurs when "different facets of a person's life, such as friends, family members, and co-workers, are lumped together under the rubric of "friends." (p. 8) [13].

Brandtzaeg and Luders' work on context collapse focuses not only on diminishing different audiences in online contexts, but it also contributes in adding the element of time. More specifically, it argues that Facebook timeline tends to blend past and present experiences in a way that could be described as "time collapse" [26]. Thus, we may see more clearly user's discomfort that may arise not only due to the context collapse but also due to the time collapse. In other words, millennials probably represent the first generation which can spot archived user's generated online content from youth to adulthood. This online content may represent an archived repository which can potentially cause discomfort to user's present online representation, as old Facebook stories may reveal undesired aspects of the user's past self. Time collapse and the aforementioned revelation of past elements of user's identity can be linked to users' "right to be forgotten" and thus, it refers to their right to proceed in their lives without feeling threat of potential leak of previously embarrassing posts [26]. Social discomfort that may be experienced from users makes them adopt certain privacy strategies, such as being more reluctant in sharing personal information while online [17, 25, 26]. Having studied the notion of informational privacy paradox related to location information, it gets clearer that users opt for disclosing personal information while online for different reasons which do not seem as paradoxical as one may have originally thought. At this point, it is important to examine the notion of geolocation and how users disclose their personal information in their online practice.

Both social and location attributes share the common characteristic of revealing potentially personal information, however this seems to be only one of the many common characteristics that they share. Therefore, we are going to attempt drawing an analogy among social and location attributes, which seem to be in accordance with each other's individual characteristics. In Schwartz and Halegoua work [27], authors introduce the notion of "spatial self", which represents each user through his/her geocoded online traces, revealing additional information about his/her social sphere. Social identity Theory and Geolocation Theory are intertwined to provide a definition of the notion, according to which "the spatial self is constituted from a bricolage of personal and collective, private and public meanings and narratives of place" (p. 13) [14]. More precisely, users' location data that are shared on geosocial applications may provide traces for users' social identity.

At that point, keeping Schwartz and Halegoua's rationale in mind and after having discussed location attributes, our study turned towards creating an analogy between social and spatial attributes, as we found common characteristics within two Theories. In other words, as location attributes and attributes of social identity seem to interrelate in users' online practice, we combined the aforementioned attributes, namely identity (who), position (where), time (when) [10] and user's activity (what) in order to examine new reciprocal ways in users' online representations through the combination of geospatial and social identity characteristics. Table 1 depicts this analogy.

Table 1. Attributes of social identity and location information.

Attributes of social identity	Attributes of location information	Examples
Face	Who	Father, dancer, patient, employee, tourist
Frame	Where	Working environment, dancing academy, house, hospital
Stage	Where (Frame) + When	Home at midnight, Pub at midnight
Time	When	7:04, evening, midnight
Activity/performance	What	Working, dancing, playing with children

The socio-spatial interpretation of users may shed some light in the complex and interconnected behavioral characteristics of digitally connected individuals. Drawing on Schwartz and Halegoua's Spatial Self, we contribute by showing how the personal and the private aspects of spatial self, which fall under the umbrella term of user's personal information, are publicly represented in social media. In that way, the table above represents how the Attributes of Social Identity and the Attributes of Location Information are intertwined, providing additional information about users' personal information through their online traces.

4.1 Face

The notion of face (who), which is a notion drawn from Social Identity Theory, is considered to include sensitive personal information. Users tend to perceive faces as social constructs which enable other users to interact properly with them [9]. In other words, "faces are a kind of social user's manual" (p. 18) and as a consequence they are thought to be separate from one another [8]. Each face includes different contexts which require different behaviors, thus, different needs on behalf of each user. They are also perceived as non-visible in different contexts. Non-visibility, in our analysis, is used to signify that users are unwilling to share personal information of one of their faces into another face. The more faces a user has the more challenging to guarantee non-visibility of one face into another. For example, a user may perceive a potential leak of personal information of his/her Dancer Face into his/her Employee Face as intimidating for his socially accepted and anticipated Face of an Employee which may not be compatible with such an attribute.

4.2 Frame (Space of Action)

Specific activities or public performances take place in specific frames (where) as users cover distinctive needs in different environments while following the respective social norms (faces) [8, 28]. For instance, when referring to user's frame, we may include information about his/her presence at a Working Environment, a Dancing Academy, his/her House, or a Hospital.

4.3 Stage

Stages combine attributes of where (frame) and when (time). User's faces are used in different settings, which are called frames (where) by Social Theory. Time can provide additional information on user's logging in during an activity or presence in a place. Stage can prove to be a very important notion in geolocation theory as it combines both user's attributes, where and when, and it can be more descriptive than disclosing each attribute distinctively. Presence in a place at a specific time of the day may also cause additional privacy concerns. For example, being home at midnight or being at the pub at midnight may trigger different conclusions when leaked during an important meeting at your working environment the following day.

4.4 Activity/Performance

User's activity is also descriptive for his/her identity as it can provide information of user's frame as well. For example, when a user discloses information about his/her activity, i.e. working, dancing, playing with children, this information can potentially be linked to a space of action, work, dancing academy or home respectively.

After meticulously examining Social Identity and Location Information attributes, namely face, frame (space of action), stage and activity or performance, we may summarize that our contribution is mainly based on the interdisciplinarity of our study, which aims to enhance literature for addressing the reciprocity and additional inter-relations among location and identity attributes and to provide further evidence for the explanation of the informational privacy paradox. The aforementioned interrelation may disclose more personal information than user's initial intention. In that essence, it is important to consider users' concerns in various social or location contexts.

Combining Location Privacy and Identity Theories creates new possible affiliations by opening up new dimensions in addressing privacy and security issues while designing systems' requirements. Bridging together those two Theories, researchers may identify not only shared characteristics between the two of them, but more importantly, they may examine a new aporetic space for further research. This space which is filled with innovative questions may convey new approaches which will contribute in the way that designers could possibly handle location and identity attributes in designing systems' requirements [8–10, 29]. In that way, those new affiliations will establish a brand-new spectrum, under which researchers intend to provide alternative methodologies and privacy strategies in designing requirements towards protecting users' unintentional disclosure of personal information.

5 Conclusion

Users seem quite concerned about potential personal information disclosure, however, they are willing to disclose information (both identity and location information) in order to engage themselves in social media's sphere [2–6]. Location data are part of the umbrella term of personal information, which are disclosed for reasons, such as social belonging, adding social capital, benefiting from online applications and entertainment purposes [2–7]. Having in mind the informational privacy paradox, as it has already been widely explored, our analysis tries to adopt a new approach in addressing that issue while at the same time provides additional possible explanations for this complex phenomenon.

Addressing users' concerns requires taking into consideration a variety of different parameters which are linked to different Theories, therefore interdisciplinary approaches are needed [8–10, 29]. The contribution of this paper focuses on bridging Social Identity and Location Privacy Theories by examining their shared characteristics. In that way, new affiliations among identity and location attributes were created, opening up new dimensions in this domain. The combination of location and identity attributes enabled our study to shed light upon new possible explanations on users' location privacy concerns which are in accordance with the principles of social-driven location sharing. This type of information which can be linked both to identity and location information may more often than not provide more information than users originally intended. Analyzing the disclosure of personal information and the privacy issues that may derive from it, we provide software developers with more information about users' personal information. This knowledge can transcribe users' identity and location privacy concerns into more socially aware privacy frameworks and requirements on behalf of the software developers.

At this point, despite our contribution, it is vital to underline the limitations of our paper. Focusing on the notion of face to analyze social identity, we often encountered semantic misconceptions as it proved to be a rather complex notion which needs further analysis. In addition, social researchers often refer to the notion of face in different naming devices, so despite the careful examination of the terminology and affiliations among different terms we may still lack papers that relate to our subject but use keywords that cannot be spotted for the time being. Considering the importance of validation approaches in such type of studies, we have already designed a quantitative tool for validation and testing. A potential further expansion of this study will include this tool.

Future research, apart from handling social identity notions, should also focus on addressing users' privacy concerns based on interdisciplinary approaches [8–10, 29], which will combine identity and geolocation attributes before reasoning about systems' requirements. Additionally, we also intend to further support and provide more solid framework in our effort to bridge social and technical aspects of privacy, taking into consideration parameters, such as not deceived by design in making selections relevant to location or identification data and refusing to provide services without granting relevant permissions. In other words, apart from examining social identity and location attributes, along with the reciprocal relationships among their characteristics, we are also planning to apply our findings in addressing users' privacy concerns with appropriate privacy frameworks.

Our study intends to shed light upon the way users handle their personal information in their effort to make themselves visible in the social media sphere to provide a better understanding of their needs to systems' designers. In that way, users' online representation can be dynamically adapted in space and time through an optional notification system. The notification system will provide recommendations which will be easily disregarded in case the user intends to make his/her post available to the online community. Last but not least, additional privacy strategies will be further explored to address users' needs appropriately in everyday social media practices. Thus, under this interdisciplinary spectrum, our future work will support designers' choices in setting requirements for socially aware information systems.

References

1. Acquisti, A., Gross, R.: Imagined communities: awareness, information sharing, and privacy on the Facebook. In: Danezis, G., Golle, P. (eds.) PET 2006. LNCS, vol. 4258, pp. 36–58. Springer, Heidelberg (2006). https://doi.org/10.1007/11957454_3
2. Duckham, M., Kulik, L.: A formal model of obfuscation and negotiation for location privacy. In: Gellersen, H.-W., Want, R., Schmidt, A. (eds.) Pervasive 2005. LNCS, vol. 3468, pp. 152–170. Springer, Heidelberg (2005). https://doi.org/10.1007/11428572_10
3. Tang, K.P., Lin, J., Hong, J.I., Siewiorek, D.P., Sadeh, N.: Rethinking location sharing: exploring the implications of social-driven vs. purpose-driven location sharing. In: Proceedings of the 12th ACM International Conference on Ubiquitous Computing, pp. 85–94. ACM (2010)
4. Herrmann, M.: Privacy in Location-Based Services, p. 284 (2016)
5. Myles, G., Friday, A., Davies, N.: Preserving privacy in environments with location-based applications. IEEE Pervasive Comput. 2(1), 56–64 (2003)
6. Birnholtz, J., Fitzpatrick, C., Handel, M., Brubaker, J.R.: Identity, identification and identifiability: the language of self-presentation on a location-based mobile dating app. In: Proceedings of the 16th International Conference on Human-Computer Interaction with Mobile Devices & Services, pp. 3–12. ACM (2014)
7. Duckham, M., Kulik, L.: Location privacy and location-aware computing. Dyn. Mob. GIS: Invest. Change Space Time 3, 35–51 (2006)
8. Lahlou, S.: Identity, social status, privacy and face-keeping in digital society. Soc. Sci. Inf. 47(3), 299–330 (2008)
9. Lenberg, P., Feldt, R., Wallgren, L.G.: Behavioral software engineering: a definition and systematic literature review. J. Syst. Softw. 107, 15–37 (2015)
10. Liu, B., Zhou, W., Zhu, T., Gao, L., Xiang, Y.: Location privacy and its applications: a systematic study. IEEE Access 6, 17606–17624 (2018)
11. Puttaswamy, K.P.N., Wang, S., Steinbauer, T., Agrawal, D., Abbadi, A.E., Kruegel, C., et al.: Preserving location privacy in geosocial applications. IEEE Trans. Mob. Comput. 13 (1), 159–173 (2014)
12. Mascetti, S., Freni, D., Bettini, C., Wang, X.S., Jajodia, S.: Privacy in geo-social networks: proximity notification with untrusted service providers and curious buddies. arXiv:10070408 [cs] (2010)

13. Marwick, A.: The Public Domain: Surveillance in Everyday Life. https://www.researchgate.net/publication/279673507_The_Public_Domain_Surveillance_in_Everyday_Life

14. Snekkenes, E.: Concepts for personal location privacy policies. In: Proceedings of the 3rd ACM Conference on Electronic Commerce, pp. 48–57. ACM, New York (2001)

15. Consolvo, S., Smith, I.E., Matthews, T., LaMarca, A., Tabert, J., Powledge, P.: Location disclosure to social relations: why, when, & what people want to share. In: Proceedings of the SIGCHI Conference on Human Factors in Computing Systems, pp. 81–90. ACM (2005)

16. Grice, H.P.: Logic and Conversation, p. 10 (1975)

17. Marwick, A.E., Boyd, D.: Networked privacy: how teenagers negotiate context in social media. New Media Soc. **16**(7), 1051–1067 (2014)

18. Kokolakis, S.: Privacy attitudes and privacy behaviour: a review of current research on the privacy paradox phenomenon. Comput. Secur. **64**, 122–134 (2017)

19. Miguel, C., Medina, P.: The Transformation of Identity and Privacy through Online Social Networks (The CouchSurfing Case) (2011)

20. Liu, L.: From data privacy to location privacy: models and algorithms. In: Proceedings of the 33rd International Conference on Very Large Data Bases. VLDB Endowment, pp. 1429–1430 (2007)

21. Ruiz Vicente, C., Freni, D., Bettini, C., Jensen, C.S.: Location-related privacy in geo-social networks. IEEE Internet Comput. **15**(3), 20–27 (2011)

22. Bao, J., Zheng, Y., Mokbel, M.F.: Location-based and preference-aware recommendation using sparse geo-social networking data. In: Proceedings of the 20th International Conference on Advances in Geographic Information Systems - SIGSPATIAL 2012, p. 199. ACM Press, Redondo Beach (2012)

23. Biddle, B.J.: Recent Developments in Role Theory, p. 26 (1986)

24. Bernstein, G., Zvi, H.T.: Over-Parenting. https://lawreview.law.ucdavis.edu/issues/44/4/articles/Bernstein.pdf

25. Beam, M.A., Child, J.T., Hutchens, M.J., Hmielowski, J.D.: Context collapse and privacy management: diversity in Facebook friends increases online news reading and sharing. New Media Soc. **20**(7), 2296–2314 (2018)

26. Brandtzaeg, P.B., Lüders, M.: Time collapse in social media: extending the context collapse. Soc. Media + Soc. **4**(1), 205630511876334 (2018)

27. Schwartz, R., Halegoua, G.R.: The spatial self: location-based identity performance on social media. New Media Soc. **17**(10), 1643–1660 (2015)

28. Jenkins, R.: Social Identity. Routledge, London and New York (2008)

29. Storey, M.-A., Treude, C., van Deursen, A., Cheng, L.-T.: The impact of social media on software engineering practices and tools. In: Proceedings of the FSE/SDP Workshop on Future of Software Engineering Research, pp. 359–364. ACM (2010)

I Agree: Customize Your Personal Data Processing with the CoRe User Interface

Olha Drozd$^{(\boxtimes)}$ and Sabrina Kirrane

Vienna University of Economics and Business, Vienna, Austria
{olha.drozd,sabrina.kirrane}@wu.ac.at

Abstract. The General Data Protection Regulation (GDPR) requires, except for some predefined scenarios (e.g., contract performance, legal obligations, vital interests, etc.), obtaining consent from the data subjects for the processing of their personal data. Companies that want to process personal data of the European Union (EU) citizens but are located outside the EU also have to comply with the GDPR. Existing mechanisms for obtaining consent involve presenting the data subject with a document where all possible data processing, done by the entire service, is described in very general terms. Such consent is neither specific nor informed. In order to address this challenge, we introduce a consent request (CoRe) user interface (UI) with maximum control over the data processing and a simplified CoRe UI with reduced control options. Our CoRe UI not only gives users more control over the processing of their personal data but also, according to the usability evaluations reported in the paper, improves their comprehension of consent requests.

Keywords: Consent request · GDPR · Privacy · User interface

1 Introduction

The General Data Protection Regulation (GDPR) as well as EU member state laws (e.g., Austrian "Datenschutzgesetz", German "Bundesdatenschutzgesetz", etc.) require, except for some cases[1], data subjects' consent for the personal data processing. The GDPR conditions the processing of personal data to a set of principles, among which is the principle of lawfulness (GDPR Art.5(1)(a)). The consent is listed as one of the lawful bases for data processing in GDPR Art.6(1)(a). What constitutes as legally valid consent is defined in GDPR Art. 4(11); complemented by GDPR Art. 7, when it comes to the conditions of consent; and clarified in the Article 29 Working Party Guidelines on consent under Regulation 2016/679. According to said sources, the consent of the data subject should be: (i) *freely given*, i.e., it provides real choice and control for data subjects; (ii) *specific*, i.e., it is separate from information about other matters, is tied to a purpose, and provides separate opt-in for each purpose; (iii) *informed*, i.e., it

---

[1] In GDPR such cases are defined in Article 6(1)(b-f).

© Springer Nature Switzerland AG 2019
S. Gritzalis et al. (Eds.): TrustBus 2019, LNCS 11711, pp. 17–32, 2019.
https://doi.org/10.1007/978-3-030-27813-7_2

includes elements that are crucial to understand personally identifiable information (PII) processing and make a choice; and (iv) *unambiguous indication of the data subject's wishes* by which they, by a statement or by a clear affirmative action, signify agreement to the processing of personal data relating to them.

One of the key challenges is the development of consent user interfaces (UIs) that adhere to said requirements, while being mindful of the potential for cognitive overload from the data subjects perspective [15]. Currently the predominant mechanism for obtaining consent is to present the data subject with a verbose description of the current and future data processing, where processing is described in some very general terms. Although there are a couple of papers that examine consent in the form of notice and choice, whereby data subjects are provided with more transparency and control [1,4], we highlight that the cognitive limitation of end users is a major issue, which needs to be addressed.

In this paper, we present our consent request (CoRe) UIs, that, to some extent, overcome such cognitive limitations. Although our UIs could be used for a variety of applications, in this paper they are tailored to our exemplifying use case scenario, whereby a young business administration student purchases a wearable appliance for fitness tracking and wishes to control how her data are used. Our use case is based on the GDPR because the GDPR provides concrete and legally binding requirements for consent, however, this does not preclude the CoRe UIs from being used all over the world. Companies outside the EU also have to comply with the GDPR and obtain a valid consent, if they want to process personal data of their EU citizens. The attributes of the consent request that form the fundamental basis of the CoRe UIs are derived from the GDPR and questions routinely asked by lawyers when they are charged with assessing the lawfulness of personal data processing in the EU: (i) the type of personal *data* collected from the data subject; (ii) the *processing* performed on the personal data; (iii) for what *purpose* the data are processed; (iv) where the data are *stored* and for what duration; and (v) if the data are *shared* who are the recipients.

The contributions of the paper can be summarised as follows: (i) we propose CoRe UI with maximum control[2] over the data processing and simplified CoRe UI[3] with reduced consent customization options; (ii) we conduct user evaluations of the proposed interfaces and provide pointers for addressing the uncovered shortcomings in terms of usability and understandability. The remainder of the paper is structured as follows: *Sect.* 2 provides an overview of the state of the art. *Section* 3 presents our use case scenario and provides an overview of the methodology used to guide our work. *Section* 4 describes CoRe UI, which has been designed for maximum control, and the respective user evaluation. *Section* 5 details our simplified CoRe UI and the corresponding user evaluation. Finally, we present our conclusions and identify directions for future work in *Sect.* 6.

---

[2] The online version of the prototype is available at: https://bit.ly/2Z1yrKs.

[3] The online version of the prototype is available at: https://bit.ly/2U6TkQw.

2   Related Work

Consent can be viewed in terms of a spectrum ranging from *no consent* to *blanket consent* [20]. Where, *no consent* means that all data usage is prohibited; *specific consent* means that consent must be tightly coupled with the purpose or context; *dynamic consent* provides autonomy and transparency to data subjects with respect to data usage; *broad consent* involves consenting to a framework whereby data are categorized according to type and ethical monitoring is used to determine if new processing is relevant under the existing framework or if additional consent needs to be provided by data subjects; and *blanket consent* refers to the granting of virtually unlimited (including future) use of the data.

As for consent in more general settings, much of the focus to date has been on privacy policies as opposed to consent interfaces, however, it is well known that users regularly agree to privacy policies without actually reading them. One potential explanation is the time and effort required to go through such policies in detail [15]. Other literature, related to obtaining consent from the data subjects, concentrates on analyzing privacy control UIs, such as app permissions [13,23]. When compared to a consent request, app permissions only provide users with an overview of the type of access the app requires. No information is provided about what could be done with the data, for example, in the background; where the data are stored; how they are processed, etc.

In terms of privacy policy visualization, Friedman et al. [9] describe their cookie-watch tool that should improve users' understanding of cookies and their management. However, they still use text, as in classical privacy policy, to provide details on cookies to the users. Kelley et al. [12] describe the process for constructing privacy policies based on labels. Although, based on their evaluation, the label approach helps users to find information more quickly and accurately, they fail to visualize the full data flow. Costante et al. [8] offer a solution to browse the privacy policy content and automatically assess its completeness. Though they group privacy policy content into categories, the text of the privacy policy still remains the same as in a typical privacy policy.

As for general analysis of privacy policies and notices, McDonald et al. [16] contrasted six companies' privacy policies and evaluated layered policies, privacy finder reports and conventional human-readable policies. They report that all formats and policies were similarly disliked. Schaub et al. [18] survey the literature on privacy notices and identify challenges, requirements and best practices for privacy notice design. Google's and Facebook's approaches to obtaining consent, according to a Norwegian Consumer Council report[4], employ dark patterns that trick users into providing consent for the processing of more information and intentionally make it harder to customize users' consent.

Although the GDPR provides some guidelines in terms of obtaining valid consent, one of the key challenges is the development of consent interfaces that satisfy relevant requirements of the GDPR, while at the same time being mindful of the potential for data subject cognitive overload. In this paper, we explore

---

[4] Norwegian Consumer Council Report. https://bit.ly/2N1TRRC.

two consent request UIs, and evaluate their effectiveness not only in terms of usability but also with respect to the understandability and task performance.

3   Background and Methodology

Before describing our CoRe user interface prototypes and the respective usability evaluations, we first provide the necessary background information with respect to our exemplifying use case scenario. Following on from this we present the methodology used to guide our work.

3.1   Exemplifying Use Case Scenario

For the development of our CoRe UI prototypes we used the following exemplifying use case scenario. Sue, a business administration student, buys a wearable appliance for fitness tracking from BeFit Inc. To be able to use the device's features she has to agree to the processing of her data. She browses to BeFit's website and is presented with a BeFit's consent request that is using the CoRe UI. For the purpose of our research the content for the CoRe UI was derived from the analysis of four smart devices (FITBIT, Apple Watch, GARMIN Vivomove, and GARMIN ForRunner) and two cloud based analytic services (Runkeeping and Strava). We use a representative data flow for our use case and, as a result, also for the CoRe UIs. Thus, there is no need for a highly complex use case for the purpose of the initial UI design and subsequent usability evaluations.

3.2   Methodology

Our UI design process is guided by Action Research (AR) [7]. AR is an iterative process where the problem is first identified; then, action is taken to solve it; and in the end, the outcomes of the action are evaluated. If the evaluation results are not satisfactory and the proposed solution is not well received, the solution is improved taking into account what was learned from the evaluation. This process continues until the problem is solved or the researcher concludes that solution cannot be found.

In order to make our usability evaluations as realistic as possible, as opposed to those performed in lab settings, we developed online prototypes to remotely test the usability [22] of our CoRe UIs, as that enabled the participants to give their consent from any place comfortable for them. Additionally, we ensured ecological validity [5] by: (i) deriving the content for the consent from the popular wearable appliances for fitness tracking; (ii) developing cross-platform prototypes that allowed users to test them on any device, operating system and browser of their choice; and (iii) testing our prototypes with a broad segment of population. We selected an observational method to test usability of our prototypes because we wanted to focus more on the why and how aspects of the user interaction, rather than on what, where, or when [14]. The evaluation of our UIs was done in an asynchronous remote way [2] using a think aloud method [6,19], where users recorded the video of their screen, combined with performance measurement [11] and post-evaluation remote questionnaire [10].

Before the actual UI testing started, the respondents were asked to imagine themselves buying BeFit's wearable appliance for fitness tracking. As a second step they were presented with BeFit's information about the consent request. After the participants read this information they were asked to activate the device, in order to start the process of giving their consent for the processing of their personal data, and were forwarded to the CoRe UI prototype for the actual evaluation. During the usability evaluation, the participants first completed a set of predefined tasks, that allowed us to measure the performance of the UI. After these predefined exercises, they were asked to simply give their own consent, as they would have done if they bought the BeFit smart watch: "Now, that you got acquainted with how the consent request works, please imagine that you decided to use the BeFit device and give your consent according to your own preferences." Users' own consent was used to assess if participants understood what they consented to. The participants recorded the video of their screen and the audio of their spoken thoughts during the whole assignment. Additionally, all the interaction of the users was recorded into the log file. After finishing their assignments, each participant filled in a questionnaire[5] containing single choice, multiple choice, rating scale and open-ended questions providing us with their demographic data as well as their impression of the CoRe UI. In the questionnaire the users were prompted to select adjectives that they would use to describe the UI prototype. We used the list of adjectives from Microsoft Desirability Toolkit, developed by Joey Benedeck and Trish Miner [3]. Since the original list consists of large amount of words, it is recommended to shorten and adapt the list, which we did in our usability evaluation.

4   CoRe UI with Maximum Control

Generally speaking, current consent requests follow all or nothing approach, where users either agree to the whole data usage policy or they cannot use services and devices. In our first UI prototype we decided to start at the other extreme and gave users full customization possibilities for their consent to data processing. We based the functionality of the CoRe UI on the GDPR requirements (see *Sect.* 1) adapted to the BeFit use case introduced in *Sect.* 3. Figure 1 depicts our first CoRe prototype for BeFit's consent request. To make our prototype more realistic and more suitable for usability testing, we developed its fully functional online version[6]. The source code of the prototype is available online[7] for a review. The design of the UI was guided by Jackob Nielsen's usability heuristics for user interface design [17]. From a technology perspective, we used Angular Material and D3.js for the front-end development of the online version and Firebase, with its real-time database and hosting, for the server side.

---

[5] Our questionnaire is available at: http://tiny.cc/z6d14y.

[6] The online version of the prototype is available at: https://bit.ly/2Z1yrKs.

[7] The source code of the maximum control UI is available at: http://tiny.cc/rh2z4y.

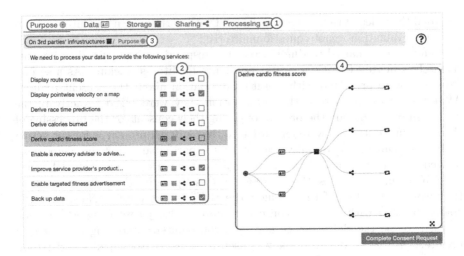

Fig. 1. CoRe UI prototype that offers maximum control to the data subject. (1) Tabs. (2) Drill down. (3) Breadcrumbs. (4) Graph.

4.1 CoRe UI Prototype Description

The first version of the CoRe UI prototype incorporated the following features: *Categorization.* We grouped information according to the five categories, namely purpose, data, storage, sharing and processing, which could be used by customers to understand how their data are processed and with whom they are shared. This grouping is realized in the form of tabs (see Fig. 1(1)). We chose this interaction design pattern to lessen the complexity of the interface and the information overload from the content of the consent request. Tabs are broadly used in desktop interfaces and websites, so that users aren't confused by the way they work. Additionally, grouping in general is a very effective way to declutter the interface [21]. To support the UI interaction, in addition to the name of the category on the tab, we added icons for each category. In the purpose tab, we display the services that are offered by BeFit that require personal data processing. The data tab lists personal data that could be processed by BeFit, if the user consents to data processing. In the storage tab we provide information on where BeFit stores the data subject's data. The sharing tab gives insights into third parties with whom BeFit may share personal data of the data subject. In the processing tab we describe how personal data could be processed.

Customization. The most prominent feature of our first CoRe UI prototype is the full customization of data subject's consent. In contrast to the usual all or nothing approach, the user can fully adjust their consent specifically to their wishes. Our consent request gives the possibility to review information or give consent according to the five categories mentioned in the categorization feature above. Any tab category can be a starting point for giving consent. The user is also given the possibility to drill down a concrete path and agree only to that path. This means that the data subject can also give permission to process only specific data categories for chosen purposes, etc. For example, users can allow BeFit to process their resting heart rate (data) to be displayed to them in BeFit's app (purpose) by performing on-device calculations (processing) and saving the data on their device (storage) without sharing it with anybody. The drill down feature is implemented by placing clickable icons of possible drill-down options near each item in the tab list (see Fig. 1(2)). Icons are especially effective when there is not much space available[8]. The users can drill down through each item in the list by clicking on an icon that corresponds to the category they want to select. In this way the users can create a unique path to consent to. The unique path is displayed and can be navigated with the aid of breadcrumbs that are displayed under the tabs (see Fig. 1(3)). This design pattern helps users to know where they are at all times. Breadcrumbs are especially important when a drill-down process is involved. This pattern is often used for filtering and in the applications with hierarchical structures [21]. The users give their consent just by selecting checkboxes (see Fig. 1(2)) that correspond to their preferences. The check box is placed near each category item beside the icons for the drill-down options. We elected to go with checkboxes as they are simple, consume little space and the choices are immediately visible to the user [21].

Understandability. To increase understandability and ease of use of the consent request we are using plain language and standard icons for the content. Every user action is backed up by feedback. To help the data subjects understand the implications of their consent, our consent request is supported by a graph (see Fig. 1(4)). The graph has a tree form and shows every possible unique path that goes through the selected item. The paths that the user consented to are highlighted in red. Each item in the graph is represented with the help of already mentioned icons. More information, in the form of a tooltip, is shown upon hovering over each icon. The user can also enlarge the graph to full-screen size by clicking the corresponding button in the lower right corner. By trying out different organizational models that are typically used to represent hierarchies, we decided that the graph was the most suitable model for our content. We also added a summary feature to our prototype. After users finish consenting, they are presented with an overview of all the information relating to the consent they had provided to BeFit.

Revocation. According to GDPR Art.7(3), the data subjects should be able to withdraw their consent for future processing and sharing of all (or a part) of their data at any time and the withdrawal of consent should be as easy as granting it. CoRe UI enables users to withdraw their consent at any time by removing the selection in a checkbox (see Fig. 1(2)). In our use case the consent is given for the first time before using the device and the consent withdrawal in our interactive UI wireframe is tailored to this use case.

---

[8] Welie.com, Patterns in interaction design. https://bit.ly/2uWvFsf.

4.2 Results of the User Evaluations

In order to gain feedback from real users as to the effectiveness of our interface we conducted a usability evaluation of the CoRe UI. Our participants were recruited among students who attended a course entitled "Intelligent Customer Interaction Design" for the first usability evaluation. This sample of participants suited well for the evaluation, because the persona (Sue) in our use case scenario was a student. This evaluation provided us with the initial feedback. In subsequent usability evaluations we planned to test the improved versions of CoRe UI prototype with a broader segment of the population.

Twenty-seven participants, between 16 and 35 years old, took part in our usability evaluation. Most of them graduated from high school and have either information technology or education as their background. 63% of the participants are male and 37% are female. The participants consider themselves competent, proficient or experts in Internet surfing. Almost half of the participants (44%) spend 3–6 h on the Internet and only 4% spend less than one hour. All participants have no difficulty using computers and half of them prefer laptops for Internet browsing, 32% preferably use desktop computers, only 11% would choose smartphones to surf the Internet and 7% would use tablets.

During the evaluation, the participants, first, completed a set of predefined tasks[9]. Then they gave their own consent, as they would have done if they had purchased the BeFit smart watch. The assignments were video recorded. After finishing their assignments, the participants were automatically redirected to a questionnaire where they answered rating scale and open-ended questions regarding their experience. The results of the analysis of the video recordings and the questionnaire answers are described below.

Video Recordings. The analysis of the 27 video recordings provided by our participants showed that having the option to customize everything was very time consuming, annoying and confusing. 74% of the participants were confused by the drill-down process and as a result did not complete the tasks correctly. Although the participants understood the icons and recalled their meaning very well, they did not understand that the drill-down functionality was only available via icons and kept using icons and tabs to drill down interchangeably, thinking that both approaches could be used to create unique paths for their consent. 22% understood the creation of the unique path partially and only 4% completed the assignment successfully. The participants required, on average, 15 min to finish all the tasks and another 15 min to give their own consent.

Comprehension Testing. To assess if participants remembered and understood what they agreed to, we asked users in the post-evaluation questionnaire to describe what they consented to in the previous task where they elected what they would personally consent to. Since the participants were confused by the functionality and overwhelmed with the customization options, 96% did not describe correctly what they consented to and, therefore, gave their consent without understanding what they were consenting to.

---

[9] Usability evaluation tasks are available at: https://bit.ly/2IaRUDk.

Time Perception. When asked to assess the time it took to give or withdraw the consent, the users confirmed our video recording observations about time consumption. Almost half of the participants (48%) answered that it took them too long to give or withdraw the consent. 22% selected too long, but it was worthwhile as their answer. For the rest of the users it took either less time (11%) or about the right amount of time (19%).

Adjective Description. Unsurprisingly, a lot of the users (67%) found the UI prototype "complex" and the whole process "time consuming". 55% of the participants found the consent representation to be "confusing". For 52% of them the UI was "hard to use". 44% of the users thought the UI was "annoying" and 41% were "frustrated" when using the CoRe UI prototype. Apart from the negative adjectives, we also received some positive feedback. 33% of the participants described the UI as being "organized", 30% as "effective", 26% as "innovative", 22% as "flexible" and 19% as "valuable".

Prototype vs Traditional Consent Request. When comparing our prototype to the classic consent request in the form of privacy policy and an "Agree" button at the bottom of the web page, a lot of the users highlighted that they liked the flexibility and customization features (e.g., I liked that: "I could choose", "I could change the settings", "I could actually decide...", "I was able to shape everything to my needs", "I could withdraw the consent at any time"). The respondents mentioned that they found the graph functionality very useful and they liked the summary in the end of the process of giving their consent. The participants replied that they liked the readability of the consent (e.g., "I liked the language - there were no problems understanding the consent request"). The users also mentioned that they found the division of information into tabs very good, because it provided some structure and contributed to understandability (e.g., "Everything is clear structured").

Ease of Use. The participants named four features that were the easiest for them to use, namely the graph, the summary, the tabs navigation and the structure, as well as giving and withdrawing consent. The hardest part was not to be lost in all the options available to the users. Many of the participants also mentioned that it was the hardest to keep all the information in mind.

Tab Usefulness. Since we anticipated that providing very detailed information to the users and giving them such a detailed control over the data processing would be overwhelming for them, we included a question in the post-evaluation questionnaire regarding the usefulness and importance of the information provided by the tabs, in order to identify which tabs could be, for example, hidden in the UI and shown only on demand or removed from the customization options. 35% of the participants think that information on all tabs is important. 38% voted for the tab *processing* to be removed.

Graph. We asked the participants two questions regarding the graph to find out if they understood it and if they found it useful. For the most of them the graph was slightly, moderately, very or extremely understandable (78%) and useful (70%) (e.g., "The graph was the only thing I really understood", "A very nice form to give the overview"). 22% of the users could not understand the graph and 30% found it to be not useful.

Overall Satisfaction. When we asked users if they were satisfied overall with the UI prototype, 41% of the participants reported satisfaction (11% - very satisfied, 30% - somewhat satisfied). 15% of the users remained neutral towards the consent request, 44% of the participants were not satisfied (33% - somewhat dissatisfied, 11% - very dissatisfied) with our UI prototype. The question "how well the consent request meets your needs?" received only 15% of negative answers. Most of the users selected somewhat well (41%), very well (29%) or extremely well (15%) as their answers.

Prototype Improvement Suggestions. The main reasons why one might not use our consent request, according to the usability evaluation, are information overload, complexity and too detailed customization. Since a lot of the participants were overloaded with the information, they suggested simplifying the information representation, offering fewer options to choose from and using color-coding.

As can be seen from the evaluation results, the data subjects were overwhelmed with such detailed consent information and with too much control over their data processing. Thus, highlighting the fact that there is a clear need for the simplification of the UI prototype and the reduction of the consent options.

5   Simplified CoRe UI

We developed a second CoRe UI prototype taking into account the evaluation results of the first version. Since the graph functionality was well received by the users in our usability testing, we decided to use the graph as the basis for our next version of the CoRe UI. The second version of the CoRe UI is depicted in Fig. 2. For the purpose of the second usability evaluation we developed an online prototype with two localizations: English[10] and German[11]. The source code of the prototype is available online[12]. As before, we used Angular Material and D3.js for the front-end development of the online version and Firebase, with its real-time database and hosting, for the server side.

5.1   CoRe UI Prototype Description

The participants of the first UI evaluation liked the categorization of the consent information into purpose, data, storage, processing and sharing, so we kept this categorization in the second version of the UI. They also highly appreciated the customization and the flexibility of the consent request. However, they expressed their frustration with too many options. In our second CoRe UI prototype we retained the customization feature, but we reduced the options by presenting

---

[10] English version of the prototype is available at: https://bit.ly/2U6TkQw.

[11] German version of the prototype is available at: https://bit.ly/2G2V6gR.

[12] The source code of the simplified UI is available at: https://bit.ly/2uWtHYM.

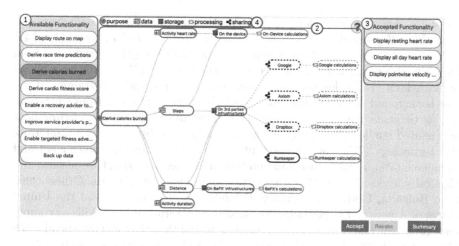

Fig. 2. The simplified CoRe UI prototype.(1) Functionalities to select from. (2) Required data processing for the selected functionality. (3) Accepted functionalities. (4) Color-coding by data category.

users with the list of available device functionalities and providing a possibility to browse just the functionalities by simply clicking on them (see Fig. 2(1)). All the data processing that is required for the selected functionality is represented as a graph (see Fig. 2(2)) showing the connections between data categories. If there are any optional items in the graph, they are highlighted with the clickable dashed line in the graph path. After the selection, the dashed line becomes a solid one. If the data subject accepts the offered data processing for the functionality, the corresponding functionality is moved from the "Available Functionality" column to the "Accepted Functionality" column (see Fig. 2(3)).

From an understandability perspective, the participants of the usability testing positively evaluated the way the consent request was formulated. Since they liked the shortness, the plain language and the icons, we reused the consent text from the first version of the prototype. Every user action is, again, backed up by feedback. In the second prototype we added color-coding to the graph (see Fig. 2(4)), as it was suggested by many participants in the usability evaluation. A summary feature was also included in the simplified UI. The pop-up with a graph-based overview of the data processing, the users consented to, is always available under the "Summary" button.

In terms of revocation, CoRe UI provides the possibility to withdraw consent at any point in time by selecting functionalities in the "Accepted Functionality" column and clicking the "Revoke" button at the bottom of that column.

5.2   Results of the User Evaluations

The second CoRe UI prototype was evaluated by 73 participants. This time we targeted a broader segment of the population. 56% of the participants are male and 44% - female. They belong to different age groups (32% - 16 to 25 years old, 36% - 26 to 35 years old, 12% - 36 to 45 years old, 16% - 46 to 55 years old, and 4% - 55 years old and over). Almost half of the participants (44%) graduated from high school. Others have no degree with some college (17%), Master's (16%) or Bachelor's (15%) degree, and trade, technical or vocational training (6%). The background of 53% of the participants is education. Apart from education, the participants have a wide range of backgrounds: agriculture, environment and related studies (10%), engineering and related technologies (7%), information technology (7%), society and culture (7%), health (6%), management and commerce (5%), architecture and building (3%), creative arts (1%), natural and physical sciences (1%). 63% of the participants come from Austria. Others come from Bulgaria, Germany, Hungary, Poland, Slovakia, Turkey, and the United States of America. The participants rated their Internet surfing skills as competent, proficient and expert. Most of them reported that they usually spend 3–6 h (40%) or 1–3 h (29%) on the Internet per day and preferably use a laptop (53%) or a desktop computer (26%) for the surfing.

In the second usability evaluation the users were given the same tasks as in the first usability testing, albeit slightly adapted to the updated prototype[13]. The same protocol was followed as in the first evaluation. The participants recorded their screen during the testing, and completed the same questionnaire. Our analysis of both the videos and the questionnaires is presented below.

Video Recordings. In each of the 73 videos we observed that the UI was very easy to use. The participants made less mistakes than in the maximum control UI. We did not observe any confusion or misunderstanding of the UI. The users immediately noticed the clickable dashed parts in the graph. It took users, on average, only three minutes to complete all the tasks. For their own consent they needed approximately one minute. The videos showed that reducing customization complexity highly improved the performance of the users.

Comprehension Testing. When describing what data processing the participants consented to, most of them (80%) provided correct information. This finding was further confirmed via open questions (e.g., "There were no problem understanding...", "... shows you exactly what you are consenting to").

Time Perception. The way the users rated the time they spent on the tasks confirms what we observed in the videos. 38% of the participants were satisfied with the time it took them to complete the tasks and for 15% it took even less than they expected. 19% of the users think that it took them too long, but it was worthwhile. The rest (28%) still considered the process to be time consuming.

Adjective Description. The users' interaction in the video left a very good impression about the prototype usability. Surprisingly, users still described the prototype as being "confusing" (40%), "annoying" (33%), "complex" (26%), "frustrating" (18%). From the video analysis and questionnaire answers we can infer that this was caused by the absence of bulk consent withdrawal functionality.

---

[13] Usability evaluation tasks are available at: https://bit.ly/2KChPpF.

Users were first confused and then irritated that they had to repeat the same action. On the other hand, for 15% of the participants the UI was "easy to use", 14% of the respondents considered the UI to be "flexible", 12% - "innovative", and 11% - "effective" and "friendly".

Prototype vs Traditional Consent Request. The respondents named three main points why they liked the CoRe UI prototype better than traditional consent requests. The CoRe UI is: (i) more understandable (e.g., "It was very clear", "It is visual", "The consent request is not long, only few text and symbols for quick processing"), (ii) provides customization (e.g., "It's much better, because it is not just the text to read and then accept everything - you can decide what you accept"), and (iii) transparency (e.g., "I am more aware that my data are used by so many applications", "It shows you exactly what you are consenting to"). We did not receive any negative feedback, however, 2 out of 73 participants wrote that they liked the traditional consent request because it is possible to consent to personal data processing using just a single button.

Ease of Use. The easiest part for the users was to browse the available functionalities. Some of the participants mentioned that the prototype was in general easy to use after one became familiar with the UI (e.g., "The whole prototype is fairly easy, once one has familiarized himself with the options"). The hardest part was the fact that the prototype did not allow for the withdrawal of consent for multiple functionalities at once (e.g., "... I cannot revoke more functionalities at the same time"). This issue can easily be fixed by adding a feature where the users can select the functionalities in bulk.

Icons and Color-Coding. More than two thirds of the participants appreciated having icons in the graph. 23% of the respondents did not see the need in icons. The participants positively evaluated the color-coding as well. 82% found it useful and only 18% reported that they did not see any usefulness in it.

Summary Graph. Most of the respondents to some extent (6% extremely, 11% very, 34% moderately, 26% slightly) understood the summary graph. 23% of the users did not understand the graph at all. 37% of the participants did not find the tree graph in the summary useful, 29% thought the graph was slightly useful, 22% selected "moderately useful" as their answer. Only a small percentage of the users 7% and 5% found the graph very and extremely useful respectively. The only issue the users mentioned regarding the summary graph was that the icons were too small (e.g., "Please put bigger icons").

Overall Satisfaction. Although the CoRe UI prototype was very easy to use as evidenced in the video recordings, 39% of the participants still reported dissatisfaction with the prototype (18% - very, 21% - somewhat). 36% (31% - somewhat, 5% - very) of the users were satisfied and 25% were neither satisfied nor dissatisfied with the UI. 37% (26% - not so well, 11% - not at all well) of the participants reported that the way the consent request is presented does not meet their needs. The others were satisfied with the representation. Two thirds of the participants liked the UI prototype enough to want to recommend it to their friends. For 30% of the users it is not likely that they would do so.

Prototype Improvement Suggestions. A lot of the participants did not suggest any improvements. They pointed out that they understood the difficulty of the information visualization for the consent request, however, they did not know how the prototype could be improved (e.g., "I think it is pretty difficult to give a short overview of all the consent information covered on one page, therefore, I have no advice"). For others everything seemed to work well and the prototype did not need any adjustments (e.g., "No improvement necessary").

6 Conclusion

In this paper, we propose an innovative consent request user interface, which gives data subjects more control over the processing of their personal data. During the research process we developed two CoRe UI prototypes based on the GDPR requirements and questions usually asked by lawyers when assessing the lawfulness of the personal data processing in the EU. The first prototype gave maximum control over personal data processing to the users, while the second prototype was simplified and provided less customization options. In both cases the consent request content was formulated as short phrases using plain language. The first UI was not well received by the participants of the usability evaluation. Users struggled with the evaluation tasks and as a result were not satisfied with the UI in general. The main issue for the users was too much control and complexity connected to it. Although the UI was perceived as complicated, the users liked the graphical visualization of the data processing as it made it easier for them to understand the implication of their consent. Additionally, the participants highly appreciated the customization feature, but they suggested to reduce its complexity.

Based on the insights gained from the first usability evaluation, we developed a simplified UI prototype. In this prototype the customization options were reduced to two actions: (i) browsing device's features and (ii) selecting third party data sharing options. All other information was just shown to the user in a graph form. In contrast with the previous evaluation, the users performed all tasks quickly, easily and almost without errors. The users liked the visualization and plain language and they appreciated the customization. The second round of testing indicated improvement in terms of performance and comprehension. However, in some cases, the users still complained about the amount of the information they had to digest.

All the materials used in the evaluations are available online, so that other consent UIs can be benchmarked against ours. Both evaluations showed that the users did not want to spend extra time on reading information in the consent request and suggested to simplify the customization feature. In order to address this issue the CoRe UI could be amended such that the functionalities or purposes for data processing are grouped into more general categories and allow consenting to a category but still retaining a more granular customization as well as detailed overview of the data processing available on demand.

Acknowledgments. This paper is supported by the European Union's Horizon 2020 research and innovation programme under grant 731601. We would like to thank our colleagues from SPECIAL and WU for their legal support and help with the user studies.

References

1. Acquisti, A., Adjerid, I., Brandimarte, L.: Gone in 15 seconds: The limits of privacy transparency and control. IEEE Secur. Priv. **11**(4), 72–74 (2013)
2. Bastien, J.C.: Usability testing: some current practices and research questions. Int. J. Med. Inform. (2010)
3. Benedek, J., Miner, T.: Measuring desirability: New methods for evaluating desirability in a usability lab setting. In: Proceedings of UPA (2002)
4. Borgesius, F.Z.: Informed consent: We can do better to defend privacy. IEEE Secur. Priv. **13**(2), 103–107 (2015)
5. Brewer, M.B., Crano, W.D.: Research design and issues of validity. In: Handbook of Research Methods in Social and Personality Psychology, pp. 3–16 (2000)
6. Charters, E.: The use of think-aloud methods in qualitative research: An introduction to think-aloud methods. Brock Educ. J. **12**(2) (2003)
7. Checkland, P., Holwell, S.: Action research. In: Kock, N. (ed.) Information Systems Action Research. ISIS, vol. 13, pp. 3–17. Springer, Boston (2007). https://doi.org/10.1007/978-0-387-36060-7_1
8. Costante, E., Sun, Y., Petković, M., den Hartog, J.: A machine learning solution to assess privacy policy completeness: (short paper). In: Proceedings of the 2012 ACM Workshop on Privacy in the Electronic Society, pp. 91–96. ACM (2012)
9. Friedman, B., Howe, D.C., Felten, E.: Informed consent in the Mozilla browser: Implementing value-sensitive design. In: Proceedings of the 35th Annual Hawaii International Conference on System Sciences, pp. 10–pp. IEEE (2002)
10. Hartson, H.R., Castillo, J.C., Kelso, J., Neale, W.C.: Remote evaluation: the network as an extension of the usability laboratory. In: Proceedings of the SIGCHI Conference on Human Factors in Computing Systems, pp. 228–235. ACM (1996)
11. Ivory, M.Y., Hearst, M.A.: The state of the art in automating usability evaluation of user interfaces. ACM Comput. Surv. (CSUR) **33**(4), 470–516 (2001)
12. Kelley, P.G., Bresee, J., Cranor, L.F., Reeder, R.W.: A nutrition label for privacy. In: Proceedings of the 5th Symposium on Usable Privacy and Security. ACM (2009)
13. Liccardi, I., Pato, J., Weitzner, D.J.: Improving mobile app selection through transparency and better permission analysis. J. Priv. Confidentiality **5**(2), 1–55 (2014)
14. MacKenzie, I.S.: User studies and usability evaluations: from research to products. In: Proceedings of the 41st Graphics Interface Conference, pp. 1–8. Canadian Information Processing Society (2015)
15. McDonald, A.M., Cranor, L.F.: The cost of reading privacy policies. ISJLP **4** (2008)
16. McDonald, A.M., Reeder, R.W., Kelley, P.G., Cranor, L.F.: A comparative study of online privacy policies and formats. In: Goldberg, I., Atallah, M.J. (eds.) PETS 2009. LNCS, vol. 5672, pp. 37–55. Springer, Heidelberg (2009). https://doi.org/10.1007/978-3-642-03168-7_3
17. Nielsen, J.: Enhancing the explanatory power of usability heuristics. In: Proceedings of the SIGCHI CHI, pp. 152–158. ACM, New York (1994)
18. Schaub, F., Balebako, R., Durity, A.L., Cranor, L.F.: A design space for effective privacy notices. In: 11 Symposium on Usable Privacy and Security (2015)

19. Seidman, I.: Interviewing as Qualitative Research: A Guide for Researchers in Education and the Social Sciences. Teachers College Press (2013)
20. Steinsbekk, K.S., Myskja, B.K., Solberg, B.: Broad consent versus dynamic consent in biobank research: Is passive participation an ethical problem? EJHG **21** (2013)
21. Tidwell, J.: Designing Interfaces: Patterns for Effective Interaction Design. O'Reilly Media Inc. (2010)
22. Tullis, T., Fleischman, S., McNulty, M., Cianchette, C., Bergel, M.: An empirical comparison of lab and remote usability testing of web sites. In: UPAC (2002)
23. Wijesekera, P., et al.: The feasibility of dynamically granted permissions: aligning mobile privacy with user preferences. In: 2017 IEEE Symposium on Security and Privacy (SP), pp. 1077–1093. IEEE (2017)

I Did Not Accept That: Demonstrating Consent in Online Collection of Personal Data

Vitor Jesus[✉] and Shweta Mustare

School of Computing and Digital Technology, Birmingham City University,
Birmingham, UK
vitor.jesus@bcu.ac.uk

Abstract. Privacy in online collection of personal data is currently a much debated topic considering, amongst other reasons, the incidents with well known digital organisations, such as social networks and, in Europe, the recent EU/GDPR regulation. Among other required practices, explicit and simply worded consent from individuals must be obtained before collecting and using personal information. Further, individuals must also be given detailed information about what, how and what for data is collected. Consent is typically obtained at the collection point and, at a single point in time (ignoring updates), associated with Privacy Policies or End-User Agreements. At any moment, both the user and the organization should be able to produce evidence of this consent. This proof should not be disputable which leads us to strong cryptographic properties.

The problem we discuss is how to robustly demonstrate such consent was given. We adapt fair-exchange protocols to this particular problem and, upon an exchange of personal data, we are able to produce a cryptographic receipt of acceptance that any party can use to prove consent and elicit non-repudiation. We discuss two broad strategies: a pure peer-to-peer scheme and the use of a Trusted Third Party.

Keywords: Privacy · Fair exchange · Consent

1 Introduction

Online privacy has always been a challenging problem that, nevertheless, has been exacerbated with technological advances in data processing and the proliferation of sensors and mobile technologies. Individuals find hard to not only track the flows of personal data but also to establish exactly what organisations (the Data Controllers or Processors) are collecting and possess about them. Furthermore, the conditions in which consent was given are also, more often than not, unclear. The EU General Data Protection Regulation (EU/GDPR), effective in May 2018, is seen as an advance in the control individuals have over their

© Springer Nature Switzerland AG 2019
S. Gritzalis et al. (Eds.): TrustBus 2019, LNCS 11711, pp. 33–45, 2019.
https://doi.org/10.1007/978-3-030-27813-7_3

personal data and covers European citizens. Recently, multiple well-known digital organisations have also been under the spotlight for collecting and sharing information in ways that, at best, are unclear to individuals. This motivates our work.

The central concept at stake is *consent*. Even if not sufficient in many cases, it is consensually necessary before personal information is collected. Among others, a key requirement of EU/GDPR is that individuals need to explicitly consent with the treatment and purpose of the collected personal data (i.e. opt-in). This further includes revealing which third parties (the Data Processors) will have access to the personal data. Communication with the user must also be clear and simple. The organisation needs to put effort in simplifying how it is communicated to the user, e.g., when explaining their Privacy Policy or Terms of Agreement.

The problem we tackle in this paper is the following: when a User sends personal data under a Privacy Policy, and after a user gives consent, and in case of dispute, how can both the online Service and the User prove (i) what data was collected, (ii) how it was collected and (iii) the terms that both parties consented with at the time? Note the problem is not only on the User side, e.g:

- a dishonest User claims to never have given consent to a particular set of Terms or Privacy Policy or even to never have given Personal Data at all, thus accusing the Service of abuse or theft; or
- a dishonest online Service claims the User consented with extra conditions, i.e., agreed to a specific Privacy Policy which is different to the ones the User truly accepted.

Note that, nowadays, the common practice is to simply rely on local records (e.g. log files) managed by each party. In case of a dispute, they prove very little as these records can be easily manipulated.

The scenario we discuss in this paper is widely common: a User creates an account, using a web browser, with an online Service (e.g., a social network, a mobile application or an email provider) by sending personal data (such as identity, address, etc.) and the personal data is regulated by jointly agreed terms of service and privacy policy. After the User reviews policies and terms, and then accepts, personal data is sent over. Two key elements are involved at this stage about the Agreement: (i) it must be clear, detailed and simple enough for any average user to understand and (ii) it should not be specific to any user unless there is a good reason, i.e., everyone in the same conditions (say, at around the same time and location) should obtain the same Terms. We will further assume there will be Third Parties that are reviewing such Terms so that users already are aware of its major implications and, above all, get reviews when the Terms are updated.

The key problem we tackle is how a User or a Service can prove that, at some past point in time, there was consent regarding a specific agreement. The problem is akin to non-repudiation with two challenges: (i) the whole interaction and process must be protected and (ii) users must be allowed to be anonymous to any level of degree which means the scheme cannot rely on legal identity.

The main contribution we offer is a practical scheme for both parties to generate *non-repudiation of receipt* (not origin) and thus demonstrate if and how consent was obtained and offered. It has thus extreme current relevance. To the best of our knowledge, this is the first publication to discuss this practical and abundantly common aspect.

The reminder of this paper consists of the following. In Sect. 2 we review the background of the technologies used. In Sect. 3 we define the problem, its requirements and provide a threat model. In Sect. 4 we propose two broad strategies (peer-to-peer and using a Trusted Third Party) and in Sect. 5 we present an implementation and evaluate key metrics. Section 6 concludes our paper.

2   Background

To the best of our knowledge, this is the first time to specifically address the problem of proving consent when an exchange of personal data occurs when registering for online services. In this section we provide a background on online consent (largely non-technical), user identity on the Internet and fair-exchange protocols.

2.1   Online Consent

Consent is a legal concept and therefore difficult to capture with technology [1]. The familiar experience of clicking and accepting terms of service is what legal experts call *click contracts* or *web-wrap agreements* [2]. At least since the EU/GDPR came in force in May 2018, consent now has a tighter formulation especially regarding its validity. In a nutshell, the data collected, the purpose and means of collection require clarity and simplicity. In the United Kingdom, and one would expect in most countries if not all, implicit trust is the key element: the user *trusts* the service will deliver as promised in exchange for what the user is passing over such as personal data [3].

The problem we face here is how to obtain cryptographic evidence of non-repudiation of receipt and under conditions that were clear for both parties before the exchange happened. In other words, the problem we discuss is, once a dispute has arisen, how both User and Service can prove, beyond any doubt, (i) what data was shared, (ii) how it was (technically) collected and (iii) under which Terms of Agreement. For example, the Service will not be able to trick the user into accepting hidden conditions and, at a future moment, claiming those conditions were exposed to the user. The User will not also be able to claim to have received a different Privacy policy which has importance to organisations.

2.2   User Identity

The current Internet is largely identity-less. At best, an online identity (say, an account) can be linked to a real identity when legal documents are available; sometimes, it can only be linked to a payment method. Most often, there is no linkage at all, except contextual ones, and the account is only valid locally to the service. This creates problems when attempting to design a non-repudiation protocol as all that parties can rely on is transaction receipts.

If we had legal identities on the Internet, the identity problem could be trivial. Nowadays, many identity systems support Public Key Infrastructure and identity cards are even, physically, smart cards holding certificates and keys issued by a government, stored in secure hardware and under a standardised security programme. Such keys would, at first sight, resolve the problem if all parties were able to digitally sign transactions. However, even in that case, they may not be legally valid. As the techno-legal community has been debating, using such cryptographic material presents several challenges such as [4]:

- Revoking certificates is problematic. If a breach of a private key is detected, it would invalidate all past transactions from a forensics perspective because it will always be difficult to assert when the keys were breached.
- Timestamping, despite seemingly simple, requires a Time authority that has to be delegated from a government.
- Public keys, even in case of a breach, can never expire as they would invalidate past valid transactions.
- In most countries, digital certificates have no legal value and evidence can only be based on declarations.

The net effect is that plain old signatures, or *acts of will* [4] (such as clicking a button), is still the only way to lawfully prove acceptance of something [5] in most parts of the world. This is aligned with Privacy regulations when requiring acceptance of terms to be explicit.

Considering that such legal elaborations is outside the scope of our paper, and in order to keep our approach as generic as possible, we simply make no assumptions on the source of user identity. To this regard, the user is whoever will be running the protocols we present in this paper at the moment of exchange. All we require is that

- there are means to contact the User outside the real-time transaction for the duration of the agreement; and
- there is a globally unique identifier for the User, or a username compounded with a globally unique identifier for the service such as a Fully Qualified Domain Name (such as an email address).

2.3 Fair-Exchange Protocols

Fair-exchange protocols are such that parties who do not trust each other, but wish to exchange something electronically, mutually generate digital evidence that satisfies proof of non-repudiation of receipt [6]. To note that *fair non-repudiation* is probably more accurate for our scenario but we chose to use the more widespread term. In our case, we exchange Personal Data for access to a service and under certain Terms of Agreement. Fair-exchange protocols have found different applications such as delivery of software against payment, delivery of invoices [7], certified email delivery [8] or consumer card payments [9]. The problem also shares similarities with multi-party computation [10].

Proven approaches exist that cover, broadly, two key requirements: multi-party [11] and whether there is a need for a Trusted Third Party [13,14]. To note, however, that it seems to be an impossibility to achieve strong non-repudiation and fairness in the sense that all parties are at the same starting point and obtain what was intended at the end, if we require no involvement of a commonly trusted mediating agent, a Trusted Third Party (TTP) [15]. A simple analogy is that, when exchanging something (say, software for a payment) someone has to go first and so the party that goes second can always exit the protocol and the first party could hardly prove it sent anything. Approaches such as gradual exchange [7], where parties exchange shares iteratively, do not strictly meet the fairness requirement in conditions such as asymmetric computing power [11]. This problem is nowadays solved with escrow parties that act as a TTP.

3   Consent Model

In this section we formalise our problem, discuss what we mean by Consent (and Agreement) and present our Trust model.

3.1   Agreement Model

We consider the following common scenario – see Fig. 1. A User (the Individual) is creating an account online which requires personal data to be collected and sent to a Service.

The key components are

- *Private Data*, the personal data that the User is about to share, D
- *Policy or Terms*, the Terms of using the Service that the Service imposes, T_S
- *Collection Logic*, the mechanism by which data is collected, L, which can be as simple as a HTML form and a POST method or a JavaScript script
- *Receipt*, a (cryptography-based) receipt proving the exchange of data and its context, R

Together, these elements create what we call an Agreement $A = (D, T_S, L)$ for which evidence of acceptance is receipt $R_A^t(U)$ generated at time t for user U. The generation and handling of the receipt is the central contribution of this paper.

Furthermore, we include in the model a Trusted Third Party (TP) that is optional. The TP has three functions:

- First and most important, it serves as a trusted medium when neither user of service trust each other and neither wish to be in an unfair position such as sending first something. In other words, and in simple terms, each sends their contributions to the TTP and only when both completed their parts of the protocol the TTP releases to each the desired contribution. In practice, we will use an offline TTP which is only used in case a party exits the protocol prematurely. This will be detailed later.

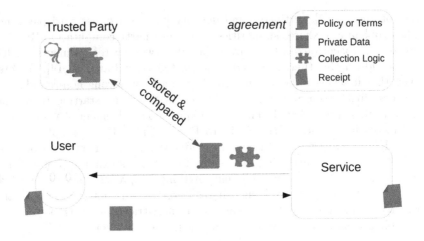

Fig. 1. Agreement model.

- In a real-world scenario[1], a TTP publicly reviews (and possibly more) the Terms offered by the Data Controller to all equivalent users. We assume users, in practice, will not review in detail all the Privacy Policies and Terms of Service they come across. No matter how simplified and well communicated they might be, we assume users will mainly use reputation mechanisms and external reviews to fully understand the implications of how their personal data is used [12] and, if needed, to revoke at a later time the given consent, especially upon an update of the terms. Note that revoking consent will use the same mechanisms as described in this paper. Such entities already exist nowadays in some form (even if specialised news websites[2]) but we envision they will become more important with national regulations that impose clarity requirements and force online services to open they practices in more detail for external scrutiny.
- It has the capability of monitoring and recording the generic Terms of a given online Service; it may, further, as in one of our strategies, store the offered Terms to a particular user and can later be checked whether the user was offered the same conditions as any other user in the same conditions. This will mitigate the risk that the Service cheats by crafting a special Agreement at a given moment for a particular user thus misleading the user into accepting different Terms, for example, by manipulating the Terms are shown to the user revisit this aspect – see next section.

---

[1] We are working with Privacy organisations towards piloting the ideas on this paper in a real-world scenario.

[2] See https://tldrlegal.com/ for software licenses.

3.2   Collection Logic

We here make a simplification that, nevertheless, still defines an overwhelming common problem: we will assume the negotiation between user and service is conducted online and over common Web technologies. In particular, we assume the user interface is implemented in HTML and Javascript and the communication protocol is HTTP. This greatly helps for two reasons:

– *HTTP is stateless.* This means that capturing outgoing and incoming data is not dependent on any previous state. Very often the overall application is stateful as the back-end application servers store information which creates a session context. However, we assume that, upon exchanging personal data, the communication is truly stateless – even if it is designed for the sake of clarity. The result is that one should be able to completely capture the negotiation and the agreement and each end can save it for future records.
– *Implementation code is open.* We simply assume, as is virtually any case today, that the collection logic is based on Javascript (so running on a web browser) which, by nature, is completely auditable by the user as javascript arrives in source-code and is available for inspection. This means that, the combination of stateless HTTP and open source-code, together with the data (personal data and, say a privacy policy in the form of a file) provides a complete record of the transaction.

It should be noted that this is not the case for, for example, mobile apps. To give a practical example, the mobile application can intercept and modify, without the user knowledge, information (such as tricking the user to accept invisible terms); further, because it is not always possible to completely reverse-engineer or decompile a mobile application, one is never sure of what the actual collection logic was which creates room for disputes between the user and the service. The mobile app case, and generalising to any collection logic, is open for future work.

3.3   Trust Model

The problem we discuss is mutual: both User and Service need to prove the agreement they claim has been accepted. At any point in the future, both the User and Service can dispute what was agreed. The following lists the key threats and assumptions in our Trust model:

– *Service tricks the user into accepting non-generic Terms.* In other words, the Terms sent to the User, under the disguise of being the generic ones for any equivalent user, contain specific obscure conditions that the User is unaware of. The Service thus cheats by crafting a special Agreement.
– *Service shows correct Terms but invisibly modifies immediately after technically obtaining consent.* This involves how consent is recorded such as in a webpage form. It is trivial to display the user a document that is then invisibly manipulated without the User being aware of.

– *Dishonest user claims consent to different Terms.* We assume it is ultimately up to the Service to make sure the User is fully aware of all Terms which includes the user interface; for example, the user's device must be able to display the page properly and this check should be done programmatically as much as possible. The User can always argue that she or he never accepted some Terms or that they were visually manipulated or hidden.

The following are outside the scope of this paper:

– *Modification of in-flight packets.* We simply assume that all parties are communicating over secure channels such as HTTP/TLS.
– *Impostor using someone else's Data.* As said, we cannot verify the user at any level and as such we can only define the User as the person engaging the Service behind a particular device at a given time.
– *Impairment of User's device.* We also leave out of scope the possibility of the user's device, deliberately or not, not having the expected functionality. For example, a component (such as a browser add-on) might be interfering in the way the Agreement is executed.

4   Strategies

We propose two strategies that differ when considering the trade-off between usability and hardness of guarantees.

– *peer-to-peer (p2p).* We have a simpler 2-party, peer-to-peer scenario, between the User and the Service collecting personal information. No other party is involved. As discussed, there is no known and fair way to obtain hard assurances between two parties that need to exchange something. In simple words, someone has to send first and, as discussed, progressive schemes (where parties exchange shares incrementally) only provide some level of assurance. In the p2p case, we assume the User is not particularly concerned if, after sending the personal data, the service does not send a receipt.
– *Trusted Third-Party.* If the User is concerned about sending personal data without guarantees, one can use a Trusted Third Party (TTP). In essence, the personal data can be first sent to the TTP, for which an evidence of submission is issued. The Service will then send evidence of *commitment to receive* the personal data on which the personal data is released. Several types of TTPs exist but we assume the risk of it being a bottleneck is not acceptable and therefore an offline TTP (who is only engaged if a party cheats) is used.

4.1   Peer-to-Peer

The peer-to-peer case assumes that a user U accepts the risk that service S will not return the expected service and only exists to collect personal data disappearing immediately after. This relaxation simplifies the problem but is not strictly a fair exchange.

User U starts by gathering and locally storing Agreement $\mathbf{A}_u = \{D_u, L, T\}$ where D_u is the user's personal data, L is a representation of the collection logic and T is the Privacy Policy or Terms of Agreement. U then applies a one-way, collision resistant, function to produce $H_u = hash(\mathbf{A}_u)$. U then generates a pair of public/private keys, K_u^{pub} and K_u^{priv}. This pair is, effectively, what binds the physical person to the consent.

User U then sends message $M_u = \{\mathbf{A}_u, Enc_{K_u^{priv}}(H_u, t_u, r_u), t_u, H_u, r_u,$ $K_u^{pub}\}$. This message consists of the agreement $\mathbf{A}_u$, its hash H_u, a timestamp t_u and a sufficiently long random nonce r_u. The message is further encrypted with K_u^{priv} and is sent along with the corresponding public key K_u^{pub} so S can verify. The role of r_u is that, along with another that S will send, r_s, provides a (with high likelihood) unique identifier of the particular context of this agreement. Further note that, from the perspective of S, the user is completely identified as the person who owns K_u^{priv}. In this sense, encryption is here used to create a notion of identity and provide authenticity in the short-lived session during which this agreement is negotiated.

Service S runs a similar procedure. It starts by gathering $\mathbf{A}_s$ independently and then calculating a hash $H_s = hash(\mathbf{A}_s)$. It then verifies H_u matches H_s. S is now assured U returned the offered agreement. S further generates K_s^{pub} and K_s^{priv} as, respectively, a pair of public and private keys. In a common scenario, these keys could be those associated with a PKI certificate which fairly resolves the problem of S's identity. For example, if the negotiation is over HTTPS, the keys associated with the TLS certificate could be used.

Similarly, S sends $M_s = \{\mathbf{A}_s, Enc_{K_s^{priv}}(H_s, t_s, r_s), t_s, r_s, K_s^{pub}\}$. U becomes assured S signed the expected agreement. U verifies H_s matches its own H_u which assures U that S returned the expected agreement. At this stage, we define $H = H_s = H_u$ as both parties verified.

U sends evidence $E_u = \{Enc_{K_s^{pub}}(H, r_u, r_s, t_u, t_s)\}$ and attaches its signature $S_u = Sign_{K_u^{priv}}(E_u)$. Together with the agreement gathered at the first step, S generates $\mathbf{R}_s^t = \{\mathbf{A}_s, E_u, S_u\}$ which is the receipt that S must hold as proof of consent.

Symmetrically, S sends evidence $E_s = \{Enc_{K_u^{pub}}(H, r_u, r_s, t_u, t_s)\}$ and attaches its signature $S_s = Sign_{K_s^{priv}}(E_s)$. Together with the agreement gathered at the first step, U generates $\mathbf{R}_u^t = \{\mathbf{A}_u, E_s, S_s\}$ which is the receipt that U must hold as proof of consent.

4.2 Using an Optimistic TTP

Using a TTP TTP has the advantage that user U does not have to send personal data before obtaining confirmation of receipt and risk a cheating service S that does not continue the expected protocol. It is also easy to design a scheme where TTP also does not have access to the personal data and serves merely as a trust binding channel that is called upon only if any party does not complete the protocol – hence called optimistic. It is still possible for a cheating S to obtain the personal data and not deliver the expected service but U will have evidence of it, contrary to the pure peer-to-peer. Our scheme is inspired in [13].

U runs the first steps of the previous strategy but instead of sending the agreement $\mathbf{A}$ in plaintext, it is sent encrypted with a symmetric key chosen for the session k. This key is also sent but encrypted with TTP's public key, K_{TTP}^{pub}. U sends therefore $M_u = \{Enc_k(\mathbf{A}_u), Enc_{K_u^{priv}}(H_u, t_u, r_u),$ $t_u, H_u, r_u, K_u^{pub}, Enc_{K_{TTP}^{pub}}(k)\}$. Note that the TTP has no access to the personal data.

If S responds with a receipt, U sends k which S should then acknowledge with a final receipt. In case S does not send the final acknowledgment, U submits (k, r) to TTP which then sends to both U and S a receipt of submission.

4.3   Analysis

Assume that at a point in the future, either U or S challenge the agreement in place, by fully or partly denying it.

In the p2p case, the scenario is symmetric so we will look only at U denying ever accepting, in whole or in part, the agreement. S can trivially prove, or force U to withdraw the challenge, by requesting the evidence on U's side. On producing evidence, with a signature based on S's public certificate, the nonce r, timestamps and identity of the service will uniquely identify the session. U can produce the agreement that was signed on its side and, along with signatures and hashes, uniquely identify both the collection logic, the personal data sent and the terms. Either S produces a consistent agreement or refuse to produce evidence at which point S has to be considered at fault.

In the TTP case, U will have evidence of submission since it shared the symmetric key k demonstrating it followed the protocol yet S did not. U has evidence of early submission so S either admits breaking the protocol or must produce its own evidence at which point the TTP will be able to open with its private key.

5   Evaluation

We implemented the peer-to-peer protocol in order to understand its impact on usability. The User was presented with a simple form as shown in Fig. 2. Upon submitting the personal data and running the protocol, a button for a Quick Response (QR) code is to be available in order to both download a file containing all the components of the agreement and the cryptographic material (evidence of agreement) as detailed in section.

We used a common mid-spec laptop to run the protocol: Windows 10 Pro, Intel Core i5, 8 Gb RAM. The browser running the javascript implementing the protocol on the client side was Google Chrome 72. We used open-source cryptographic libraries for javascript: Cryptico, Node-forge, js-sha256 and js-md5.

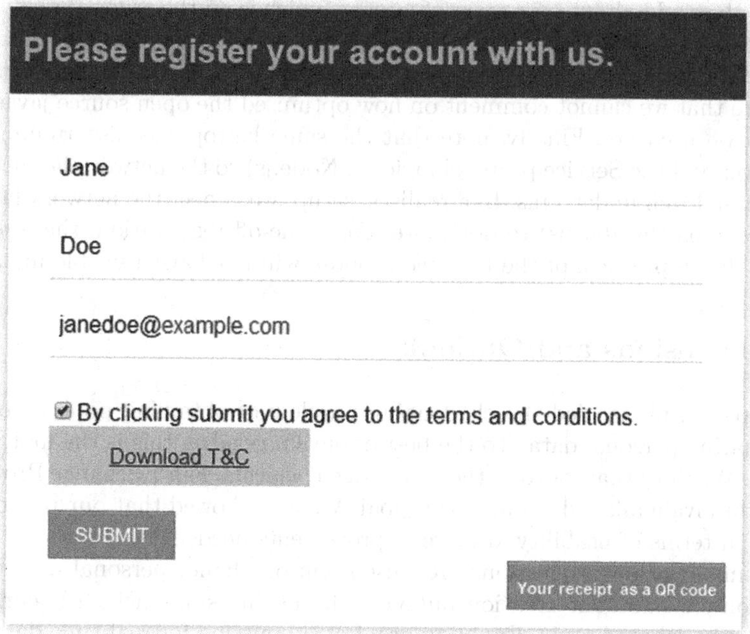

Please register your account with us.
Jane
Doe
janedoe@example.com
By clicking submit you agree to the terms and conditions.
Download T&C
SUBMIT
Your receipt as a QR code

Fig. 2. User interface.

We tested different sizes of both the HTML and documents involve such as a Privacy Policy. The results we obtained are showing in Fig. 3. We used two common hashing functions, SHA-256 and the older MD5. Results show that the impact in usability are minimal and fairly independent of the size of the agreement.

Time to complete protocol (ms)
1800
1600
1400
1200
1000
800
600
400
200
0
SHA-256
MD5
size of agrement (Bytes)
0
20000
40000
60000
80000
100000
120000

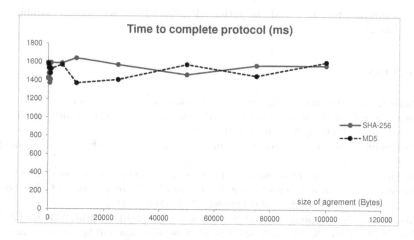

Fig. 3. Latency added by the fair exchange protocol.

All values add about 1.5 s more of latency which is on the order of magnitude of network latency for web pages. The size of the agreement does not seem to play a major role, at least in the range we considered (up to 100 kB of files). Also note that we cannot comment on how optimised the open source javascript libraries we used are. Finally, note that the same laptop was also running the web server and the Service protocol logic (in Node.js) so the network latency was minimal and well under 1 ms. In a realistic setup, we expect the network latency (commonly on the 100 ms) to dominate. For a one-off registration, these results suggest that a protocol of the kind we propose will not have a visible impact.

6   Conclusions and Outlook

In this paper, we tackled the challenging problem of obtaining poof of consent when sharing personal data. To the best of our knowledge, this is the first paper to do so. We show that, beyond the techno-legal aspects, Fair Exchange Protocols can be an invaluable aid towards this goal. We also showed that our proposal is feasible in terms of usability, despite improvements needed.

A number of open questions are raised. On one hand, personal data is not shared only on account creation but virtually at any stage, which is currently an intensely debated topic. Enabling proof of submission for real-time data may use the same approach as we do here (in a rather static scenario) but raises usability and manageability challenges - for example, an ultimately, each data packet could be the subject of a receipt which would dramatically impact the performance of the current Internet. Another direction we will be pursuing is how to completely encapsulate an Agreement when the collection logic is not open as it happens with mobile apps. Finally, our scenario, despite overwhelmingly used, considers only web applications. Work should be done at a larger scale with other types of applications, from mobile applications to machine-to-machine.

Acknowledgments. We would like to thank Professor Peter Sommer, of Birmingham City University, for his insights into the legal aspects.

References

1. Millett, L.I., Friedmann, B., Felten, E.: Cookies and web browser design: toward realizing informed consent online. In: Proceedings of the Conference on Human Factors in Computing Systems (2001)
2. Sandholm, T.W.: Unenforced E-commerce transactions. IEEE Internet Comput. **1**(6), 47–54 (1997)
3. Rajaretnam, T.: The problem to consent to the collection, use, and disclosure of personal information in cyberspace. In: International Conference on Cyber Security, Cyber Warfare and Digital Forensic (CyberSec) (2012)
4. Maurer, U.: New approaches to digital evidence. Proc. IEEE **92**(6), 933–947 (2004)
5. Laurie, B., Bohm, N.: Signatures: an interface between law and technology, January 2003. http://www.apache-ssl.org/tech-legal.pdf

6. Zhou, J., Gollmann, D.: A fair non-repudiation protocol. In: Proceedings of the 1996 IEEE Conference on Security and Privacy, SP 1996, Washington, DC, USA (1996)

7. Watrobski, J., Karczmarczyk, A.: Application of the fair secret exchange protocols in the distribution of electronic invoices. Proc. Comput. Sci. **112**, 1819–1828 (2017)

8. Paulin, A., Welzer, T.: A universal system for fair non-repudiable certified e-mail without a trusted third party. Comput. Secur. **32**, 207–218 (2013)

9. Neville, W., Horie, M.: Efficiently achieving full three-way non-repudiation in consumer-level ecommerce and M-Commerce transactions. In: IEEE 10th International Conference on Trust, Security and Privacy in Computing and Communications, Changsha (2011)

10. Garbinato, B., Rickebusch, I.: Secure multiparty computation vs. fair exchange: Bridging the gap, Technical Report DOP-20070123, University of Lausanne, DOP Lab (2007). http://www.hec.unil.ch/dop/Download/articles/DOP-20070123.pdf

11. Onieva, J.A., Zhou, J., Lopez, J.: Multiparty nonrepudiation: a survey. ACM Comput. Surv. **41**(1), 5:1–5:43 (2009). https://doi.org/10.1145/1456650.1456655. ISSN: 0360-0300

12. McDonald, A., Cranor, L.F.: The cost of reading privacy policies. J. Law Policy Inf. Soc. **4**(3), 543–568 (2008). Privacy Year in Review issue I/S

13. Markowitch, O., Kremer, S.: An optimistic non-repudiation protocol with transparent trusted third party. In: Davida, G.I., Frankel, Y. (eds.) ISC 2001. LNCS, vol. 2200, pp. 363–378. Springer, Heidelberg (2001). https://doi.org/10.1007/3-540-45439-X_25

14. Zhou, J., Deng, R., Bao, F.: Evolution of fair non-repudiation with TTP. In: Proceedings of the 4th Australasian Conference on Information Security and Privacy, ACISP 1999, London, UK (1999)

15. Garbinato, B., Rickebusch, I.: Impossibility results on fair exchange. In: Proceedings of the 6th International Workshop on Innovative Internet Community Systems, I2CS 2006, vol. LNI. German Societyof Informatics (2006)

Privacy Policy Specification Framework for Addressing End-Users' Privacy Requirements

Nazila Gol Mohammadi[✉], Jens Leicht, Nelufar Ulfat-Bunyadi, and Maritta Heisel

paluno - The Ruhr Institute for Software Technology,
University of Duisburg-Essen, Duisburg, Germany
{nazila.golmohammadi,jens.leicht,nelufar.ulfat-bunyadi,
maritta.heisel}@uni-due.de

Abstract. Privacy policies are a widely used approach in informing end-users about the processing of their data and collecting consent to such processing. These policies are defined by the service providers and end-users do not have any control over them. According to the General Data Protection Regulation of the European Union, service providers should make the data processing of end-users' data transparent in a comprehensible way. Furthermore, service providers are obliged to provide the end-users with control over their data. Currently, end-users have to comprehend a lengthy textual policy in order to understand how their data is processed. Improved representations of policies have been proposed before, however these improvements do mostly not empower the end-users in controlling their data. This paper provides a conceptual model and a proof of concept for the privacy policy specification framework that empowers end-users' when using online services. Instead of having to accept predefined privacy policies, end-users can define their privacy preferences and adjust the applied privacy policy for a specific service.

Keywords: Privacy · Requirements engineering · Privacy policies · Sticky policy · Cloud computing

1 Introduction

Privacy policies play an important role for the protection of privacy-relevant data. The protection of data and privacy preservation are the main goals of legal regulations like the *General Data Protection Regulation (GDPR)* of the European Union. Due to the GDPR, service providers are obliged to provide insights into the processing of personal data for their end-users. The GDPR applies to all companies and institutions that process data of individuals located in the EU. If any infringements are detected, service providers can expect a financial penalty [4]. To comply with data protection legislation, an informed consent to privacy policies is the most important legal foundation for data handling on the

© Springer Nature Switzerland AG 2019
S. Gritzalis et al. (Eds.): TrustBus 2019, LNCS 11711, pp. 46–62, 2019.
https://doi.org/10.1007/978-3-030-27813-7_4

Internet. Therefore, privacy policies should make the service provider's data processing transparent for end-users in a comprehensible way. However, a variety of studies revealed that most of the end-users are overwhelmed with the amount of information they are confronted with in a privacy policy [9,13]. Furthermore, the GDPR specifies the right for end-users to object to the processing of their data, which may result in the obligation for the service provider to delete their data or at least to stop processing them. Current implementations of privacy policies do not support empowering end-users, e.g. with providing a possibility to withdraw the consent to data processing.

The difficulty in the cloud environment is the number of parties involved in handling the end-user's data, and the fact that every involved party may be using a different policy with a variety of different goals. In most cases, the end-user does not know how many parties are involved and how his/her data is handled. For the end-user it is also difficult, if not impossible, to know if the parties involved are trustworthy. Even if the companies handling the data are known, it is impossible to know which part of the private data each company handles. To overcome the difficulty in handling data through different parties involved in a cloud computing environment, a possible solution is the use of *sticky policies* [12,14], which have been proposed in various versions. Since the policy is transferred together with the end-users' data, every party knows how to handle the data. Sticky policies are data-oriented instead of service-oriented, allowing end-users to introduce their privacy requirements when using a service.

Although, when using sticky policies, the end-users are enabled to specify their privacy requirements, generation of sticky policies is not user-friendly and not usable for all end-users. These sticky policies are only considering end-users privacy preferences without considering a specific service. On the one hand, end-users might tend to provide a rather strict sticky policy as they want their data to be protected. However, this restricts the service providers too much, even making service provisioning impossible for them. On the other hand, service providers are interested in getting the most benefit by using their end-users' data as freely as possible. Thus, they exploit the legal limits as far as possible in privacy policies with vague statements. This situation results in conflicts between the two parties.

We provide a framework that resolves the conflicts between the two parties. Our framework makes use of the concept of sticky policies and uses them for the specification of privacy preferences of end-users. This allows the end-user to adjust the privacy policy that is provided by the service provider. However, the framework restricts the adjustments the end-user can make to allow all data processing necessary for service provisioning. The resolution of the conflicts will allow the enforcement of the end-user's privacy preferences. In this way, our approach addresses the transparency as well as intervenability. Consequently, the end-users are no longer obliged to consent to privacy policies that contain unnecessary processing of their data. This results in a better privacy protection in conformance to the GDPR. To improve the representation and user-friendliness, in the user interface of our privacy policy specification framework, we use existing patterns from the state of art and practise. The fact that similar user interfaces have been used before is advantageous to our development, because these are well-established, and end-users know how to operate them.

Our framework focuses on capturing users' privacy preferences. Hence, this paper does not address the monitoring and enforcement of sticky policies or data security mechanisms e.g. through encryption.

The remainder of this paper is structured as follows. Section 2 describes background information on which our work is based. Afterwards, Sect. 3 presents the results of the state-of-the-art analysis, followed by the conceptual model and the process of our proposed framework. The process is illustrated with an application example. Section 4 presents related work. Finally, Sect. 5 contains a discussion and conclusion.

2 Background and Fundamentals

In this section, we briefly introduce the fundamental techniques and concepts for the framework that is described in Sect. 3.

Privacy Protection. In a privacy context, three additional goals, accompanying the goals of the security context (confidentiality, integrity, and availability), are important [16]: unlinkability, transparency, and intervenability. *Confidentiality* refers to the non-disclosure of data, i.e. keeping it private. *Integrity* refers to avoiding the manipulation and corruption of data. *Availability* means that the data is available for access at any time. *Unlinkability* aims at the separation of privacy-relevant data from any other data, privacy-relevant or not. It should be impossible or at least infeasible to find a link between the privacy-relevant data and any other data, not directly belonging to that set of data. This also means that the privacy-relevant data should not be usable in any context other than the one it is intended for. Thus, assuring unlinkability also leads to purpose-binding, where a set of data is only used for a specific purpose. *Transparency* allows the involved parties to understand the processes of handling the privacy relevant data at any point in time and to be able to reconstruct this information at any time. It describes the transparency of the system, i.e. there is no black boxing allowed, as this would mean that the involved parties are not able to understand the handling of the data. Transparency includes planned processing as well as the time after processing. A possible method of proving transparency is the availability of source code. However, availability of source code also requires the end-user to be able to understand the source code, which makes it an unrealistic method of providing transparency. *Intervenability* allows all involved parties to interfere with the data processing. This allows corrections in the system and countermeasures in the case that something does not work as intended. This also allows the erasure of data and the withdrawal of consent to any privacy policy.

Note that we carefully distinguish between privacy protection goals and the measures and mechanisms that are used to achieve them. For example, pseudonymity is a mechanism to achieve the privacy goal of unlinkability. Hence, we do not consider pseudonymity as a goal in our work.

Privacy Policies. In order to fulfil these goals, privacy requirements are used. These refine the goals of privacy protection by forming rules that directly apply to some data or service. The privacy requirements are combined to a privacy policy, which contains all rules that apply while handling the data or using the service.

Privacy policies are the standard approach used by nearly all service providers in the world wide web. They consist of statements describing how the data provided by the end-user is handled and what kind of data is collected. Each statement contains obligations, which the service provider has to fulfil. Each statement contains an action stating what type of processing is restricted by the statement. Additionally, each action is combined with a purpose. This purpose defines whether the processing of the data is needed for service provisioning or whether it is done for marketing or analysis. Every statement also refers to the data that is handled in the context of the statement. Privacy policies are provided in textual form and are written in a language that is difficult to understand from an end-user's point of view. Typically, policies are written in a language that is useful for lawyers but not for the end-user of a service [13].

The approach of privacy policies, as they are used today, is service-oriented. This means the end-users have to agree to different policies for each service they want to use. This approach follows the *"Take it or leave it!"* principle. It means that end-users can only use the service if they agree to the privacy policy provided by the service provider. The end-users have no chance of changing the policy to restrict the usage of their data. End-users can only decline the privacy policy, by not using the service. If so, they have to find another service provider who provides a similar service with an acceptable privacy policy.

Privacy policies are subject to regulations, e.g. the General Data Protection Regulation (GDPR) [4] of the European Union. The GDPR defines rules that have to be followed by service providers. A major rule is to inform the end-user about the handling of her/his data, which is done by defining privacy policies.

Sticky policies represent a special kind of privacy policy that uses a different approach than the privacy policies defined by service providers. Instead of having a privacy policy for each service, end-users can define a policy for each set of data they provide to any service provider. Sticky policies are, therefore, data-oriented, whereas standard privacy policies are service-oriented. Data-orientation is achieved by sticking the policy with all its statements to the data itself. This leads to the benefit that all parties involved in handling or storing the data can access the policy that is attached to it and, thus, every party knows how the data has to be handled. The approach also leads to the ability to reuse a sticky policy on multiple services. This means that end-users can create a sticky policy containing all their privacy requirements and stick it to all data that they send to different service providers.

Sticky policies were proposed in different versions by Pearson et al. [12] and Spyra et al. [14]. In all versions, the sticky policies approach relies on a trust-based system. The end-user generates the policy and sticks it to the encrypted data that the policy shall protect. The service provider receives both, data and sticky policy, and has to contact a trusted authority to get the key necessary for decrypting the data. If the service provider does not have a bad reputation, the trusted authority provides the key for decryption. The service provider must acknowledge that it follows the policy. Then it receives the decryption key from the trusted authority. With the key, the service provider can access the data and start processing it. If another service provider is involved in processing the data, it will be forwarded in its encrypted form together with the sticky policy, and every service provider has to request the decryption key from scratch.

3   Privacy Policy Specification Framework

In this section, we first present the results of a state-of-the-art analysis we performed, in order to design our proposed framework according to the challenges revealed by the analysis. Afterwards, the framework is presented, followed by the description of the process of our framework and an application example.

3.1   Challenges in Addressing End-Users' Privacy Requirements

The following state-of-the-art analysis was conducted through a literature review and observations of the authors of this paper. The state-of-the-art analysis revealed that there are still some challenges with both approaches (standard policies and sticky policies) regarding the definition of the end-users' privacy requirements:

(1) *Take-it-or-leave-it attitude of service providers:* Privacy policies as defined by service providers are not user-oriented and are provided with a *"Take it or leave it!"* attitude. End-users have no options and cannot change the policies to protect their privacy. The *"Take it or leave it!"* attitude is an observation that is not backed by literature. This problem can be solved by using sticky policies. However, the following challenges arise when using sticky policies.

(2) *Lack of knowledge for defining sticky policies:* When using sticky policies, the responsibility for defining a privacy policy is handed over to the end-user. The end-user now has to actively define a sticky policy and not every end-user is capable of defining his/her privacy requirements in a sticky policy, as technical know-how is needed. Already in 2004, a survey showed that most end-users are not willing to spend much effort in order to protect their privacy [5]. Although this seems to be a major issue with sticky policies, end-users would only have to define their privacy requirements once and could stick the resulting sticky policy to every data leaving their device, thus resulting in much less work compared to reading and understanding a privacy policy for each service the end-user wants to use.

(3) *Trust in service providers:* Another difficulty with the sticky policies approach is the fact that it is trust-based [12,14]. This means that a malicious service provider can easily request the decryption key pretending to be a legitimate service provider following the sticky policy. But instead it just

decrypts the data to use it in a malicious way. The trusted authority will only be able to stop the then blacklisted service provider after getting to know the malicious behaviour. However, this does not protect the data of the first user in this example. Only future users will be protected.

(4) *Too strict sticky policies:* Strict policies represent another problem that arises when the end-users can define the policies on their own. Too strict policies prohibit the service provider from accessing necessary data, thus making the service unusable for that end-user. The end-users do not know which data is actually needed to provide the service when they define the sticky policy. The sticky policies approach provides no means for telling the end-user which data is actually needed by the service provider for the provision of the service, e.g. a banking service needs to have access to the account details of the end-user. However, when end-users do not know which data is actually needed, they could define that no processing of any data is allowed, resulting in the problem that the service cannot be provided to the end-user. This challenge was revealed when developing our framework and thus has not been backed by literature.

We aim at addressing all these challenges by the framework that we present in the next subsection.

3.2 Conceptual Model

Figure 1 illustrates the different stakeholders and items related to the described problem. The *Service provider* provides a *service* together with the *privacy policy* for the service. The privacy policy as well as the service itself are restricted by *legislators* due to *regulations* such as the GDPR. These regulations state the rights and duties with regard to the end-user's privacy. The service provider is interested in adhering to the data protection regulations because substantial penalties are the consequence of disobeying the regulations. The *End-Users* use the service and provide data to the service that needs to be protected. With

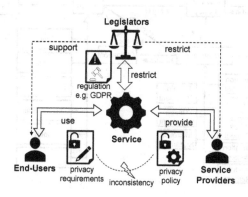

Fig. 1. Motivational problem

the sticky policies approach end-users can express their *privacy requirements* to the service providers. However, the service providers' policies and the end-users' preferences will most likely contain *inconsistencies*.

To create a conceptual framework, we considered not only the papers resulting from the state-of-the-art analysis but also two formal documents that define privacy principles and help to identify the important actors and entities. On the one hand, we considered the privacy framework as defined in the international standard ISO/IEC 29100 [1]. On the other hand, we considered the EU GDPR [4], which is the currently binding legal framework in the EU member states. ISO/IEC 29100 and the EU GDPR partly overlap but do not use the same terminology.

To avoid ambiguities, we use the following definitions for the most important actors relevant for our policy specification framework (see Fig. 2):

– A *data subject* is "an identifiable natural person, who can be identified directly or indirectly, in particular by reference to an identifier such as a name, identification number, location data, online identifier or to one or more factors specific to the physical, physiological, genetic, mental, economic, cultural or social identity of that natural person" [4]. This term is called personally identifiable information (PII) principal in ISO/IEC 29100. In this paper, a data subject represents a person whose data is stored and/or processed in the cloud. The data subject has, with respect to the personal data, the rights stipulated by the GDPR. In this paper, we consider end-users as data subjects.

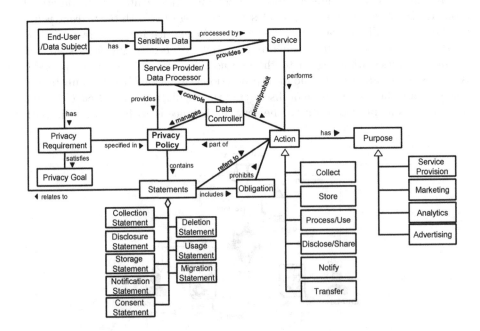

Fig. 2. Conceptual model

- The *data controller* is "the natural or legal person, public authority, agency or other body which, alone or jointly with others, determines the purposes and means of the processing of personal data" [4]. This term is called PII controller in ISO/IEC 29100. In this paper, a data controller represents a legal entity providing a cloud service which stores and/or processes personal data. The data controller has, with respect to the stored/processed personal data, the obligations stipulated by the GDPR. We consider the service provider at the first interaction point with the end-user as the data controller.
- The *data processors* are all other involved service providers that do not play the role of the data controller, but process end-users' data. In the context of cloud computing many parties can be involved as data processors, but only one of them is responsible for managing the policy as the data controller. The processing of the data shall be controlled by a binding contract between controller and processor. The processor may only process the data in the way the controller specified in the sticky policy. This restriction can be made legally binding by integrating it into the aforementioned contract.
- We define *sensitive data* in a wider manner compared to personal data. The focus of the GDPR is on personal data. Personal data "means any information relating to an identified or identifiable natural person (data subject)" [4]. This is called personal identifiable information (PII) in ISO/IEC 29100. We, however, consider sensitive data as any data stored in the cloud that needs to be protected, according to the data protection preferences of the affected data subject. In particular, we extend the notion of sensitive data to also include confidential business data.
- A *service* represents a cloud service that works with end-users' data. The data controller is responsible for the legal and compliant operation of the services.

The *data subject* has *sensitive data* that is *processed by* a *service* performing *actions* on it. These *actions* are part of the *privacy policy* that will be specified using the policy specification framework. The different *actions* define what can be done with the *sensitive data* that is provided to the *service*. Available actions are:

- Collect: Collection of *Sensitive Data* that is not directly supplied by the end-user
- Store: Storing data supplied by the end-user
- Process/Use: Processing of data resulting in new data.
- Disclose/Share: Sharing data with other parties
- Notify: Notification of the end-user at specific events
- Transfer: Transferring data to other locations

Every *action* has a *purpose* that defines whether the *action* is necessary for *service provision* or whether it is used for *marketing, analytics,* or *advertising*. Using this purpose-binding of the *actions*, it is possible to decide whether the usage of the *sensitive data* is actually necessary to provide the service or whether the end-user can decide not to allow this action. Our framework distinguishes four purposes: *service provision* means that the *action* is necessary for providing the service, e.g. account information for online banking. *Marketing, analytics,* and *advertising* are optional purposes, stating that the action is not actually necessary for the service to function. *Marketing* means the usage of the end-user's data to inform new end-users about the *service*. *Analytics* addresses the usage of *sensitive data* for the creation of statistics, and *advertising* means the usage of the data to provide advertisements to the end-user that provides the data.

Using the privacy policy specification framework, end-users can communicate their *privacy requirements* to the *service provider*. These *privacy requirements* satisfy the *privacy goals* mentioned earlier. The *privacy policy* generated from the end-users input contains *statements* including *obligations* regarding the handling of the data that the end-user provides to the service. These *obligations* can, for example, prohibit the processing (*action*) of the data for *marketing* purposes.

Each *statement* relates to the *sensitive data* provided by the end-user and is stuck to the data using the sticky policies approach. A *statement* is one of the core elements of our conceptual model. *Privacy policies* consist of one or several *statements*. The *statement* implies conditions and rules that refer to the *action* that is performed by the *service*. The associations of *sensitive data, action,* and *purpose* are important because it is necessary to track which *actions* are allowed to be performed for what *purpose*.

Generic statements can aggregate one or more specific statements. A *collection statement* is a statement that specifies which data is allowed to be collected by the *service provider*. This means it will restrict the *collect action* of the *service provider*. *Disclosure statements* define the rules and conditions specifying which data of the end-users is allowed to be disclosed to which audience. A *storage statement* specifies how long the data will be stored. *Usage statements* specify for which *purpose* the end-users' data is allowed to be used and processed. A *notification statement* specifies the rules and conditions regarding the question about what the end-user needs to be informed and how. *Consent statements* describe where and under which condition the end-users are required to give their consent. A *migration statement* describes the rules and conditions for the migration of the data to different locations.

The data controller manages the policies together with the data and controls the other involved service providers, so that the services provided by these providers only perform actions that the data controller permits.

The data controller manages both types of privacy policies, the one provided by the service provider and the sticky policy created from the end-user input. Based on the purpose, the controller can decide whether a statement given by the service provider is necessary to provide the service or whether it is used for additional purposes. In this way, the end-user is given the possibility to make choices and too restrictive policies, which would conflict with the data processing needed to provide the service, are avoided.

The GDPR requires a contract between the data controller and the data processor. As mentioned in the description of "data processor" above, part of this contract could be the application of the sticky policies. Whether this is enough to fulfil the GDPR may not be elaborated in this paper as the focus of this work is the end-user's point of view.

3.3   Process of Privacy Policy Handling

Our policy specification framework informs the end-user about processing that is necessary for service provisioning, e.g. storing of files when using a file sharing service. All other actions and purposes can be either permitted or rejected by the end-user. The framework finds a trade-off between the unconstrained policy provided by the service provider, who wants to process/collect more data than necessary in order to get the most value out of the end-user's input, and the end-user's stricter policy. All statements of the privacy policy, that are not stated to be necessary for the provisioning of the service, are considered optional. Service providers can specify a processing as necessary by using the purpose *Service Provision* when specifying the privacy policy for a service. Optional statements are displayed to the end-user as a modifiable input, allowing the end-users to enter their privacy preferences.

Figure 3 shows the relations of the components involved in our proposed policy specification framework. *Privacy policies* are in a first step provided by the *service providers* and are adjusted by the *end-users*. *End-users* specify their *privacy requirements* in the *privacy policies* by adjusting them. The resulting *privacy policies*, which contain the end-users' *privacy requirements* are then encoded in *sticky policies*. These are attached to the *sensitive data* that is going to be processed by the *service* provided by the *service providers*. A *sticky policy* is accessed by a *service* when processing the *sensitive data*. By doing so the *service*

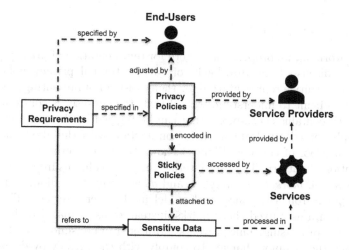

Fig. 3. Policy handling overview

can check whether the processing that is going to be started is allowed on the *sensitive data* it handles or not.

With the components and their relations given in Fig. 3, the following process can be established for the privacy policy specification framework. At first, the service provider creates a privacy policy for the service he/she wants to provide. This policy contains statements, as explained in Sect. 3.2, which in turn contain a purpose for every action they restrict. The privacy policy is then processed to retrieve the information, which statements are necessary for service provisioning and which ones the end-users can adjust according to their preferences. End-users are afterwards confronted with an interface that informs them about the processing that cannot be rejected, e.g. by showing disabled input fields for the affected statements. For all other actions and purposes the interface shows modifiable input fields. The modifiable input allows the end-user to give consent to an action with a specific purpose or to restrict the service from performing an action for a purpose. A new privacy policy containing the statements supplied by the service provider and the end-user's preferences is created from the input. This policy is encoded in a sticky policy, which is then attached to the sensitive data that is provided to the service. The sticky policy is stored in a triplestore, allowing the service to access the statements by action and/or by purpose. A triplestore is a purpose-built database for the storage and retrieval of triples through semantic queries. A triple is a data entity composed of subject, predicate, and object. This technique is used in our approach to store the service-side policies as well as end-users' sticky policies in a machine-processable format. The Resource Description Framework (RDF) specifies such a triple store [8]. To reduce the effort of end-users in providing their preferences, a locally stored copy of these preferences could be used to automatically adjust the privacy policies for new services. Then end-users only need to review the automatically adjusted preferences. However, the end-users must also have the ability to modify their preferences at any time, by reopening the user interface if they need to.

3.4   Proof of Concept

In another work [6], we proposed a pattern for representation of privacy policies. Therein, we discussed the drawbacks of current textual privacy policies and suggested an intuitive representation for them. Instead of presenting a very long and mostly difficult to understand wall of text, the end-user is confronted with a table which contains check-boxes that can be toggled by the end-user.

We implemented our framework in conjunction with the above-mentioned pattern as a proof of concept. Figure 4 shows the user interface that uses the above-mentioned pattern. The user interface uses the columns from left to right: *service provision, marketing, analytics,* and *advertising*. This allows a direct use of the purposes from the conceptual model in the user interface. The service provision column uses fixed check marks, instead of using disabled check boxes for mandatory processing. This prevents end-users from misunderstanding check boxes, which they cannot change. To comply with the privacy-by-default principle of the GDPR all optional processing is disabled (unchecked) by default.

Fig. 4. Example user interface

We consider it possible to assign any processing purpose to one of our main purposes. However, an additional purpose called "other" could be added to the system, that is used in cases where the processing does not fit any of our predefined purposes. The actual information about the processing is stored in the description, thus enabling the use of a "other" purpose.

The data is grouped in nine categories to simplify the interface. The categories are taken from an example that was part of the aforementioned work. Figure 4 also visualises the different states of the input cells.

Cells in the *service provision* column use fixed check marks, which will be displayed in orange, when the end-user did not yet consent to the processing. After submitting consent, the colour of the check marks changes to green to clarify that the end-user has already consented the processing.

The *marketing* column shows disabled check boxes, which represent processing that is not requested/provided by the data controller, meaning the end-user cannot consent to this cell, as there is no data in this category that is used for this purpose.

The *analytics* column contains active check boxes that are not ticked. This means the data controller wants to process data in a category for analytics purposes. The end-user either did not yet specify preferences for these cells or prefers that no processing is done in this category.

The last column for the purpose *advertising* shows ticked check boxes, which correspond to active consent of the end-user, as these check boxes must actively be selected by the end-user.

All cells in the grid and the headlines for each row represent more detailed information. This information is presented to the end-user through the use of tooltips. The tooltips contain information about the data that is referenced by the usages of each row or cell. The data and data type are combined with a description of the usage, which allows end-users to better understand whether they want to allow this usage or not.

The restriction of active check boxes to actually available processing partially fulfils Article 13 and 14 of the GDPR, by informing the end-user about the processing that may occur. Especially the fixed check marks for service provision inform the end-user about what data processing is mandatory.

The user interface presented was implemented as a Windows 10 app. It loads the service providers' privacy policy, containing all data processing that the data controller intends to perform. The policy is loaded from an RDF triple store using SPARQL, a query language for triple stores. When the end-user submits consent, all preferences, expressed by ticked and unticked check boxes, are stored in a second triple store. The data controller can then define the sticky policies for the end-user, in a policy definition language that is understood by the policy system used by the data controller and data processors. This eliminates the problem of different policy definition languages with incompatibilities. Instead of letting end-users encode a policy in a language of their choice, the data controller can use a compatible definition language to define the sticky policy.

This work is a work-in-progress. Our implementation has still some limitations and does not provide all features mentioned in [6]. The implemented interface currently provides no way of showing a textual policy for the end-user to read.

4   Related Work

Pearson and Casassa-Mont [12] as well as Spyra et al. [14] propose different versions of the *sticky policies* approach and thus strengthen the user-orientation in the context of privacy policy specification. However, both approaches concentrate mainly on user-orientation and do not include the service provider's side in their concept. This introduces the problem of over-specifying the end-user's privacy requirements (as described in Sect. 3.1), which we address with our framework.

The EnCoRe project provides components that enable the end-users to specify their sticky policy as described by Pearson and Casassa-Mont [12]. However, the project's website is no longer available and there is no further information about the elicitation of the end-users' privacy requirements. We provide a pattern for the presentation of modifiable privacy policy statements [6]. However, the pattern presented there does not provide any functionalities. The user interface of our framework is instantiated from this pattern. The idea of using a table for representing a privacy policy is based on the "Nutrition Label" approach suggested by Kelley et al. [9]. They first proposed the "Nutrition Label" approach as a way of better presenting privacy policies and later evaluated this approach in comparison to other existing approaches like the ubiquitous full text privacy policy and more structured ones [10]. We use pictograms in the design of the user interface. Hansen [7] compares different approaches on pictograms in the field of privacy.

Formal methods for privacy policies could be used for the back-end of our proposed policy specification framework or to improve the sticky policies approach by solving the problem of diverse policy specification languages. Berthold [3] provides a formal approach and Agrafiotis et al. [2] address resolving ambiguities in privacy requirements that are revealed by the development of their formal method for privacy [15]. Formal methods can also be used to resolve conflicts between the policies from end-users and service providers. This policy negotiation has also been addressed in work by Kolter [11].

5 Conclusions and Future Work

In this section, we first discuss our approach and then conclude our paper with a summary and an outline of the future work.

Discussion. As seen in Sect. 4, it is not easy to address the data protection goals especially with regard to transparency and intervenability. Although researchers have dealt a lot with privacy policies, they either meet the goal of transparency or the goal of intervenability, but not both. However, both goals are important privacy protection goals for privacy engineering [16]. With our framework for the specification of privacy policies, we address the asymmetry between end-users and service providers by offering a modifiable and well-structured policy layout. It can be customized to any application, but still the problem of feasibility remains. We address all the challenges mentioned in Sect. 3, but the trust in service providers is still a limitation. The *"Take it or leave it!"* principle is addressed by empowering the end-users with the ability of manipulating the privacy policy and specifying their privacy requirements. On the one hand, service providers may abuse their ability to specify that data processing is necessary for the service provisioning. Thereby, the end-users are still confronted with a *"Take it or leave it!"* policy, resulting in a limited or even no possibility to express their privacy preferences. On the other hand, the service providers are obliged to limit the data collection due to the GDPR and other regulations. Our framework can then support the service providers to conform with these regulations by limiting the data collection, consent documentation and purpose specification. Furthermore, the end-users are empowered with the ability for withdrawing their consent or adjusting their privacy preferences. The *lack of knowledge for defining sticky policies* is reduced through the proposed user interface with a structured representation of possible statements. By defining different purposes for different actions on the data, we address the *too strict policies* challenge. To solve this problem, the end-user is not enabled to disallow all actions necessary for service provisioning.

We expect that the service provider, being the data controller, already provides all necessary components to enforce the policy resulting from our framework. The data controller can access the triplestore to retrieve the statements of the policy permitting or disallowing actions.

It is not clear how service providers can be convinced to use our given privacy policy approach. As it is up to them to decide what data is essential for using their service, they could assign the service provision purpose to all actions and thus prevent any changes. One possibility to avoid problems like this would be to oblige them by law to comply with the guidelines, e.g. with the threat of high penalty.

Summary. Service providers and end-users often have a conflict concerning privacy policies. On the one hand, providers have to adhere to the data protection regulations and thus have to keep their end-users' data private. On the other hand, however, service providers rely on the collection of end-user data and exploit the legal limits, when processing data they collected whilst the end-user uses their services. Service providers are obligated to inform their end-users about the data that is collected and how it is handled. For this reason, they use standard privacy policies. The problem with the privacy policies, as they are used today, is the missing user-orientation. They adhere to existing law in borderline manner but are not matching the end-users' privacy requirements.

Not only the missing user-orientation, but also the *"Take it or leave it!"* principle are major disadvantages of textual policies. End-users are trapped in a situation of accepting privacy policies to use services they are not allowed to use until they agree (forced consent). This leads to a feeling of having no freedom of choice and the end-user has no interest in even reading privacy policies. This forced consent is also addressed by the GDPR.

Our proposed framework is more user-oriented, as end-users are able to change the policy, which is going to protect their data, and it also makes it easier for the end-users to understand the policies at all. It uses a well-structured layout in the form of a table (instead of a textual privacy policy) to inform the end-user about the processing that is going to be executed on his/her data. Our approach also makes it possible to capture input from the end-user, thus allowing the ability to adjust the policy to address the privacy requirements.

By capturing the end-user's privacy requirements once, the amount of overhead/effort that the end-user has when using new services, can be reduced. The privacy requirements (sticky policies) can be used for any future policy negotiation that the end-user needs to deal with. For this purpose, the privacy requirements could be stored on the end-user's side and used for any policy negotiation later on.

Future Work. This work is work in progress and, in future work, the proposed framework will be evaluated. In the context of real-life case studies user experiments, as part of the RestAssured project, will demonstrate our policy specification framework. It is also important to take a more in-depth look at the service provider's side to find out how to ensure that the service providers do not misuse the purpose of *service provision*. Misuse would make part of the policy unchangeable and prevents the end-users from protecting their privacy.

Acknowledgment. Research leading to these results received funding from the European Union's Horizon 2020 research and innovation programme under grant agreement number 731678 (RestAssured). We gratefully acknowledge constructive discussions with partners in the RestAssured project.

References

1. ISO/IEC 29100:2011 - Information technology – Security techniques – Privacy framework (2011). http://www.iso.org/iso/catalogue_detail.htm?csnumber=45123
2. Agrafiotis, I., Creese, S., Goldsmith, M., Papanikolaou, N.: Applying formal methods to detect and resolve ambiguities in privacy requirements. In: Fischer-Hübner, S., Duquenoy, P., Hansen, M., Leenes, R., Zhang, G. (eds.) Privacy and Identity 2010. IAICT, vol. 352, pp. 271–282. Springer, Heidelberg (2011). https://doi.org/10.1007/978-3-642-20769-3_22
3. Berthold, S.: Towards a formal language for privacy options. In: Fischer-Hübner, S., Duquenoy, P., Hansen, M., Leenes, R., Zhang, G. (eds.) Privacy and Identity 2010. IAICT, vol. 352, pp. 27–40. Springer, Heidelberg (2011). https://doi.org/10.1007/978-3-642-20769-3_3
4. Regulation 2016/679 of the European Parliament and of the Council of 27 April 2016 on the protection of natural persons with regard to the processing of personal data and on the free movement of such data, and repealing Directive 95/46/EC (General Data Protection Regulation). Official Journal of the European Union L119, pp. 1–88, May 2016. http://eur-lex.europa.eu/legal-content/EN/TXT/?uri=OJ:L:2016:119:TOC
5. Fatema, K., Chadwick, D.W., Lievens, S.: A multi-privacy policy enforcement system. In: Fischer-Hübner, S., Duquenoy, P., Hansen, M., Leenes, R., Zhang, G. (eds.) Privacy and Identity 2010. IAICT, vol. 352, pp. 297–310. Springer, Heidelberg (2011). https://doi.org/10.1007/978-3-642-20769-3_24
6. Gol Mohammadi, N., Pampus, J., Heisel, M.: Resolving the conflicting needs of service providers and end-users: a pattern for incorporating end-users privacy preferences into privacy policies (2019, accepted for publication)
7. Hansen, M.: Putting privacy pictograms into practice-a European perspective. Jahrestagung der Gesellschaft für Informatik e.V. (GI) **154**, 1–703 (2009)
8. Hayes, P., Patel-Schneider, P.: RDF 1.1 semantics. W3C recommendation, World Wide Web Consortium, February 2014. http://www.w3.org/TR/2014/REC-rdf11-mt-20140225/
9. Kelley, P.G., Bresee, J., Cranor, L.F., Reeder, R.W.: A nutrition label for privacy. In: Proceedings of the 5th Symposium on Usable Privacy and Security, SOUPS, p. 4 (2009). https://doi.org/10.1145/1572532.1572538
10. Kelley, P.G., Cesca, L., Bresee, J., Cranor, L.F.: Standardizing privacy notices: an online study of the nutrition label approach. In: Proceedings of the 28th International Conference on Human Factors in Computing Systems, CHI, pp. 1573–1582 (2010). https://doi.org/10.1145/1753326.1753561
11. Kolter, J.P.: User-centric Privacy: A Usable and Provider-independent Privacy Infrastructure, vol. 41. BoD-Books on Demand (2010)

12. Pearson, S., Casassa-Mont, M.: Sticky policies: an approach for managing privacy across multiple parties. IEEE Comput. **44**(9), 60–68 (2011). https://doi.org/10.1109/MC.2011.225

13. Pollmann, M., Kipker, D.K.: Informierte Einwilligung in der Online-Welt. Datenschutz und Datensicherheit **40**(6), 378–381 (2016). https://doi.org/10.1007/s11623-016-0618-6

14. Spyra, G., Buchanan, W.J., Ekonomou, E.: Sticky policies approach within cloud computing. Comput. Secur. **70**, 366–375 (2017). https://doi.org/10.1016/j.cose.2017.07.005

15. Tschantz, M.C., Wing, J.M.: Formal methods for privacy. In: Cavalcanti, A., Dams, D.R. (eds.) FM 2009. LNCS, vol. 5850, pp. 1–15. Springer, Heidelberg (2009). https://doi.org/10.1007/978-3-642-05089-3_1

16. Zwingelberg, H., Hansen, M.: Privacy protection goals and their implications for eid systems. In: Camenisch, J., Crispo, B., Fischer-Hübner, S., Leenes, R., Russello, G. (eds.) Privacy and Identity 2011. IAICT, vol. 375, pp. 245–260. Springer, Heidelberg (2012). https://doi.org/10.1007/978-3-642-31668-5_19

A Data Utility-Driven Benchmark for De-identification Methods

Oleksandr Tomashchuk[1,2]([envelope]), Dimitri Van Landuyt[2], Daniel Pletea[1], Kim Wuyts[2], and Wouter Joosen[2]

[1] Philips Research, Eindhoven, Netherlands
{oleksandr.tomashchuk,daniel.pletea}@philips.com
[2] imec-DistriNet, KU Leuven, Leuven, Belgium
{dimitri.vanlanduyt,kim.wuyts,wouter.joosen}@cs.kuleuven.be

Abstract. De-identification is the process of removing the associations between data and identifying elements of individual data subjects. Its main purpose is to allow use of data while preserving the privacy of individual data subjects. It is thus an enabler for compliance with legal regulations such as the EU's General Data Protection Regulation. While many de-identification methods exist, the required knowledge regarding technical implications of different de-identification methods is largely missing. In this paper, we present a data utility-driven benchmark for different de-identification methods. The proposed solution systematically compares de-identification methods while considering their nature, context and de-identified data set goal in order to provide a combination of methods that satisfies privacy requirements while minimizing losses of data utility. The benchmark is validated in a prototype implementation which is applied to a real life data set.

Keywords: De-identification · Anonymisation · Pseudonymisation · Data utility · Privacy · GDPR

1 Introduction

The rise of the Internet-of-Things (IoT) and Big Data creates unprecedented opportunities to businesses, yet also the rapid development of these technologies raises many challenges. Increasing amounts of data are being entrusted to service providers, as big data analytics capabilities are increasingly powerful. However, new business and emerging models in the context of these technological advances also create much societal concern with respect to privacy and trust. As such, methods that improve protection of sensitive data for privacy purposes are rapidly gaining importance, and their proper usage is a success factor for digital business systems.

Many privacy-enhancing technologies (PETs) and privacy building blocks exist [34], and these vary in terms of complexity, practical applicability and architectural impact. Data de-identification is one sub-class of PETs that groups

S. Gritzalis et al. (Eds.): TrustBus 2019, LNCS 11711, pp. 63–77, 2019.
https://doi.org/10.1007/978-3-030-27813-7_5

methods which involve removing associations between the gathered or processed data and the identity of the data subject. This allows extensive use of data sets while preserving the privacy of individual data subjects. There are many methods for data set de-identification, varying from simply removing identifiable data to obfuscating and adding noise.

Despite existing survey efforts (e.g. [18]), the required knowledge on peculiarities of application of different de-identification methods to structured textual/numerical data is largely missing. From this perspective, we particularly focus on de-identification of such data. De-identification of unstructured data and multimedia data (audio/video/pictures) is out of the scope of this paper. Extensive review and performance evaluation of single- and multi-shot (image and video) re-identification algorithms can be found in [12], whereas a survey study of de-identification of multimedia content can be found in [30].

In the context of software engineering, sound approaches towards selecting appropriate de-identification methods are currently lacking. This lack of expertise can lead to re-identification attacks like the AOL and Netflix re-identification examples [28]. Employing different privacy models (e.g. k-anonymity [15], t-closeness [24], etc.) can mitigate such re-identification risks. However these privacy models have limitations that can be further addressed by combining them in the right way tailored per specific data sharing purpose. Considering the shortage of de-identification experts and the fact that de-identification highly depends on their expertise, not just systematization of methods is needed, but also automation of de-identification processes is desirable.

In this paper, we introduce a benchmark system for de-identification methods. It may be considered as an extension of approaches proposed by Xiong and Zhu [26] and Morton et al. [32]. This benchmark takes into account privacy requirements, unique properties of existing methods and data utility metrics, changes of data utility triggered by the de-identification processes, and goals of de-identified data. We present the design of the benchmark system, introduce its prototype implementation and validate it in the context of realistic data sets.

The remainder of this paper is structured as follows: Sect. 2 discusses the background of the paper, whereas Sect. 3 states the problem. Section 4 provides description of the proposed benchmark, Sect. 5 demonstrates the validation that we performed for our solution. Section 6 provides an overview of related work, Sect. 7 discusses important aspects of the benchmarking process. Section 8 concludes the paper and highlights future work.

2   Background

In general, de-identification is accomplished by removing the association between the (identifying) data and the data subject. It can be achieved by applying specific methods. Section 2.1 first establishes an overview of de-identification terminology. Then Sect. 2.2 lists existing de-identification approaches and summarizes existing support for de-identification.

2.1 Terminology and Concepts

There is unfortunately no single agreed-upon definition for privacy concepts. Several commonly-used definitions exist for the overarching concept of 'privacy', yet they all have a slightly different meaning [31].

Pfitzmann and Hansen [25] have defined anonymity of a subject as '*the subject is not identifiable within a set of subjects, the anonymity set*'. Sweeney [15] was first to specify the level of anonymity: k-anonymity of information means that the information for each person cannot be distinguished from at least k-1 individuals whose information is in the data set. The General Data Protection Regulation (GDPR) [33] defines anonymous information as '*information which does not relate to an identified or identifiable natural person or to personal data rendered anonymous in such a manner that the data subject is not or no longer identifiable*'.

De-identification, anonymisation and pseudonymisation all describe the action of bringing data in an anonymous or pseudonymous state.

There is however also no consensus in terminology of, and relations between, 'de-identification', 'anonymisation' and 'pseudonymisation'. To illustrate, there are noticeable differences in the definitions of anonymisation provided by ISO and NIST:

- 'Process by which personal data is irreversibly altered in such a way that a data subject can no longer be identified directly or indirectly, either by the data controller alone or in collaboration with any other party' [2];
- 'Process that removes the association between the identifying data set and the data subject' [7];

Even more striking differences may be noticed with respect to definitions of de-identification provided by NIST [7] and Zuccona et al. [36]. Similar issues exist for definitions of pseudonymisation in the GDPR [33] and by NIST [7].

Terminological mismatch between different sources of information makes application of methods as well as understanding of fundamental concepts very challenging. In order to cope with it in this paper, we consider de-identification as a concept of a higher level, which covers both anonymisation and pseudonymisation, as follows:

- *De-identification* refers to any process of removing the association between a set of identifying data and the data subject [7];
- *Pseudonymisation* refers to processing of personal data in such a manner that the personal data can no longer be attributed to a specific data subject without the use of additional information, provided that such additional information is kept separately and is subject to technical and organisational measures to ensure that the personal data are not attributed to an identified or identifiable natural person [33]; We also find pseudonymisation as a type of de-identification as claimed in [2];
- *Anonymisation* is a process through which personally identifiable information (PII) is irreversibly altered in such a way that a PII principal can no longer

be identified directly or indirectly, either by the PII controller alone or in collaboration with any other party [1].

2.2 De-identification Methods, Privacy Requirements and Loss of Data Utility

De-identification is a process implemented by de-identification methods, aimed at the realization of privacy requirements. Due to its transformative nature, this process always incurs losses in terms of data utility.

De-identification methods are used for reducing the amount of identifying information, and attaining the privacy requirements that are typically represented in privacy models that allow reasoning about the privacy of the data subject, and ensuring compliance. To this end, data utility metrics, underestimated in the current state-of-the-art, are very important for quantifying data utility losses and thus for assessing the level of de-identification, to create a de-identified data set suited for the intended use. Examples of state-of-the-art de-identification methods, data utility metrics, and privacy models are presented in Fig. 1.

Many de-identification methods are in existence and some attempts towards their systematization have already taken place. For example, Nelson lists existing methods in [23], but his systematization has a large degree of overlap between the de-identification methods. A more recent and far more precise systematization was introduced in the ISO 20889 standard [3]. It thoroughly describes de-identification methods that are grouped into eight distinct types, based on the nature of the techniques that they use. This systematization together with [6] and [13] forms a basis of a knowledge base that is required for selecting a suitable de-identification method.

Nevertheless, there is always a probability of having removed too much or too little information from the involved data set. In order to reduce this probability, one needs to have clearly-defined privacy requirements. In most cases, the de-identification need is triggered by risks, which are the basic drivers of privacy requirements. Transforming probabilistic risks into deterministic requirements is a challenge that can be addressed with the use of privacy models. Many privacy models are in existence, such as k-anonymity [15], l-diversity [19], t-closeness [24], β-likeness [10], δ-presence [21], δ-disclosure [11], etc. The selection of such a model depends on its applicability to particular cases.

However, knowledge of requirements and methods is hardly enough for proper de-identification. This is due to the fact that almost any data set contains potentially relevant information that can be used for gaining insights into the data, while the goal of de-identification is exactly to remove the link between the data subject and that information of interest. Such a removal is always accompanied by reduction in usefulness of the information. In order to take this into consideration, one needs to use data utility metrics that are capable of quantifying the changes in the utility of the information of interest. Many data utility metrics are in existence that are aimed at measuring different properties of a data set and a tailored selection of them as well as correct usage improves the results of the de-identification process [27].

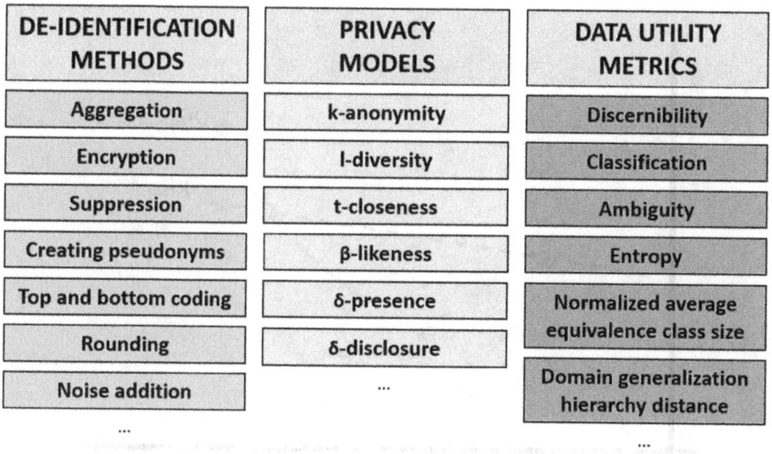

DE-IDENTIFICATION METHODS	PRIVACY MODELS	DATA UTILITY METRICS
Aggregation	k-anonymity	Discernibility
Encryption	l-diversity	Classification
Suppression	t-closeness	Ambiguity
Creating pseudonyms	β-likeness	Entropy
Top and bottom coding	δ-presence	Normalized average equivalence class size
Rounding	δ-disclosure	
Noise addition	...	Domain generalization hierarchy distance
...		...

Fig. 1. Examples of state-of-the-art de-identification methods, privacy models, and data utility metrics

3   Problem Statement

As shown in the previous section, there is a broad variety in de-identification methods and heterogeneity in different tool implementations for each of these methods. If de-identification is not done properly, re-identification may take place which can lead to financial, reputational, and other kinds of losses. However, in practice, selecting the most suited method is a non-trivial task.

Firstly, the most suitable method depends highly on the application context: the nature of the data, privacy requirements, assumptions made about data accessibility, and potential attackers and their incentives all play a role.

Secondly, this selection process depends highly on the expertise and knowledge of the de-identification expert. For example, finding good parameters for these methods requires extensive know-how. In practice however, such expertise is not always readily available.

Thirdly, the selection and configuration of a method involves complex architectural trade-offs. As mentioned by Mittal et al. [9], a de-identification scheme can be evaluated from two complementary perspectives: data utility preservation and resistance to re-identification attacks. This is also corroborated by Lee et al. [17] through their demonstration of the relation between data utility and disclosure risk (depicted graphically in Fig. 2).

Considering these facts, an algorithm for defining the most suitable de-identification methods of data sets is necessary, because each data set, depending

on the type of information that it contains and the availability of that information to attackers, needs a specific combination of de-identification methods for
bringing the level of de-identification to a satisfactory level.

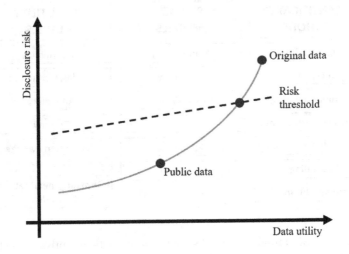

Fig. 2. Data utility vs. disclosure risk (from: [17])

4   Approach

As discussed in the previous section, selecting the most suited de-identification
method for a specific application relies on multiple factors. In this paper, we
present a systematic benchmark for de-identification methods. The benchmark
system implements an exhaustive search for the most appropriate methods and
combinations thereof in terms of two key factors: (i) adherence to the privacy
requirements and (ii) data utility loss of the transformed data set.

The benchmark implements a two-phased approach: (i) in the expansion
phase, candidate methods are generated, and (ii) in the reduction phase, these
are filtered based on the privacy requirements (which act as a cut-off) and the
data utility score.

The benchmark is exhaustive in the sense that it applies different methods
at a fine-grained level (attribute-level) and allows combining different methods
within the same data set. Furthermore, it systematically iterates over parameter
values of the different methods, and thus allows assessing the impact of these
parameters.

Figure 3 provides a graphical, flow-based representation of the proposed
benchmark system, which in turn is refined throughout the following sections.

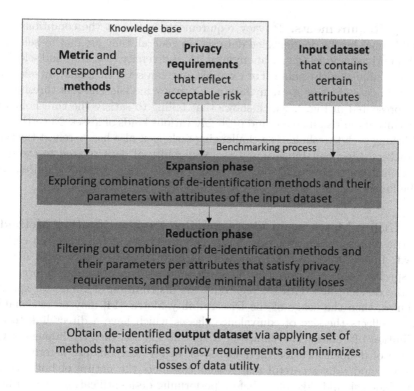

Fig. 3. Flow diagram of the proposed approach

4.1 Input and Output

The input consists of a structured data set that has to be de-identified. We expect this data set to contain attributes that represent direct and/or indirect identifiers, and a finite amount of tuples. The data set may contain any kind of information that may be de-identified using the methods introduced in [3].

The output consists of the de-identified data set obtained using the de-identification methods that satisfy the privacy requirements and maximally preserve data utility. In general, it should not contain direct identifiers or information that is not relevant for reaching de-identified data set goals.

4.2 Knowledge Base

The knowledge base is a representation of information that is necessary for execution of the benchmark. However, the base should not be treated as a part of the proposed benchmark. Considering that the knowledge base does not belong to the processing part, inputs on it are neither exhaustive nor complete, and presented here to support gaining an understanding of the proposed approach.

Privacy Requirements. Privacy requirements represent the conditions that should be met by the de-identified data set. In general, they are met by selecting a certain privacy model (e.g. k-anonymity [15], l-diversity [19], etc.) and selecting a certain value as a threshold. For example, one can set a threshold by selecting $K = 20$ in case of using k-anonymity as a privacy model. The risk threshold is also represented in Fig. 2, which shows that failing to satisfy the threshold will lead to unwanted risk increase and probably various kinds of losses. Nevertheless, establishing such thresholds is a challenging task, as it also has to reflect the type of attackers, their capabilities, and the availability of data related to the data set. Profiles of attackers that may be useful for establishing privacy requirements can be found in [16].

Data Utility Metrics and Corresponding De-identification Methods. A metric represents a way of measuring the usefulness of the data in a certain context. In our case, it has to measure changes in data utility with regards to a specific goal. For example, if one is interested in obtaining information from the de-identified data set regarding the distribution of values for specific attributes, then the usage of the Discernibility Metric [14] may be reasonable, since it reflects the size of equivalence classes which have a direct link to the distribution of values. The choice of a specific metrics directly influences the selection of de-identification methods. Most of the methods are heterogeneous in nature, and thus a careful match that considers the nature of both metric and methods should take place before performing de-identification. It is of high importance to select and apply those methods, which led to changes in data utility that are measurable by selected metric. For example, the Normalized Average Equivalence Class Size Metric [14] can precisely measure changes of data utility caused by aggregation and rounding, but it becomes impossible to extract meaningful values of data utility change by applying it after suppression or replacement of values by pseudonyms. Another example that demonstrates the necessity of tailoring the selection of methods to the types of data is that if we have a data set with attribute "Address", applying permutation will not be helpful for improving local k-anonymity, but t/b (top and bottom) coding would be helpful.

4.3 Benchmarking Process

The simplified twofold representation of the benchmarking process in Fig. 3 highlights its two main phases: expansion and reduction. In practice, the border between them is not clearly delineated, and that is why we further refine these phases in the form of pseudo-code below. For demonstration purposes, we use k-anonymity as the main privacy model, but other models (l-diversity, t-closeness, etc.) may be used as well.

input : privacy requirement K, privacy model kan, data utility metric
         M and its loss implementation dul, de-identification methods
         SM_i and their parameters SP_{ij} suitable for given M, data set D
         that contains attributes A_h which have to be de-identified;
output: combination R_h of methods with specific parameters per every
         attribute that satisfy privacy requirements and minimize data
         utility losses;

foreach A_h **do**
   foreach SM_i **do**
      foreach SP_{ij} **do**
         Obtain de-identified attribute $A'_h = SM_i(SP_{ij}, A_h)$;
         Obtain $PK = kan(A'_h)$;
         if $PK > K$ **then** compute data utility loss $dul(A'_h, A_h)$ *and*
         save it to a 3-dimensional buffer $BUF[h, i, j]$;
      end
   end
end
Obtain list $R_h \subset BUF$ that contains per every tuple h indexes of
methods i and parameters j, dul of which is minimal;

5   Validation

As the most influential part of the proposed benchmark is the reduction phase, we
decided to focus our validation explicitly on it. Considering its twofold nature, we
have crystallized two fundamental concepts of the phase for validation purposes
which can be found below:

1. Applying different methods to the very same piece of data leads to different
   results of de-identification;
2. Every de-identification method influences data utility in a unique way.

The first concept affects the part of the benchmark in which every possible
combination of methods and parameters per attributes is applied and the resulting data set evaluated against the privacy requirements. The second concept in
turn affects the part of the benchmark that involves searching for a combination
of methods and parameters per attributes that minimizes data utility losses.

5.1   Validation of the First Concept

In order to validate this concept we created a Python script that under given privacy requirements based on k-anonymity delivers a result in form of a method,
which, when applied, allows reaching the k-anonymity level closest to the target.
Our script includes implementations of the following methods: shuffling (permutation), hashing, top and bottom coding, aggregation, and suppression. We
applied the script to a Graduate Admissions data set [5] and fix parameters of

the methods to ensure that changes in results can be attributed to the nature of the applied methods, instead of changed parameters. The validation results are shown in Table 1. These results demonstrate that for reaching different levels of k-anonymity, different methods should be used.

Table 1. Methods per attributes, which, when applied, lead to obtaining k-anonymity which is the closest to needed privacy level (K – the required level of k-anonymity)

Attribute	$K = 1$	$K = 5$	$K = 50$	$K = 300$
Serial No.	shuffling	aggregation	aggregation	suppression
RE Score	aggregation	t/b coding	t/b coding	t/b coding
TOEFL Score	suppression	suppression	suppression	suppression
University Rating	shuffling	shuffling	aggregation	aggregation
SOP	shuffling	shuffling	aggregation	aggregation
LOR	shuffling	shuffling	aggregation	aggregation
CGPA	suppression	suppression	aggregation	aggregation
Research	shuffling	shuffling	shuffling	aggregation
Chance of Admission	suppression	suppression	aggregation	aggregation

5.2   Validation of the Second Concept

In order to validate this concept, we created a Python script that compares data utility before and after applying the specified methods. The measurements are done with the usage of the following metrics: the Discernibility Metric, the Normalized Average Equivalence Class Size Metric, and the Probability Distribution Metric. As in the previous section, our script includes implementations of the following methods: t/b coding, aggregation, and rounding. Similarly to the approach that we used for the previous concept, we applied the script to the same data set and kept parameters of the methods constant in order to assure that changes in results originate from the nature of methods, but not from the changes of parameters.

The results are presented in Fig. 4, and they demonstrate that if we measure data utility with a certain metric after applying some de-identification methods, losses in data utility are quite different in every case. Even if the nature of metrics is quite similar (both Discernibility Metric and Normalized Average Equivalence Class Size Metric measure properties of equivalence classes), the pattern which can be observed on the corresponding graphs is not identical. Also, the results of applying the Probability Distribution Metric show that these methods in question do not perform well on attributes such as Serial No., University Rating, and SOP, while being measured by the given metric.

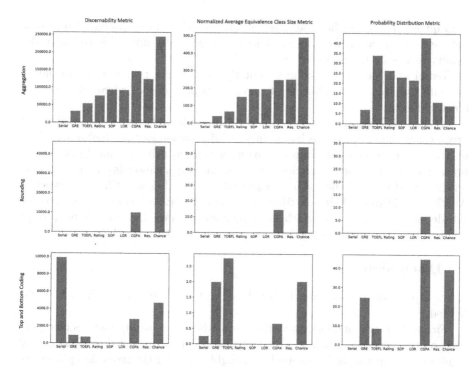

Fig. 4. Visualization of data utility losses per attribute under specific metric. The losses occur due to application of given de-identification methods. X axis represents the attributes of the data set. Y axis represent data utility loss (Discernibility Metric: min = 0, max = 250,000 (for given data set); Normalized Average Equivalence Class Size Metric: min = 0, max = 500 (for given data set); Probability Distribution Metric: min = 0%, max = 100%)

6   Related Work

Previous work in this field is mostly focused around utility and quality metrics. For example, LeFevre et al. [14] consider the Discernibility and Normalized Average Equivalence Class Size Metrics as measures of quality of anonymization in case of applying generalization or perturbation to the input data set. Goldberger and Tassa [8] contemplate loss, ambiguity, probability distribution, mutual information, and classification metrics as a way of measuring data utility. Also, there were some proposals for measuring data utility and level of de-identification through the application of game theory and entropy-based models [35]. However, these proposed metrics are relatively complex and applying them demands strong expertise in corresponding fields.

The importance of utility metrics is extensively discussed in [27]. Podgursky highlights that it is not clear whether a single metric which can accurately measure anonymization quality across all data sets and use-cases may exist, and that it is quite possible that a general metric will not accurately capture the data quality for a specific case. Also, he stresses that if any potential uses of a data set are known before anonymizing, it is generally advisable to tailor the quality metric on the expected use.

Templ and Meindl [20] complement this by stating that it is beneficial to evaluate the gain in explanation of parameters or variables when releasing de-identified data.

Xiong and Zhu in [26] tried to cope with the trade-off between data utility and privacy, but their approach is based only on information loss as a measure of data utility reduction, and data impurity as a measure of privacy gain. Ignoring the broader variety of existing metrics, methods, and privacy models puts restrictions on the added value of their work for practitioners and de-identification experts. Another problem of their contribution is that it does not consider the goal of the de-identified data set which is of high importance for performing proper de-identification. Similar consideration were also made in [4, 22, 29, 32].

7   Discussion

A few aspects of the benchmark introduced in this paper are worth to be highlighted.

Firstly, tailoring of de-identification methods to data utility metrics is important, as this otherwise leads to situations in which methods reduce data utility significantly, but this is not properly highlighted during the reduction phase. As a result, the quality of the output may suffer significantly.

Secondly, it supports the use of multiple metrics simultaneously. This allows the usage of the benchmark when the utility of the information of interest in the de-identified data set may be quantified with different metrics. The output of the benchmark is a combination of methods that satisfies privacy requirements and minimizes losses of data utility, but it is possible to provide a ranking. This may be useful for cases when requirements are not strict, and allows exploration of these intermediate results for finding the optimal solution. This is due to the fact that slight strengthening of some requirements may lead to huge data utility losses or vice versa. While it makes the computations heavier, it may bring added value given that the relations between privacy requirements and the benchmark results are not linear in most cases.

Thirdly, privacy requirements, metrics and methods do not reflect the presence of direct identifiers, and so we expected them to be removed during the process of de-identification by other means.

Fourthly, the proposed benchmark is expected to be applied to real life IoT solutions during the process of their development. However, two requirements need to be satisfied for applying the benchmark: (i) it is necessary to have a dataset that is equal to the one that has to be de-identified at a predefined point of the solution's architecture, and (ii) the element that will be responsible for applying de-identification methods should have enough computational power for executing them. In case these requirements are met, the output of the benchmark will enable extension of the element's software by the most suitable de-identification methods.

8 Conclusion and Future Work

In this paper we introduced a data utility-driven benchmark for selection of de-identification methods. This benchmark implements an exhaustive exploration of all combinations of de-identification methods that satisfy two key factors: adherence to the privacy requirements and minimization of data utility losses.

The benchmark provides direct support to practitioners and developers for selecting de-identification methods and making de-identification-related decisions. It also sheds light on the usage of de-identification methods and contributes to automation of de-identification processes.

Altogether, our benchmark enables better opportunities for businesses to cope with privacy-related challenges that are originating from the nature of IoT and big data.

In future steps, we will strengthen the approach with a more exhaustive overview of applicability between methods and metrics which also may consider related trade-offs and the specific nature of the data (non-structured, free text, etc.). In addition, further extension of the knowledge base, assessment of performance, investigation of opportunities for performance improvements, and conducting further evaluation of the benchmark through field tests will also be of benefit.

Acknowledgements. This research is funded by Philips Research, Research Fund KU Leuven, and the HEART project (www.heart-itn.eu). This project has received funding from the European Union's Horizon 2020 research and innovation programme under the Marie Skłodowska-Curie grant agreement No. 766139. This publication reflects only the authors' view and the REA is not responsible for any use that may be made of the information it contains.

References

1. ISO/IEC 29100 Information technology - Security techniques - Privacy framework (2011)
2. ISO 25237 - Health informatics - Pseudonymization (2017)
3. ISO/IEC 20889 - Privacy enhancing data de-identification terminology and classification of techniques (2018)
4. Abdou Hussien, A., Ramadan, N., Hefny, H.A.: Utility-based anonymization using generalization boundaries to protect sensitive attributes. J. Inf. Secur. **6**(03), 179–196 (2015). https://doi.org/10.4236/jis.2015.63019
5. Acharya, M.S.: Graduate admissions. https://www.kaggle.com/mohansacharya/graduate-admissions. Accessed 18 Apr 2019
6. Article 29 Data Protection Working Party: 0829/14/EN WP216 opinion 05/2014 on anonymisation techniques (2014)
7. Garfinkel, S.L.: NIST IR 8053: De-identification of personal information (2015)
8. Goldberger, J., Tassa, T.: Efficient anonymizations with enhanced utility. Trans. Data Priv. **3**, 149–175 (2010)
9. Ji, S., Mittal, P., Beyah, R.: Graph data anonymization, de-anonymization attacks, and de-anonymizability quantification: a survey. IEEE Commun. Surv. Tutor. **2**, 1305–1326 (2016)

10. Cao, J., Karras, P.: Publishing microdata with a robust privacy guarantee. Proc. VLDB Endow. **5**, 1388–1399 (2012)
11. Brickell, J., Shmatikov, V.: The cost of privacy: destruction of data-mining utility in anonymized data publishing. In: Proceedings of the 14th ACM SIGKDD International Conference on Knowledge Discovery and Data Mining (2008)
12. Karanam, S., Gou, M., Wu, Z., Rates-Borras, A., Camps, O., Radke, R.J.: A systematic evaluation and benchmark for person re-identification: Features, metrics, and datasets. arXiv preprint arXiv:1605.09653 (2016)
13. Limniotis, K., Hansen, M.: Recommendations on shaping technology according to GDPR provisions - an overview on data pseudonymisation (2018)
14. LeFevre, K., De Witt, D.J., Ramakrishnan, R.: Mondrian multidimensional k-anonymity, p. 25 (2006)
15. Sweeney, L., Samarati, P.: Protecting privacy when disclosing information: k-anonymity and its enforcement through generalization and suppression (1999)
16. Sion, L., Yskout, K., Van Landuyt, D., Joosen, W.: Risk-based design security analysis. In: 2018 ACM/IEEE 1st International Workshop on Security Awareness from Design to Deployment (2018)
17. Lee, Y.J., Lee, K.H.: What are the optimum quasi-identifiers to re-identify medical records? In: 2018 20th International Conference on Advanced Communication Technology (ICACT), pp. 1025–1033. IEEE (2018)
18. Liu, Z., Qamar, N., Qian, J.: A quantitative analysis of the performance and scalability of de-identification tools for medical data. In: Gibbons, J., MacCaull, W. (eds.) FHIES 2013. LNCS, vol. 8315, pp. 274–289. Springer, Heidelberg (2014). https://doi.org/10.1007/978-3-642-53956-5_18
19. Machanavajjhala, A., Gehrke, J., Kifer, D.: L-diversity: privacy beyond k-anonymity. In: 22nd International Conference on Data Engineering (ICDE 2006). IEEE (2006)
20. Templ, M., Meindl, B.: Robust statistics meets SDC: new disclosure risk measures for continuous microdata masking. In: Domingo-Ferrer, J., Saygın, Y. (eds.) PSD 2008. LNCS, vol. 5262, pp. 177–189. Springer, Heidelberg (2008). https://doi.org/10.1007/978-3-540-87471-3_15
21. Nergiz, M.E., Atzori, M., Clifton, C.: Hiding the presence of individuals from shared databases. In: Proceedings of the 2007 ACM SIGMOD International Conference on Management of Data (2007)
22. Salari, M., Jalili, S., Mortazavi, R.: A utility preserving data-oriented anonymization method based on data ordering. In: 7th International Symposium on Telecommunications. IEEE (2014)
23. Nelson, G.S.: Practical implications of sharing data: a primer on data privacy, anonymization, and de-identification. In: SAS Global Forum Proceedings (2015)
24. Li, N., Li, T., Venkatasubramanian, S.: t-closeness: privacy beyond k-anonymity and l-diversity (2007)
25. Pfitzmann, A., Hansen, M.: A terminology for talking about privacy by data minimization: anonymity, unlinkability, undetectability, unobservability, pseudonymity, and identity management, v0.34 (2010). http://dud.inf.tu-dresden.de/literatur/Anon_Terminology_v0.34.pdf
26. Xiong, P., Zhu, T.: An anonymization method based on tradeoff between utility and privacy for data publishing. In: International Conference on Management of e-Commerce and e-Government. IEEE (2012)
27. Podgursky, B.: Practical k-anonymity on large datasets. Master's thesis. Vanderbilt University, Nashville, Tennessee, May 2011

28. Porter, C.C.: De-identified data and third party data mining: the risk of reidentification of personal information. 5 Shidler J.L. Com. and Tech. 3 (2008)
29. Tang, Q., Wu, Y., Liao, S.: Utility-based k-anonymization. In: 6th International Conference on Networked Computing and Advanced Information Management. IEEE (2010)
30. Ribaric, S., Ariyaeeinia, A., Pavesic, N.: De-identification for privacy protection in multimedia content: a survey. Signal Process. Image Commun. **47**, 131–151 (2016)
31. Solove, D.J.: A taxonomy of privacy. Univ. PA Law Rev. **154**(3), 477 (2006)
32. Morton, S., Mahoui, M., Gibson, P.J., Yechuri, S.: An enhanced utility-driven data anonymization method. Trans. Data Priv. **5**, 469–503 (2012)
33. The European Parliament and the Council of the European Union: Regulation (EU) 2016/679 General Data Protection Regulation. Official Journal of the European Union, pp. 1–88, May 2016
34. UC Berkeley School of Information: Privacy patterns (2018). https://privacypatterns.org/
35. Wan, Z., Vorobeychik, Y., Xia, W., Clayton, E.W., Kantarcioglu, M., Ganta, R., Heatherly, R., Malin, B.A.: A game theoretic framework for analyzing re-identification risk. PLoS ONE **10**(3), e0120592 (2015)
36. Zuccona, G., Kotzur, D., Nguyen, A., Bergheim, A.: De-identification of health records using Anonym: effectiveness and robustness across datasets. Artif. Intell. Med. **61**, 145–151 (2014)

DEFeND Architecture: A Privacy by Design Platform for GDPR Compliance

Luca Piras[1]([⊠]), Mohammed Ghazi Al-Obeidallah[1], Andrea Praitano[2,3],
Aggeliki Tsohou[4], Haralambos Mouratidis[1], Beatriz Gallego-Nicasio Crespo[5],
Jean Baptiste Bernard[6], Marco Fiorani[6], Emmanouil Magkos[4],
Andrès Castillo Sanz[7], Michalis Pavlidis[1], Roberto D'Addario[2],
and Giuseppe Giovanni Zorzino[2,3]

[1] Centre for Secure, Intelligent and Usable Systems,
University of Brighton, Brighton, UK
{l.piras,m.al-obeidallah2,h.mouratidis,m.pavlidis}@brighton.ac.uk
[2] Maticmind SpA, Rome, Italy
{andrea.praitano,roberto.daddario,giuseppe.zorzino}@maticmind.it
[3] UNIHermes, Rome, Italy
{andrea.praitano,giuseppe.zorzino}@unihermes.org
[4] Ionian University, Corfu, Greece
{atsohou,emagos}@ionio.gr
[5] Atos, Madrid, Spain
beatriz.gallego-nicasio@atos.net
[6] Gridpocket SAS, Valbonne Sophia Antipolis, France
{jean-baptiste.bernard,marco.fiorani}@gridpocket.com
[7] International University of La Rioja UNIR, Madrid, Spain
andres.castillo@unir.net

Abstract. The advent of the European General Data Protection Regulation (GDPR) imposes organizations to cope with radical changes concerning user data protection paradigms. GDPR, by promoting a Privacy by Design approach, obliges organizations to drastically change their methods regarding user data acquisition, management, processing, as well as data breaches monitoring, notification and preparation of prevention plans. This enforces data subjects (e.g., citizens, customers) rights by enabling them to have more information regarding usage of their data, and to take decisions (e.g., revoking usage permissions). Moreover, organizations are required to trace precisely their activities on user data, enabling authorities to monitor and sanction more easily. Indeed, since GDPR has been introduced, authorities have heavily sanctioned companies found as not GDPR compliant. GDPR is difficult to apply also for its length, complexity, covering many aspects, and not providing details concerning technical and organizational security measures to apply. This calls for tools and methods able to support organizations in achieving GDPR compliance. From the industry and the literature, there are many tools and prototypes fulfilling specific/isolated GDPR aspects, however there is not a comprehensive platform able to support organizations in

© Springer Nature Switzerland AG 2019
S. Gritzalis et al. (Eds.): TrustBus 2019, LNCS 11711, pp. 78–93, 2019.
https://doi.org/10.1007/978-3-030-27813-7_6

being compliant regarding all GDPR requirements. In this paper, we propose the design of an architecture for such a platform, able to reuse and integrate peculiarities of those heterogeneous tools, and to support organizations in achieving GDPR compliance. We describe the architecture, designed within the DEFeND EU project, and discuss challenges and preliminary benefits in applying it to the healthcare and energy domains.

Keywords: Privacy by design · Privacy engineering ·
Security engineering · Data protection · GDPR

1   Introduction

Information and Communication Technologies (ICT) playes a significant role in the every-day life. New technological advances such as Cloud Computing, Internet of Things and Big Data provide benefits and have changed the way we store, access and exchange information. The rapid development and advances in ICT have led to their adoption by organizations (enabling them to transform business to digital services, increasing efficiency), public authorities (enabling them to provide new services to citizens and to reduce complexity) and individuals (enabling them to communicate and share personal information faster and efficiently).

However, together with all the benefits that such technologies bring, opportunities (deliberate or accidental) for misuse of citizen data are also created mostly due to lack of control over management and privacy issues of citizen data. To react to such challenge, organizations have to adopt solutions that support with an end-to-end data protection governance, which can adapt to the specific characteristics of different sectors. To cover these regulatory gaps, and to force organizations to guarantee citizens rights, the European General Data Protection Regulation (GDPR) has been proposed. Even though GDPR aims to enforce and guarantee data subjects (e.g., citizens, customers) rights - for instance, enabling data subjects to be more aware regarding the usage of their data, and taking decisions over them (e.g., revoking usage permissions, asking for a fast data removal) -, it is important to note that it introduced also important challenges and difficulties for organizations, which led in many cases, since GDPR is in force, organizations to pay heavy fines for not being fully GDPR compliant [3].

Organizations are facing those problems for many reasons. Most of them are related to the nature of GDPR, which is a very long, complex regulation, covering many aspects, not providing details concerning technical and organizational privacy and security measures needed, and therefore it is difficult for organizations to be fully GDPR compliant. In fact, GDPR, by promoting a Privacy by Design and Privacy by Default approach, obliges organizations, in a not clear way, to change heavily their methods regarding the acquisition, management, processing of user data, as well as the monitoring of data breaches, notification, and definition of prevention plans for reducing the possibility that breaches happen, and to reduce also the potential damage. To be GDPR compliant, organizations are required also to trace precisely activities performed on user data, and are required to supply authorities with detailed information on this. Thus, authorities are enabled to monitor and to sanction more easily the organizations.

Therefore, organizations need tools and methods able to support and guide them in achieving full GDPR compliance [11]. This means, for instance, a support for: **(i)** analysing and understanding the current GDPR compliance level of an organization; **(ii)** selecting which GDPR aspects should be fulfilled by the organization (i.e. not all GDPR aspects should be satisfied by all the organizations; in fact it depends on the current situation, business and needs of the specific organization, and, thus, the challenge is to understand which subset of GDPR should be addressed); **(iii)** understanding which are the actions required to achieve GDPR compliance, preparing a plan for this, and having ready-to-use items and guidance for carrying out this complex process; **(iv)** providing the user with functionalities for exercising her rights; **(v)** being prepared to provide authorities with the documentation expected, and to interact with them.

Within a European project[1], we reviewed tools and prototypes from the industry and the literature, and found that there are many tools and prototypes able to fulfil specific/isolated GDPR aspects, however a comprehensive platform able to support organizations in being GDPR compliant in relation to all the GDPR requirements does not exist. In this work, we propose the design of an architecture for such a platform, able to reuse and integrate peculiarities of those heterogeneous tools, and to support organizations in achieving GDPR compliance. This paper presents an architectural solution to this challenge, which empower organizations to protect personal data according to GDPR, and that is applicable to heterogeneous sectors. Specifically, in this work, we describe the architecture that has been designed within a EU project, the Data govErnance For supportiNg gDpr (DEFeND (See footnote 1), and discuss challenges and preliminary benefits in the application of it to the healthcare and energy sectors.

The rest of the paper is organized as follows: Sect. 2 presents the conceptual idea around the DEFeND platform and the methodological and technical approach adopted. The architectural design and functionalities of the DEFeND platform are explained in Sect. 3. Section 4 presents multi sectors piloting of the platform, and Sect. 5 provides the related work, and compares it with the DEFeND solution. Finally, conclusions and future work are discussed in Sect. 6.

2 The Conceptual Foundations of the DEFeND Platform

We start illustrating conceptual aspects and challenges of the DEFeND platform. Then, we describe our methodological and technical approach for tackling this.

---

[1] DEFeND is a EU H2020 project: https://www.defendproject.eu/.

2.1 The DEFeND Concept and Challenges

DEFeND (See footnote 1) is an Innovation Action project focusing on improving existing software tools and frameworks, designing and developing new integration software, driven by market needs, to deliver a unique organizational data privacy governance platform, for facilitating data scoping, processing, data breach management, by a privacy by design approach, and supporting organizations for GDPR compliance. To comply with GDPR, organizations have to implement in their processes different tools, solutions, and practices, as to inherently integrate privacy in those ones. Thus, it is fundamental for the DEFeND platform to provide a solution that not only supports compliance of the relevant GDPR articles, with a privacy by design approach, but also that fulfils specific organizations' needs.

GDPR considers many different aspects, and calls for the collaboration of heterogeneous professionals, with different skills and responsibilities in the organization. Professionals receive GDPR compliance support by different tools, each one covering only a small subset of GDPR aspects. Thus, the main challenge for the DEFeND platform is to provide support for all the different aspects for achieving GDPR compliance, according to the specific requirements of an organization. Main goals of DEFeND are to have: (i) a comprehensive platform able to support the organization in whole GDPR compliance; (ii) a platform able to fit heterogeneous contexts and dimensions of organizations; (iii) a modular, extensible platform that the organization can extend through tools and solutions based on its needs.

2.2 Methodological and Technical Approach

The DEFeND Platform is based on a novel technical approach we call Data Privacy Governance for Supporting GDPR (DEFeND) (See footnote 1). To support the modular approach and the GDPR compliance, we designed the platform architecture with a series of software components based on solutions that focus on each of the areas of GDPR [1] (e.g. conceptual languages to support privacy-by-design [11] or automated tools to support consent management). The DEFeND platform works as an orchestrator of the functionalities provided by the different components. We follow a Model-Driven Privacy Governance (MDPG) technical approach that enables building and analysing, from an abstract to a concrete level, privacy related models by following a Privacy-by-Design approach that spans over two levels, the Planning Level and the Operational Level, and across three management areas, i.e. Data Scope, Data Process and Data Breach as shown in Fig. 1. The DEFeND platform at the planning level (Fig. 1) focuses on supporting the development of models of the Organizational Data, which capture information required for GDPR compliance such as identification of Data and Assets, Organizational Info and Establishments, Data Transparency, Lawfulness and Minimization, Personal Data Consent and Data Breach Information [3]. At the operational level, the platform supports the transformation of planning models to operational models, which are used to perform analysis

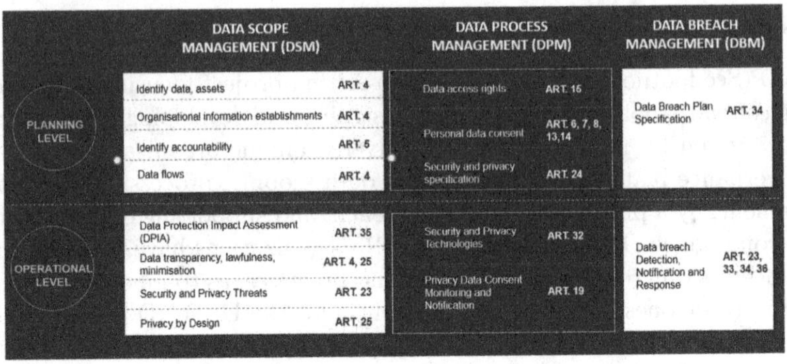

Fig. 1. Three management areas and two operational levels of DEFeND platform

for Data minimisation, Data Protection Impact Assessments, Privacy-by-Design and Privacy-by-Default principles [3]. The platform includes also functionalities to support GDPR reporting and notifications to data controllers/processors, consent and data breach notifications to Data Subjects, and GDPR Organizational Reporting to relevant authorities.

Moreover, we designed the DEFeND platform and architecture also on the basis of four procedural pillars: (i) *User Engagement* of heterogeneous kinds of stakeholders [14] (i.e. local public administration authorities, employees and citizens) from early stages of platform development, definition of functional and non-functional requirements (e.g., privacy, security, legal and acceptance requirements [14]), specification of realistic pilots and software validation; (ii) *Integration* of the various components through interconnected activities via implementation of appropriate interfaces and linkage mechanisms; (iii) *Piloting*, i.e. validation via real-life pilots in the healthcare, energy, banking, public administration sectors; (iv) *Training* via a program based on deep analyses of pilot organizations and their needs (e.g., software acceptance needs [14]), for creating awareness of privacy issues and privacy culture in the organization.

3   The Architecture of the DEFeND Platform

The architecture of the DEFeND Platform, shown in Fig. 2, is composed of 5 main services: *Data Scope Management Service, Data Process Management Service, Data Breach Management Service, GDPR Planning Service and GDPR Reporting Service.*

Each one assists organizations to collect, analyse and operationalize different aspects and articles of GDPR [1], and provides appropriate reporting capabilities. To support those services, the platform consists of 5 back-end components: Data Assessment Component, Data Privacy Analysis Component, Privacy Specification Component, Privacy Implementation and Monitoring Component, Data Breach Component. Each component includes modules that are the result of the extension of software tools, services and frameworks (described in the related

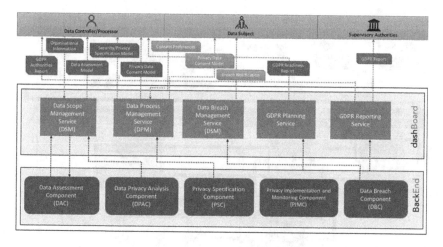

Fig. 2. The DEFeND platform architecture with dashboard, services and components

work section), developed within national and international projects. The platform has a dashboard working as front-end among the platform and its users.

We designed the platform in a modular, flexible way, by following a Model-Driven Privacy Governance (MDPG) technical approach, and our novel DEFeND approach, we call Data Privacy Governance for Supporting GDPR (DEFeND (See footnote 1), Sect. 2.2). Its modular, flexible architecture helps to increase the possibility to employ it in as many as possible heterogeneous domains, with different organizational needs. While, our DEFeND approach helped us in designing an architecture that, through its components, covers each areas of GDPR [1] (Fig. 2). Furthermore, its MDPG components support a privacy by design workflow, by employing conceptual languages and automated tools [11]. Moreover, thanks to our DEFeND and MDPG approaches, we designed architectural components supporting a privacy by design workflow able to guide, from abstract to concrete levels, the analysis of privacy related models spanning over 2 levels, the Planning Level and the Operational Level, and across 3 management areas, i.e. Data Scope, Data Process and Data Breach (Figs. 1 and 2). The next subsections describe the architectural components, modules, interactions, workflow, and dashboard.

3.1 Data Assessment Component (DAC)

DAC (Fig. 3) supports the elicitation of organizational information and transforms them for the Data Analysis Privacy Component. DAC is based on next modules.

Organization Data Collection (ODC) Module. ODC, extending BE-Assess tool[2], provides an Organizational Data Questionnaire collecting information

---

[2] https://www.maticmind.it/.

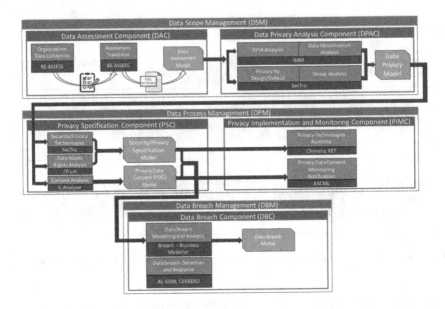

Fig. 3. Main components of the DEFeND platform and their interactions

related to organizational scope, list of data processing, status of privacy processes and activities. It is used by the organization (data controller and data processor/s) to evaluate the status of the organization regarding parts relevant to GDPR. Moreover, ODC allows organizations to create a self-characterisation (e.g., size, available privacy/GDPR expertise) for recommending specific modules of the DEFeND Platform that the organization requires.

Assessment Translator (ATr) Module. ATr, extending BE-Assess tool (See footnote 2), takes as input the Organizational Data Questionnaire from ODC, and translates it into an XML schema used to create the Data Assessment Model (DAM). DAM is a goal-based requirement engineering model of organizational data, including information concerning organization actors, assets, establishments and data flows.

3.2 Data Privacy Analysis Component (DPAC)

On the basis of DAM, DPAC performs Data Protection Impact Assessment, Data Minimisation analysis and Privacy-by-Design/Default and Threat analysis (Fig. 3). Analysis results are used for creating the Data Privacy Model. Such model provides a strategic conceptual model that clearly defines operational aspects of Data Scope Management and supports organizations to deal with GDPR [3]. DPAC can perform these activities on the basis of the RAM (See footnote 2) and SecTro tools [11], and by extending them with the next modules.

DPIA Analysis (DPIA) Module. It is based on the RAM (See footnote 2) tool. It enables organizations to measure and review their privacy level, and if necessary proposes design changes. Moreover, it includes safeguards privacy/security measures for mitigating potential risks. Its analysis results are used to create DPM.

Privacy-by-Design/Default (PbD) Module. This is based on the state-of-the-art goal-oriented security and privacy requirements engineering method Secure Tropos [11]. The method and its tool are extended to support the GDPR privacy by design/default requirement. PbD supports organizations in understanding security and privacy requirements, and design systems and services fulfilling those requirements. This "forces" organizations to deeply consider privacy since first phases of the software engineering process and not as an afterthought.

Data Minimisation Analysis (DMAn) Module. DMAn extends RAM (See footnote 2) for supporting the analysis of data usage for ensuring the application of the data minimisation principle of GDPR, fostering organizations to process only personal data needed to achieve processing purposes.

Threat Analysis (ThAn) Module. This enables the modelling and analysis of privacy threats on personal data held by organizations. Threat analysis includes identification of relevant vulnerabilities, attack methods and potential malicious actors. ThAn, extending SecTro [11] and RAE[3] tools, supports threat assessment through combining different sources of information such as vulnerability scans and real-time monitoring of the infrastructure.

3.3   Privacy Specification Component (PSC)

PSC processes DPM through the following modules.

Consent Analysis (CAn) Module. This takes the organizational privacy information included in DPM and data subject consent preferences from data subjects (requested through the DEFeND Platform dashboard). CAn extends CAnalyzer[4] and Privacy Level Agreements to support elicitation, analysis and specification of data subject consent and creates a Data Privacy Consent (DPC) Specification in the form of Data Privacy Consent Model (DPCM). DPCM is used by the Privacy Implementation and Monitoring Component (PIMC) to visualize, monitor and enforce data subject consent.

Data Access Rights Analysis (DARA) Module. DARA extends JTrust [11] and EPICA (See footnote 3) tools supporting generation of policies for controlling data access, usage and information processing. It supports elicitation, modelling and analysis of data access rights scenarios by analysing potential access requests, how these are processed within the organization, and how information is provided to the data subject. Analysis results feed the Security/Privacy Specification Model.

Security/Privacy Technologies (STT) Module. This supports the selection of optimal security/privacy configurations with respect to criteria such as security/privacy requirements priorities and the severity of threats. Specifically, it extends SecTro [11] supporting expressions related to mitigation level of threats

---

[3] https://atos.net/en/.
[4] https://www.visioneuproject.eu/.

and goals of the systems (e.g., cost and performance) as cost-functions to be optimized. STT output feeds the Security/Privacy Specification Model.

3.4 Privacy Implementation and Monitoring Component (PIMC)

PIMC leverages the Privacy Data Consent Model and the Security/Privacy Specification Model for supporting run-time implementation of privacy technologies and monitoring, enforcement and notification of the Privacy Data Consent. PIMC has been designed with the next modules.

Privacy Technologies Runtime (PCR) Module. On the basis of models, obtained via PSC, this module guarantees the execution of the relevant security/privacy technologies across three main areas: encryption (extending KET (See footnote 3)), authorisation (extending EPICA (See footnote 3)) and anonymization (extending CHIMERA[5]). In terms of encryption, it supports key management and encryption of relevant sensitive data using a wide range of different encryption strategies to fulfil needs of as many as possible heterogeneous organizations. Regarding authorisation, it controls access based on the specification derived from the Data Access Rights Analysis, covering also location and time aspects. Concerning anonymization, PCR supports ingestion of data (structured and non-structured) and a high-level Domain Specific Language for data transformation and anonymization.

Privacy Data Consent Monitoring and Notification (PDCMN) Module. It is based on the XACML (See footnote 3) and EPICA (See footnote 3) tools, and includes a Privacy Data Consent Monitoring enforcer and notifier. It supports organizations to enforce and monitor the Privacy Data Consent Model, by automatically filtering traffic and removing data that the data subject has not consented to share. Furthermore, if there is an attempt to share data without appropriate consent, PDCMN provides a notification to both data controllers and data subjects.

3.5 Data Breach Component (DBC)

DBC is responsible for modelling, analysing, detecting and responding to data breaches. On the basis of the Security/Privacy Specification Model and the Privacy Data Consent Model, provided by PSC, it enables organizations to develop, at planning stage, a data breach model, which is then used at run-time to detect, notify and respond to data breaches. It includes next modules (Fig. 3).

Data Breach Modelling and Analysis (DBMA) Module. By extending the Business Modeller tool [11], DBMA supports organizations to create the Data Breach Model. A model including a representation of the organization business processes, along with data flows and relevant security and privacy requirements. DBMA also supports analysis, on the model, for the definition of response plans to potential threats and data breaches.

---

[5] https://www.pdmfc.com/.

Data Breach Detection and Response (DBD) Module. It is based on the XL-SIEM[6] and CERBERO[7] tools, for providing an information management system receiving input from various sources (both from the platform, for instance DBM, and from external sources such as threat identification websites), evaluating such information and detecting, notifying and responding to potential data breaches. DBD generates a data breach bulletin offering information concerning potential data breaches, and notifies organizations about data breaches.

3.6 Platform Dashboard

The platform dashboard (top of Fig. 2) acts as a front-end between users (Data Controllers/Processors, Data Subjects and Supervisory Authorities) and platform back-end components. On the one hand, it provides organizations with control over creation, deployment, and monitoring of data privacy governance strategies helping them to achieve GDPR compliance. On the other hand, it enables data subjects to use the platform offering consent related activities required by GDPR.

Specifically, the dashboard provides organizations with privacy related capabilities to: (**i**) *Input organizational Info into the platform*, supported by DAC through an easy to understand and interactive questionnaire; (**ii**) *Create, View and modify organizational Privacy related models*, concerning the Data Assessment Model, Data Privacy Model, Security/Privacy Specification Model, Privacy Data Consent Model, and Data Breach model; (**iii**) *Implement Privacy Technologies*, enabled through PIMC; (**iv**) *Monitor and Receive notifications about data subject consent and data breaches*, supplied by PIMC and DBC; (**v**) *Monitor and evaluate GDPR compliance readiness*, supported by PIMC and DBC.

The dashboard provides data subjects with functionalities to: (**i**) *Define Consent Preferences*, allowed through the Consent Analyzer of PSC; the input is taken into account on the creation of the Data Privacy Consent model, which is used to monitor and enforce data subject consent management; (**ii**) *Receive Notification about Consent violations*, obtained through the Privacy Data Consent Monitoring and Notification module of PIMC; (**iii**) *Receive notifications about data breach*, offered through the Data Breach Component (DBC).

Finally, the dashboard includes specific GDPR supporting modules: (**i**) a *GDPR Planning Service* that supports the collection of information from the platform models, and its visualisation based on GDPR requirements; the result is a visual representation of the GDPR readiness of the organization and the ability to define a plan of action to achieve compliance; (**ii**) a *GDPR Reporting Service* that supports the collection of information required for GDPR reporting purposes; such information is encapsulated in the platform models, and can be visualised through the dashboard and shared with authorities.

---

[6] https://atos.net/en/.
[7] https://www.maticmind.it/.

4   Multi Sectors Piloting of the Platform

In the next 2 subsections, we discuss challenges and preliminary benefits in the application of the DEFeND platform to the healthcare and energy sectors.

4.1   Challenges and DEFeND Benefits in the Energy Sector

The recent and massive deployment of Smart Meters in many EU countries has raised many questions linked to privacy and data protection rights. Smart meters are a new generation of energy consumption readers, capable of connecting via digital networks, sending real time information back to energy grid consumption systems, and monitoring companies with a high temporal resolution rate [16]. The appearance of this technology has been relatively controversial. Part of the population sees it as a remarkable tool to control and improve energy efficiency. The other part of the population sees it as a sensitive tool, able to save and report critical information regarding household behaviour and life.

Ensuring privacy and security of smart meter data is a major challenge for energy companies, due to the degree of privacy and data protection that is mandated by GDPR. This is a difficult task for many reasons: first, the deregulation of the market in many EU countries created a lot of new energy data management companies including many Small and Medium-sized Enterprises (SMEs). SMEs, even more than big companies, have lots of difficulties with GDPR, and are missing a complete platform able to support them in being GDPR compliant concerning all the GDPR requirements. Second, utility companies often need to involve third service providers to collect, process and display to end-users the large amount of information sensed by smart meters.

The DEFeND platform is expected to provide a strong technical support for companies from the energy sector concerning achieving GDPR compliance. In particular, utility companies expect DEFeND to be able to identify their needs in terms of security and personal data. This can be done based on preliminary assessments to evaluate the structure and the nature of data, processes, roles of different controllers/processors of involved companies. DEFeND will be able also to identify decisive security measures thanks to its new methodological and technical approach. The challenge is to satisfy GDPR aspects for heterogeneous actors, with different needs, among customers, end-users, and third parties.

4.2   Challenges and DEFeND Benefits in the Healthcare Sector

GDPR defines health data as personal data relating to physical or mental health of a natural person, including provision of health care services, which reveal information concerning health status. Thus, medical information is high sensitive personal data (e.g. a disease, a disability). Due to the nature of this data, GDPR requires additional security measures for processing such information. Within those processes fundamental elements are to be considered such as the consent, quality of data, information to patients and confidentiality. The main legal basis for the treatment of sensitive data is the consent [3]. According to GDPR, this should be explicit and cannot be collected in unfair or fraudulent ways.

Within the DEFeND healthcare pilot, documentation referring to clinical-statistic sheets, entry authorization and urgency report will be considered. In the related processes, patients must be informed of the existence of these files, related purposes, possible recipients of information, the identity and address of maintainers and the possibility of exercising their rights. It is mandatory, in each health centre, the existence of an information sheet, at disposal of the patient, where authorization for data processing can be requested. It includes, for instance, name of the professional, the centre where the patient has been treated, purposes, and should express the publication agreement of the clinical case directed to health professionals. The professional secret is mandatory and medical centres must adopt necessary measures to guarantee confidentiality and legal access procedures for staff members.

To guarantee the correct recollection and storage of all this documentation, a platform directly designed for the healthcare domain is needed. Thus, the DEFeND platform will be integrated in the hospital information system to help privacy officers of health centres to comply with GDPR. For example, consent management has been always a big issue due to the vast paperwork involved. Thus, it is needed to complement existing software for health records with a platform that allows, patients and the clinicians, to be sure regarding the correspondence among health data treatments and the consent given. DEFeND consortium is developing the platform in collaboration with data protection officers of hospitals. Privacy by design will be applied with the concrete needs of healthcare institutions and patients. DEFeND will grant patients, and their tutors, the actual exertion of rights regarding data concerning their health, which is stored usually in a distributed way over several centres.

5   Related Work

The next two Subsections describe the novelty of the DEFeND platform and its architecture compared respectively to the industry situation and the literature.

5.1   Industry Comparison

According to the 2018 Privacy Tech Vendor Report from IAAP [2], the number of vendors providing privacy management technologies has doubled in one year, and some of the existing ones have enhanced offerings with new services. Despite the remarkable increase in the market offering, the report highlights also: "there is no single vendor that will automatically make an organization GDPR compliant" [2].

Solutions are classified in the IAAP's report into 2 main categories: Privacy Program Management and Enterprise Privacy Management, considering overall business needs. The first are grouped into 6 subcategories: assessment managers, consent managers, data mapping, incident response, privacy information managers and website scanning. The second are grouped in 4 subcategories: activity monitoring, data discovery, de-identification/pseudonymity and enterprise communications. None of the listed vendors is able to provide solutions that cover all the 10 sub-categories. AvePoint is the most complete vendor according to IAAP's report, offering numerous solutions that provide functionalities covering all sub-categories except for the enterprise communications. Functionalities offered by the DEFeND platform also cover 9 subcategories: all except the privacy information management subcategory. Contrary to AvePoint, DEFeND provides organizations with the capability to employ 1 platform for all GDPR compliance issues, during GDPR assessment, implementation, monitoring and response.

Forrester [1] released a report evaluating the 12 most significant providers in the market of EU GDPR compliance and privacy management. Providers offer privacy management platforms supplying services across geographies and reporting capabilities associated to a dashboard. Platforms are evaluated against 10 criteria. One important conclusion of the report is that a functionality such as data discovery across systems, is a key feature to avoid bad consequences of doing such task manually (i.e. inaccuracies, guesswork), and increases assurance in terms of accountability. DEFeND supports this functionality via the Organization Data Collection module, where organizational data is collected and automatically transformed to a Data Assessment Model. In addition, Data Privacy Impact Assessments (DPIA) functionality is considered a powerful feature by Forrester's analysis. DEFeND uniquely integrates privacy-by-design approaches with DPIA, and threat analysis, at planning level to create a set of tools enabling organizations to develop new services and systems in accordance with GDPR.

5.2   Research Novelty

The DEFeND Platform has been conceptualised around three axes of privacy protection, i.e. Privacy By Design, Consent Management and Privacy Impact Assessment and Risk Management, all related to the general obligations for controllers and processors for GDPR compliance. In the following paragraphs, we explain the novelties that DEFeND introduces in all these three areas.

Privacy by Design. Various methodologies and patterns have been developed to ensure that systems and services are designed with respect to privacy. Problem-based Security Requirements Elicitation (PresSuRE) uses problem diagrams to support modelling of functional requirements, where every functional requirement of each asset is related with possible threats and security requirements [6]. In [5], a privacy threat analysis framework for privacy requirements elicitation and selection is designed. Privacy threats were identified, related to DFD elements and prioritised through risk assessment. Privacy Safeguard (PriS) [8], a privacy requirement engineering methodology, considers privacy requirements as organizational goals and uses privacy-process patterns to describe the impact of privacy goals to the affected organizational processes. A threat based approach to elicit privacy requirements, LINDDUN, is proposed by [5], which includes a systematic methodology and catalogue of privacy related threat tree patterns. The authors propose a mapping of privacy threat types to system components that are modelled with Data Flow Diagrams (DFDs). Once privacy threat types are identified, then are further refined with the help of privacy threat tree patterns specifically developed for each threat type. Finally, authors present a mapping of privacy requirements to existing Privacy Enhancing Technologies (PETs) in order to support analysts that are not experts in privacy technologies. The PRIPARE (PReparing Industry to Privacy by Design by supporting its Application in REsearch) methodology [7] is the result of a European Union funded project, which aims to integrate existing practices and research proposals on privacy engineering. It contains 7 phases enabling analysts to consider privacy issues.

The DEFeND platform advances the above state-of-the-art by facilitating organizations to implement a privacy management approach, which takes into account Privacy by Design, enabling them to (re)design their processes with respect to their privacy requirements, at an operational level. In other words, the DEFeND platform integrates privacy recommendations and suggestions on implementing privacy requirements from the early stage of service and software development. Moreover, such privacy recommendations and suggestions are assigned to agents, but without further justification of whether the agents can be trusted to take them, they remain just assumptions, which may prove wrong and lead to privacy breaches [12]. Trust-based concepts enable the developer to identify trust relationships and to analyse the identified trust relationships so that trust assumptions regarding privacy are valid [13]. Therefore, the DEFeND project facilitates further trust analysis which is required in order to justify that privacy requirements will be met by the suggested privacy implementations.

Consent Management. Research studies have demonstrated that obtaining user consent is difficult. First, the mechanism used widely for obtaining user consent is privacy policies and notices, however users do not read them [10]. Hence, consent becomes invalid and not informed [15]. Further, even if users read the privacy policies, their understanding is hindered by the legal and technical terminology and the difficulty to follow long texts [4]. Several more factors contribute to this situation making the obtained consent not informed [15]. Considering data subjects have the right to revoke their consent at any time, organizations should provide the flexibility to them to withdraw consent as easily as they gave it, making the "rights management process" as simple as possible.

The DEFeND platform approaches Consent Management in a holistic way, delivering a Privacy Data Consent (PDC) to users which will act as a contract among the data controller and data subject, encapsulating all the necessary information regarding the consent of the processing to their personal data. At operational level, the platform, based on the PDC, will monitor and enforce data subject's preferences, and will notify users if any inconsistency will be identified.

Privacy Impact Assessment and Risk Management. Risk management is based on the experience and knowledge of best practice methods. International risk management standards are used to support risks or threats identification, as well as to assess their probabilities. To structure the process of risk assessment, there are various attempts to develop ontologies for general risk assessments [9].

Privacy Impact Assessments (PIAs) can be used to identify and reduce privacy risks of projects. The UK Information Commissioner Office (ICO) has developed a set of steps and principles of the code of practice for conducting privacy impact assessment. The code explains the key principles behind a PIA and recommends that a PIA should be undertaken for any project that will either involve the use of personal data or have other impact on the privacy of individuals. The DEFeND platform advances the current state of the art in Data Protection Impact Assessment by providing an in-depth processing analysis based on a recognized methodology and based on international standards. This analysis will be performed in a easy and user-friendly interface, and it will not need a specific knowledge and expertise in security and/or risk analysis to be performed.

6   Conclusions

This work presents the architecture of the platform developed within the Data govErnance For supportiNg gDpr (DEFeND) (See footnote 1) EU project, and discusses challenges and preliminary benefits of its application to healthcare and energy sectors.

The aim of the DEFeND platform is to support organizations in achieving compliance with the European General Data Protection Regulation (GDPR), by following a Privacy by Design approach. Obtaining GDPR compliance for organizations is a very complex, difficult and expensive task. This is due to the vastness and complexity of GDPR, covering many data protection aspects, and requiring organizations to adopt multiple heterogeneous security measures, remaining abstract and not providing organizations with clear, concrete technological indications. In the industry and in the literature, there are many tools and prototypes able to cover only a very reduced set of GDPR aspects. Thus, the DEFeND platform covers this gap, by proposing a comprehensive platform satisfying the full complexity of GDPR, through an architectural design able to integrate and reuse the most relevant peculiarities of heterogeneous available tools, making them to collaborate as architectural components providing organizations with a Privacy by Design workflow.

Finally, in this paper we discuss also challenges and preliminary benefits in the application of the DEFeND platform to healthcare and energy sectors. As future work, we will evaluate the platform also within banking and public administration pilots in real and realistic scenarios.

Acknowledgments. This work was partially supported by the DEFeND EU project, funded from the European Unions Horizon 2020 research and innovation programme under grant agreement No 787068.

References

1. The Forrester New Wave^{TM}. https://www.forrester.com/report/The%20Forrester%20New%20Wave%20GDPR%20And%20Privacy%20Management%20Software%20Q4%202018/-/E-RES142698
2. Privacy Tech Vendor Report. https://iapp.org/resources/article/2018-privacy-tech-vendor-report/
3. Regulation 2016/679 and Directive 95/46/EC (GDPR) of the EU on the processing of personal data and on the free movement of such data (2016). https://publications.europa.eu/en/publication-detail/-/publication/3e485e15-11bd-11e6-ba9a-01aa75ed71a1/language-en
4. Capistrano, E.P.S., Chen, J.V.: Information privacy policies: the effects of policy characteristics and online experience. Comput. Stand. Interfaces **42**, 24–31 (2015)
5. Deng, M., Wuyts, K., Scandariato, R., Preneel, B., Joosen, W.: A privacy threat analysis framework: supporting the elicitation and fulfillment of privacy requirements. Requir. Eng. J. **16**, 3–32 (2011)
6. Faßbender, S., Heisel, M., Meis, R.: Problem-based security requirements elicitation and refinement with pressure (2015)
7. Garcia: PRIPARE privacy by design methodology handbook. Technical report (2015)
8. Kalloniatis, C., Belsis, P., Gritzalis, S.: A soft computing approach for privacy requirements engineering: the PRiS framework. Appl. Soft Comput. **11**, 4341–4348 (2011)
9. Mayer, N., Dubois, E., Matulevicius, R., Heymans, P.: Towards a measurement framework for security risk management
10. McDonald, A.M., Cranor, L.F.: The cost of reading privacy policies. ISJLP **4**, 543 (2008)
11. Mouratidis, H., Argyropoulos, N., Shei, S.: Security requirements engineering for cloud computing: the secure tropos approach. In: Karagiannis, D., Mayr, H., Mylopoulos, J. (eds.) Domain-Specific Conceptual Modeling, pp. 357–380. Springer, Cham (2016). https://doi.org/10.1007/978-3-319-39417-6_16
12. Pavlidis, M., Mouratidis, H., Gonzalez-Perez, C., Kalloniatis, C.: Addressing privacy and trust issues in cultural heritage modelling. In: Lambrinoudakis, C., Gabillon, A. (eds.) CRiSIS 2015. LNCS, vol. 9572, pp. 3–16. Springer, Cham (2016). https://doi.org/10.1007/978-3-319-31811-0_1
13. Pavlidis, M., Mouratidis, H., Islam, S.: Modelling security using trust based concepts. Int. J. Secure Softw. Eng. (IJSSE) **3**, 36–53 (2012)
14. Piras, L., Dellagiacoma, D., Perini, A., Susi, A., Giorgini, P., Mylopoulos, J.: Design thinking and acceptance requirements for designing gamified software. In: 13th International Conference on Research Challenges in Information Science (RCIS). IEEE (2019)
15. Tsohou, A., Kosta, E.: Enabling valid informed consent for location tracking through privacy awareness of users: a process theory. Comput. Law Secur. Rev. **33**, 434–457 (2017)
16. Zheng, J., Gao, D.W., Lin, L.: Smart meters in smart grid: an overview. In: 2013 IEEE Green Technologies Conference (GreenTech) (2013)

General Data Protection Regulation and ISO/IEC 27001:2013: Synergies of Activities Towards Organisations' Compliance

Vasiliki Diamantopoulou[1(⊠)], Aggeliki Tsohou[2], and Maria Karyda[1]

[1] Department of Information and Communication Systems Engineering,
University of the Aegean, Samos, Greece
{vdiamant,mka}@aegean.gr
[2] Department of Informatics, Ionian University, Corfu, Greece
atsohou@ionio.gr

Abstract. The General Data Protection Regulation that is already in effect for about a year now, provisions numerous adjustments and controls that need to be implemented by an organisation in order to be able to demonstrate that all the appropriate technical and organisational measures have been taken to ensure the protection of the personal data. Many of the requirements of the GDPR are also included in the "ISO27k" family of standards. Consequently, organisations that have applied ISO27k to develop an Information Security Management System (ISMS) are likely to have already accommodated many of the GDPR requirements. This work identifies synergies between the new Regulation and the well-established ISO/IEC 27001:2013 and proposes practices for their exploitation. The proposed alignment framework can be a solid basis for compliance, either for organisations that are already certified with ISO/IEC 27001:2013, or for others that pursue compliance with the Regulation and the ISO/IEC 27001:2013 to manage information security.

Keywords: General Data Protection Regulation ·
ISO/IEC 27001:2013 · Information Security Management System ·
Compliance

1 Introduction

Personal data is one of the driving forces of modern enterprises and is nowadays exchanged on a broad scale [12]. Consequently, the necessity for protecting individuals' personal data is of utmost importance, especially when taking under consideration the value that personal data has for the digital economies and the interest that its collection attracts, either for public or private organisations. This necessity might have already been imposed by legal and contractual obligations, but since May 2018, is also imposed by the General Data Protection Regulation

© Springer Nature Switzerland AG 2019
S. Gritzalis et al. (Eds.): TrustBus 2019, LNCS 11711, pp. 94–109, 2019.
https://doi.org/10.1007/978-3-030-27813-7_7

(GDPR) [5]. Personal data is considered the driving force of the societies to develop, interact, take decisions. For this reason, the protection of personal data has seen a major upheaval during the last decades, concentrating the attention of politicians, developers, public and private organisations, legislators, authorities, as well as the general public.

European Union provisioned the protection of individuals' privacy by setting the general rules for the processing of personal data with the Directive 95/46/EC [4]. The scope of the Directive was to provide data subjects with a set of rights, to state the obligations of controllers and processors when dealing with personal data and to foresee supervisory authorities and mechanisms for ensuring that the rules are applied. However, the continuous growth and evolution of technology has taken place at such a pace, that the existing legal frameworks had become obsolete, calling for an adaptation of the corresponding legislation. The GDPR that replaces the Directive 95/46/EC builds on the principles and rules of the pre-existing Directive, but it is differentiated in the volume of the enhancement of the rights of the Data Subjects. Moreover, it appoints responsibility to the data controllers and processors for the protection of personal data they keep, by bringing forth the concept of self-regulation and accountability. Finally, it increases the sanctions related to the violations of its provisions.

Compliance with the GDPR comprises a challenging project for organisations for a series of reasons; the complexity of business activities and the duplication of data (in different information flows or even entire departments within an organisation) are the most important ones. However, even if organisations need to comply with the GDPR, they lack guidelines that could help them into complying with these requirements. There are already products being developed that can be used towards the compliance with the GDPR, however, none of the current technical solutions is able to capture the current security status of an organisation, identify the gaps, assess the criticality of the processing activities and the personal data they use, provide concrete solutions tailored to each organisation to finally fortify its processes and guarantee the protection of individuals' personal data [7].

The GDPR describes the responsibility of data controllers and the data processors to *implement appropriate technical and organisational measures to ensure a level of security appropriate to the risk* (Art. 32), without pinpointing specific methodology or techniques. We argue that the ISO 27k standard series can form a concrete baseline for businesses to build their "towards-compliance" strategy upon, dealing with topics such as risk definitions and assessment, continuous evaluation and appropriate documentation. An important aspect that any entity seeking compliance to current security/privacy standards should be aware of, is the fact that the (existing) ISO/IEC 27001:2013 (hereafter, ISO 27001) and the (newly brought) GDPR do not aggregately add burden (effort/costs) to an organisation. The similarities in both are quite many, and they both aim to cultivate a culture of protecting (processes/assets/data) and shaping the organisation's philosophy in this direction. Therefore, we argue that if an organisation already has an ISO 27001-based framework in place, compliance with the GDPR requires limited effort, as many processes and controls should already be in place, as well as the organisation's attitude towards protecting (processes/assets/data). The aim of this paper is to identify synergies by analysing the ISO 27001 standard and the GDPR and extracting the main concepts from both texts, and propose best practices for compliance. This work (i) maps the concepts expressed by each of these documents, (ii) identifies the common guidelines that the two documents share, and (iii) provides guidelines to organisations that are already certified according to the ISO 27001, on the actions that they need to take in order to also comply with the requirements of the GDPR. Vice versa, an organisation that satisfies current legal requirements and applies best practices on the field, constitutes also a good candidate for future certification with ISO 27001 with little effort. This should act as a motivation for these organisations to consider gaining such a certification since it leads to considerable benefits, such as more efficient and time saving processing, communication of a positive message to employees and customers, to name a few.

In this way, a transition to a new, consolidated approach to personal data protection and ISMSs, can be achieved.

2 Background: Data Protection in EU

2.1 General Data Protection Regulation (EU) 2016/679

The European Commission (EC) context for personal data protection starts in 1995, with the Directive 1995/46/EC regarding the protection of natural persons against the processing of their personal data and the free movement of such data. Moreover, the Directive 2001/58/EC [1] is related with the Processing of Personal Data and Protection of Privacy in Electronic Communications. Finally, the Directive 2006/24/EC [3] is about the retention of data generated or processed in connection with the provision of publicly available electronic communications services or of public communications networks and amending Directive 2002/58/EC [2].

The development of new types of Information Systems (IS) (e.g., interoperable IS which require the transfer of data from one system to another, possibly from one country to another, the uploading activity of personal data, etc.), as well as their rapid growth development, demand the establishment of new ways of management of the data these IS process. Since January of 2012, EC has proposed a reform of data protection rules and principles in order to increase the level of control of users' data, and thus, reduce the cost for businesses. Proposes a reform of data protection rules in order to increase the control over (personal) user data and reduce costs for businesses. Two years later, on March 2014, EC approves the proposal for the new Regulation (first draft), while on April 2015 it approves the General Data Protection Regulation 679/2016. One month later, on May 2016, the Regulation comes into effect, with a 2-year transition period. With brought us to the infamous 25th May 2018 when the Regulation is being applied, as a directly applicable law in all the member - states of European Union.

Conclusively, the GDPR is new regulation, which brings new obligations, new rights to the world formed by Information and Communication Technologies and the globalisation of information flows and services. The GDPR's orientation is to support the security of personal data so that it can then support citizens' rights. It lays down the requirements for the protection of individuals with regard to the processing of personal data and the free movement of such data. It is mandatory for public and private organisations that manage personal data of European citizens. The aim is for citizens in the European Union to gain (more) control of their personal data.

2.2   Major Breakthroughs of GDPR

The GDPR is an attempt to change stakeholders' mentality about the uncontrolled processing of their personal data. Additionally, the use of ISs to talk to each other, to exchange data between IS owners and use them for unknown processing purposes is a major problem for democracy in an information society. Consequently, the implementation of the GDPR is not tertiary, it is of major importance for the citizens' own life; this orientation was given by the European Parliament. Major breakthroughs of the GDPR are summarised in the following list:

- **Definition of Personal Data.**
  Additionally to the definition of personal data presented in the Directive 95/46/EC, which mentions that it is any information relating to an identified or identifiable natural person, the GDPR has added *location data, an online identifier*, as well as factors specific to the *genetic identity* of a natural person, besides physical, physiological, mental, economic, cultural or social identity, already included in Directive 95/46/EC.
- **Definition of Special Categories of Personal Data.** In special categories of personal data, GDPR includes the processing of *genetic data* and *biometric data for the purpose of uniquely identifying a natural person*, apart from personal data revealing racial or ethnic origin, political opinions, religious or philosophical beliefs, or trade union membership, data concerning health or data concerning a natural person's sex life or sexual orientation, already included in Directive 95/46/EC.
- **Data Controller's responsibilities:** The GDPR describes precisely the term of the data controller, its roles and responsibilities. Compared with the Directive 95/46/EC, the data controller shall now *implement appropriate technical and organisational measures* to ensure and to be able to demonstrate that processing is performed taking into account the *nature, scope, context* and *purposes of processing* as well as *the risks of varying likelihood and severity for the rights and freedoms of natural persons.*
- **Jurisdiction:** This point presents another dimension in the territorial scope of the application of the Regulation, since it applies, now, to the processing of personal data in the context of the activities of an establishment of a controller or a processor in the European Union, *regardless of whether the*

processing takes place in the Union or not. This requirement relates with processing regarding *the offering of goods or services, or the monitoring of their behaviour as far as their behaviour takes place within the Union.*

- **Consent Management:** The way that data subject's consent is given to anyone who wants to process their data changes, by meaning that the consent should be *freely given, specific, informed and unambiguous indication of the data subject's wishes by which he or she, by a statement or by a clear affirmative action.* In this way, the data subjects are given the opportunity/ability to gain control over the management of their data, and the controllers can manage the provided consent as a proof for their legal processing.
- **Breach notification:** In the Directive 95/46/EC, there wasn't any reference regarding the notification of the supervisory authorities when a data breach occurs. The GDPR describes this process as an obligation assigned to the data controller, highlighting the short time period that they should react, by informing the supervisory authorities *without undue delay and, where feasible, not later than 72 h after having become aware of it.* Reference is also made to the notification of data subjects, if there is a risk for their rights and freedoms.

In the context of the new legislation, with which many non EU based organisations need to comply, when they process EU citizens data, data protection entails new and increased security requirements. However, this new regulation is not to be taken as a new set of laws, guidelines and obligations; there already exists an internationally known and well-established framework that can stand as a baseline for conforming to information security requirements in general; with necessary extensions this could also assist in accommodating data protection requirements.

3   ISO/IEC 27001:2013

ISO 27001 [8] is part of ISO27k standards which provide recommendations on good practices for information security management, risk management and taking security measures, within the context of an Information Security Management System (ISMS). ISO27k standards provide details (e.g., ISO/IEC 27005 about the information security risk management and ISO/IEC 27018 for the protection of personally identifiable information in public clouds), while other ISO and non-ISO standards and resources provide much more information and, in some cases, propose alternative or complementary approaches and controls. It specifies the requirements for establishing, implementing, operating, monitoring, reviewing, maintaining and improving a documented ISMS within the context of the organisation's overall business risks. The objective of the standard is to thoroughly describe an ISMS, to provide definitions on the fundamental terms of information security, and for terms that are referenced in the family of ISO 27k. This standard is addressed to all types of organisations and businesses of any business sector, size, and activities.

The standard consists of two main sections, the main body of the document and the Annex A'. The main body of the document consists of ten sections/clauses. Clauses 4–10 describe the ISMS, while Annex A' presents the security modules, control objectives and controls that an ISMS shall cover at minimum. The structure of security controls includes 14 modules that expand in 35 security objectives and 114 security controls to achieve the objectives. An organisation must deal with all the security controls in the Annex, except the non-applicable ones. In this case, the exceptions are recorded in a Statement of Applicability. Each certificate states the Statement of Applicability: That is, which of the controls of Annex A' includes and which it excludes.

4   From an ISMS to GDRP Compliance

The GDPR provisions numerous personal data protection settings and controls, many of which are also recommended in ISO/IEC 27001:2013, ISO/IEC 27002: 2013, and other "ISO27k" standards. Organisations that currently have an ISMS are likely to satisfy many of the GDPR requirements already, needing a few adjustments to be made. Other organisations might decide to apply an ISMS as a general framework for the management of the personal data of data subjects that they process, in the context of: (i) the broader management of the information risks; (ii) the security of the data they process, either in hard copy or in a digital version, as well as the relevant compliance; (iii) the incident management; and (iv) addressing business continuity issues.

In this section we analyse the ISMS framework of ISO 27001 and identify synergies with the GDPR compliance efforts. In the next section we analyse the fourteen control modules of Annex A' of ISO 27001 and we then describe the necessary additional actions that an organisation is required to implement, in relation to the aforementioned controls, towards GPDR compliance. Finally, we provide suggestions to the organisations that are already certified according to the ISO 27001, on the following actions they have to conduct to also comply with the requirements of the GDPR.

4.1   Analysis: Extending the ISMS Towards GDPR Compliance

The compliance of an organisation with the GDPR can be seen as a project that follows the fundamental steps of the Deming Plan-Do-Check-Act (PDCA) cycle [11]. PDCA is an iterative four-step management method used in business for the control and continual improvement of processes and products. Although ISO 27001 in version 2013 extends in more steps, in fact, in a general perspective it is based in the PDCA cycle, as all management standards. In the project of GDPR compliance, each of these steps includes the following actions that should be conducted:

- **Plan:** In this first step we set the objectives of the project, and we identify the corresponding employees that will be involved in the process. Practically, in this step we have the initiation of the project, which is supported by the whole organisation and has the commitment of the management. Additionally, we define the organisational structure for managing data protection (i.e.

nominating a DPO, distinguishing roles related with the security of IS and data protection). Also, this step contains the identification of personal data the organisation keeps, and the classification of them. This process will facilitate the risk assessment (GDPR, Recital 76) with respect to personal data as well as the conduction of a Data Protection Impact Assessment (DPIA), if it is necessary.

- **Do:** This step allows the plan set up in the previous step to be carried out. It includes the design of the necessary controls and procedures as well as their implementation. The documentation of key processes and security controls is also included in this step. Documentation facilitates the management of the aforementioned processes and controls, and it varies depending the type, the size and the complexity of the organisation, their IS any other technologies available, as well as the requirements of the stakeholders and the relevant third parties (customers, suppliers). Furthermore, this step contains the establishment of a communication plan, as well as the set up of awareness and training sessions for the employees of the organisation.
- **Check:** This step consists of two concrete actions. The first action contains the monitoring, measurement, analysis and evaluation of the process. In order to be sure that the suggested controls, set up in the second step, are implemented efficiently, the organisation shall determine the controls that need to be measured and monitored, focusing on the activities that are linked to the organisation's critical processes. The second action refers to the internal audit that the organisation shall conduct. The objectives of the audit should be focused on the evaluation of the actions related with the GDPR requirements been implemented in the organisation.
- **Act:** The final step of the process aims at maintaining the results of the project and identification of corrective action processes as well as the continuous improvement of the established framework. The corrective actions procedure is realised through the following steps: (i) identification of the nonconformity and analysis of its impacts on the organisation; (ii) analysis of the situation, i.e. analysis of the root causes, assessment of the available options, selection of the most appropriate solution(s); (iii) corrective actions, by implementing the chosen solutions and recording the actions taken; (iv) continuous improvement, by evaluating and reviewing the actions taken.

The certification of an organisation to the ISO 27001 facilitates its compliance with the GDPR since the requirements of the latter can be compared with an already established control framework, as the one of the ISMS.

5 A Consolidated Compliance Framework: Extending Control Objectives and Controls to Achieve GDPR Compliance

ISO 27001 facilitates compliance with the GDPR because its requirements may be compared with an operational and already established control framework, such as the ISMS. Hereafter, we present the necessary controls and processes that should be implemented in order for the organisations to be compliant with the GDPR. The proposed list of those items is not exhaustive, since additional controls or processes might be required, depending on the nature and particularities of each organisation.

The following guidelines are based on the analysis of the 14 modules of the ISO 27001, where the implementation/satisfaction of them describes the ISMS. Each paragraph describes the obligations that ISO imposes to organisations, and compared to them, we propose the additional actions that the organisation has to conduct towards GDPR compliance.

5.1   Enhancing Information Security Policies with Data Protection Policies

The first control module includes one control related with the management direction for information security. The objective is the provision of management direction and support for information security in accordance with business requirements, and relevant laws and regulations.

Complying with GDPR: Since the organisation has already developed an information security policy, the requirement towards GDPR compliance for the data controller is the development and establishment of a data protection policy. This policy should meet in particular the principles of data protection by design and data protection by default [6,10]. More specifically, this policy should be distinct from the information security policy [9], providing information on:

– The lawfulness of processing (which requires legal analysis).
– The time frame that the processing/storage of personal data will take place.
– The existence of any automated decision-making process, including profiling, with information on possible consequences.
– Data collected from other sources.
– The Data Protection Officer's data.
– The procedures employed in order to satisfy all data subjects' rights.

The Data Protection Policy applies to all personal data processed by the organisation, to all operational processes that involve the processing of personal data, and to all members of the organisation who are directly or indirectly involved in the processing of personal data. It is not a static document but should be kept as up to date as possible and adjusted in line with the changes of IS and the technical and social environment. It is also updated in the event of major changes to the organisation or its IT systems.

5.2   Extending Organisation of Information Security

This control module includes two controls, (i) the internal organisation, and (ii) the mobile devices and teleworking. This control module aims at the establishment of a framework for the administration on the implementation and operation of security within the organisation, and the protection of security related with the information accessed, processed and/or stored at teleworking sites, and the use of portable devices.

Complying with GDPR: The requirements towards GDPR compliance include, firstly, specific management of personal data that the organisation keeps. More specifically, the personal data should be (Art. 5):

- Processed lawfully, fairly and in a transparent manner.
- Collected for specified, explicit and legitimate purposes and not further processed in a manner that is incompatible with those purposes.
- Adequate, relevant and limited to what is necessary in relation to the purposes for which they are processed.
- Accurate and, where necessary, kept up to date.
- Kept in a form which permits identification of data subjects for no longer than is necessary for the purposes for which the personal data are processed.
- Processed in a manner that ensures appropriate security of the personal data.

Next, the data controllers need to cooperate with the supervisory authorities when a data breach occurs (Art. 33), informing them without undue delay, when the personal data breach is likely to result in a risk to the rights and freedoms of natural persons. When the data controller realises that the data breach may pose a high risk to their rights and freedoms, they should also inform the data subjects for the violation of their data.

Additionally, the data controller needs to conduct a DPIA when particular types of processing is likely to result in a high risk to the rights and freedoms of natural persons (Art. 35). The data controller carries out DPIA in case of (i) systematic and extensive evaluation of personal aspects relating to natural persons which is based on automated processing, including profiling, (ii) processing on a large scale of special categories of data, (iii) systematic monitoring of a publicly accessible area on a large scale.

Furthermore, a data protection officer should be appointed, since (i) the processing is carried out by a public authority or body, except for courts acting in their judicial capacity, (ii) the data controller's main activities require regular and systematic monitoring of the data subjects on a large scale, the data controller's main activities are large scale processing of specific categories of personal data.

Finally, an organisation can proceed to the establishment of codes of conducts (Art. 40). Codes of conduct can contribute to the proper application of the GDPR, *taking account of the specific features of the various processing sectors and the specific needs of micro, small and medium-sized enterprises.* They are related to associations and other bodies that represent data controllers or data processors. To this direction, data controllers and data processors are encouraged by the GDPR to be certified with a certification mechanism (Art. 42). Such mechanisms may be established for the purpose of demonstrating the existence of appropriate safeguards provided by controllers or processors. They enable the mandatory monitoring of compliance either by the supervisory authority, or by an accredited organisation (demonstrating independence and expertise). Codes of conduct can be drawn up by organisations that represent data controllers or data processors and approved either by the supervisory authority of a member state or by the European Data Protection Board.

5.3 Expanding Controls on Human Resources Security to Employees' Privacy Protection

This control module consists of three of controls: (i) information security prior to employment; (ii) during employment, and (iii) termination and change of employment. The corresponding objectives of these controls are to ensure that the employees and contractors understand their responsibilities and are suitable for the roles which they are appointed; that they are aware of and fulfil their information security responsibilities; to protect the organisation's interests as part of the process of changing or terminating employment.

Complying with GDPR: Additionally to the above that mainly deal with the security of the organisation related with their employees, GDPR sets a series of actions related with the protection of data of an organisation's employees. Starting with the management of the personal data that the organisation keeps, they have to apply special restrictions to personal data concerning criminal convictions and offences (Art. 10). Moreover, data controllers have to maintain relevant documentation related with data protection, i.e. records of processing activities (Art. 30), by maintaining a list of classified corporate information - including personal data, and documentation of applied technical and organisational measures the organisation applies.

5.4 Enhancing Asset Management with Personal Data Management

This control module contains three controls: (i) responsibility for assets; (ii) information classification; and (iii) media handling. The objective for the first control is the identification of the organisational assets, and the definition of appropriate protection responsibilities. Regarding the information classification, the organisation need to ensure that information receives appropriate level of protection in accordance with its importance, and finally for the media handling control, the organisation is responsible for preventing unauthorised disclosure, modification, removal or destruction of information stored on media.

Complying with GDPR: It is clear that this control provides guidelines for the protection of any valuable for the organisation asset. Taking into account that personal data and special categories of personal data also consist a valuable asset, the organisation needs to know all location where this data is kept (Art. 5, 7, 9, 30), and under which lawful process this data has been obtained (this point is also related with the consent that the organisation should obtain by the data subject). Additionally, the data controller/processor should be in position to provide information to the data subject related to the aforementioned personal data they keep (Art. 13, 14) by developing appropriate procedures for the satisfaction of this right.

5.5   Establishing Access Control Designed Following Data Protection by Design and by Default Principles

Access control contains four controls: (i) business requirements of access control; (ii) user access management; (iii) user responsibilities; and (iv) system and application access control. All these controls are related with the access management of the users to information, preventing unauthorised access to systems and services and promoting accountability for safeguarding organisation's authentication information.

Complying with GDPR: The organisation should develop their systems with respect to data protection by design and by default principles (Art. 25) in order to protect users' privacy. Additionally, the organisation should implement process through which the data subjects can either correct, or request correction (Art. 16) of the personal data the organisation holds for them, or erase, or request the erasure (Art. 17) of such data.

5.6   Employing Cryptography

The control module Cryptography contains one control, i.e. cryptographic controls, which aims at ensuring proper and effective use of the technological measure of cryptography in order to protect the confidentiality, authenticity and/or integrity of information.

Complying with GDPR: Encryption and anonymisation are the two technical measures that the GDPR proposes (Art. 32). Moreover, for the satisfaction of the right to data portability (Art. 20), the organisation is encouraged to apply encryption to securely communicate the corresponding personal data to other organisations.

5.7   Enhancing Communications Security with Personal Data Protection Objectives

This control module contains two controls: network security management and information transfer. The objective is to ensure the protection of information in networks and its supporting information processing facilities and to maintain the security of information transferred within an organisation and with any external entity.

Complying with GDPR: Emphasis should be given to the design and development of the communication security where more than one organisations are involved and access to personal data is required (Art. 26). Appropriate roles should be given to the corresponding employees who have access to such data, accompanied with specific responsibilities. Additionally, the organisation should be able to locate and retrieve securely the personal data it keeps, satisfying thus the right of access by the data subject (Art. 15).

5.8 Acquiring, Developing and Maintaining Systems Following Data Protection Principles

This control module contains three controls: (i) security requirements of IS, (ii) security in development and support process, and (iii) test data. The requirements of this section are referred to the development process of IS. It is worth mentioning that this is the first time that we meet requirements related to the development of a system in ISO 27001. Organisations should be able to choose their working environment (framework, language, operating system, to name a few parameters) in relation to the criticality of the product they wish to develop.

Complying with GDPR: The organisation should estimate/assess the profit in relation to the cost (cost-benefit analysis) of managing a new system related to the lawful processing of data (Art. 6). This should also be covered in the risk assessment and management, in general, and taken under consideration when designing or upgrading systems and processes. This assessment may indicate, for example, that some personal data processing residual risk may be accepted or this risk should be further mitigated by applying one or more security controls. Also, the organisation should be able to identify and assess the special categories of personal data they keep. In order to avoid information risks, where feasible, the organisation needs to assess if they really need to keep personal and special categories of personal data or the aggregation of such data is also accepted (Art. 9, 11).

In addition, in order to satisfy the right of data subjects to know the outcome of requests related with the correction, completion, erasure, restriction of their personal data (Art. 19), the organisation should inform the requestor on the above, also providing that this process/application form is easy for insiders and outsiders of the organisation to follow.

5.9 Managing Supplier Relationships While Protecting Personal Data

This control module contains two controls: (i) information security in supplier relationships, and (ii) supplier service delivery management. The objective is to manage the relationship of the organisation with its suppliers, or any other third party that has access to the organisation's assets, and to set up and agreed level of information security and service delivery.

Complying with GDPR: Organisations located outside Europe that interact with European organisations must formally nominate privacy representatives inside Europe if they meet certain conditions. If an organisation uses one or more third parties to process personal info ("processors"), it must ensure they too are compliant with GDPR (Art. 27, 28). Moreover, organisations need to ensure the privacy and other information security aspects of their business partners. This might contain aspects such as jointly investigating and resolving privacy incidents, breaches or access requests, to name a few. These requirements are applied to any relationship the organisation has with external parties, such as

ISPs and CSPs, and any other third party that the organisation has exchanged (personal) data with, for example external payroll or marketing companies.

5.10 Extending Incident Management with Notification in Case of Data Breach

This control module contains one control, i.e. management of information security incidents and improvements. The objective of this control is to ensure a consistent and effective approach to the management of information incidents.

Complying with GDPR: The organisation should implement process in order to be able to notify without undue delay the supervisory authority (Art. 33) and the data subjects (Art. 35) if it is required.

5.11 Enhancing Compliance to Satisfy Lawfulness of Processing

This control module contains two controls: (i) compliance with legal and contractual requirements, and (ii) information security reviews. This last control aims at the avoidance of any kind of breaches related to information security and of any security requirements and to ensure that the information security is implemented and operated in accordance with the organisational policies and procedures.

Complying with GDPR: Additionally, the organisation should develop processes to satisfy the lawfulness of processing (Art. 5), for the consent of the data subjects (Art. 7, 8), for the satisfaction of the rights of data subjects (Art. 12–22), for ensuring the appropriate safeguards in case of a transfer of personal data to third countries or international organisation (Art. 44).

5.12 Modules that Support GDPR Compliance

This section presents modules that have no direct application to the GDPR, but can help an organisation develop a culture that will assist towards reaching GDPR compliance; they are also included here for the sake of completeness.

Enhancing Physical and Environmental Security for GDPR Compliance: This control module contains two controls: the secure areas and the equipment. The identification of secure areas can prevent unauthorised physical access, damage and interference to the organisation's information and information processing facilities, while the safeguarding of the equipment of the organisation prevents loss, damage, theft or compromise of assets and interruption of organisation's operation.

Complying with GDPR: This section applies to the general requirement of the GDPR to the organisations for implementing appropriate technical and organisational measures to ensure the level of security appropriate to the risk (Art. 24, 25, 28, 32).

Enhancing Operations Security for GDPR Compliance: This control module contains seven controls: (i) operational procedures and responsibilities, (ii) protection from malware, (iii) back up, (iv) logging and monitoring, (v) control of operational software, (vi) technical vulnerability management, and (vii) information systems audit considerations. The objective of this section is to ensure correct and secure operations of information processing facilities, protection against malware and data loss, to record events and generate evidence, to ensure the integrity of operational systems, to prevent exploitation of technical vulnerabilities and to minimise the impact of audit activities on operational systems.

Complying with GDPR: Similarly to the previous section of "physical and environmental security", an organisation is able to demonstrate that they have implemented they appropriate technical and organisational measures to safeguard the personal data they keep. Additionally, the organisation should implement procedures related with the management of the satisfaction of the data subjects' rights (Art. 12–22) and for the process of the provision of consent of the data subjects (Art. 7).

Extending Business Continuity Management to Support GDPR Compliance: This control module contains two controls: (i) information security continuity, and (ii) redundancies. The objective is the establishment of a business continuity and disaster recovery plan. The continuity of operations is indented to restore the operation of the organisation's systems within a reasonable time. In addition, staff training is required in the continuity plan, while its efficiency must be tested and managed properly.

Complying with GDPR: As a general direction for the satisfaction of the GDPR, an organisation should implement appropriate technical and organisational measures to ensure the level of security appropriate to risk (Art. 24, 25, 28, 32).

6   Conclusions

The application of ISO 27001 supports organisations in creating better business efficiency, safeguards valuable assets such as personal data or hardware, protects staff and organisations' reputation, and simultaneously facilitates the attainment of compliance objectives. Several GDPR requirements are not covered in ISO 27001, however ISO 27001 provides the means to push organisations one step closer to accomplish conformity to the Regulation, minimising the required effort.

Even for organisations that are not ISO 27001 certified, complying with the GDPR is a good catalyst for considering implementing such a scheme for higher information protection assurance. Already, by being ISO 27001 compliant, organisations demonstrate (and is the case) that the data owned and used is managed based on data protection regulations. Consequently, if organisations already have an ISO 27001 framework in place, compliance with GDPR requirements will not be necessitated a duplication of effort. In addition, compliance to the GDPR is mandatory, whereas ISO 27001 certification is not. Organisations can start from ISO 27001 certification and reach GDPR compliance, or vice versa.

The results of this work provide guidelines for practitioners, such as information security and privacy experts since it presents a roadmap on how to design a "towards GDPR compliance" project, contributing also to their awareness regarding the protection of personal data of their organisation.

Future work of this study includes the validation of the proposed guidelines towards GDPR compliance by a number of ISO 27001 certified organisations that have also reached GDPR compliance. The analysis of such feedback will further validate (or provide other perspectives to) the findings of this work. Moreover, data protection officers could also be involved in this process, providing their experiences regarding the demanded effort to reach GDPR compliance for an already ISO 27001 certified organisation.

References

1. Commission directive 2001/58/EC of 27 July 2001 amending for the second time directive 91/155/EEC defining and laying down the detailed arrangements for the system of specific information relating to dangerous preparations in implementation of article 14 of European parliament and council directive 1999/45/EC and relating to dangerous substances in implementation of article 27 of council directive 67/548/EEC (safety data sheets)
2. Directive 2002/58/EC of the European parliament and of the council of 12 July 2002 concerning the processing of personal data and the protection of privacy in the electronic communications sector (directive on privacy and electronic communications)
3. Directive 2006/24/EC of the European parliament and of the council of 15 March 2006 on the retention of data generated or processed in connection with the provision of publicly available electronic communications services or of public communications networks and amending directive 2002/58/EC
4. European commission: Directive 95/46/EC of the European parliament and of the council. http://eur-lex.europa.eu/legal-content/EN/TXT/?uri=CELEX:31995L0046. Accessed 14 May 2017
5. European parliament: Regulation (EU) 2016/679 of the European parliament and of the council of 27 April 2016 on the protection of natural persons with regard to the processing of personal data and on the free movement of such data, and repealing directive 95/46/EC (general data protection regulation)
6. Cavoukian, A., et al.: Privacy by design: the 7 foundational principles. Inf. Privacy Commissioner Ontario, Canada 5 (2009)
7. IAAP: Privacy tech vendor report. Technical report (2018)
8. ISO/IEC: ISO 27001:2013 information technology - security techniques - information security management systems - requirements. Technical report (2013)
9. Lambrinoudakis, C.: The general data protection regulation (GDPR) era: ten steps for compliance of data processors and data controllers. In: Furnell, S., Mouratidis, H., Pernul, G. (eds.) TrustBus 2018. LNCS, vol. 11033, pp. 3–8. Springer, Cham (2018). https://doi.org/10.1007/978-3-319-98385-1_1

10. Langheinrich, M.: Privacy by design—principles of privacy-aware ubiquitous systems. In: Abowd, G.D., Brumitt, B., Shafer, S. (eds.) UbiComp 2001. LNCS, vol. 2201, pp. 273–291. Springer, Heidelberg (2001). https://doi.org/10.1007/3-540-45427-6_23
11. Moen, R., Norman, C.: Evolution of the PDCA cycle (2006)
12. Spiekermann, S., Acquisti, A., Böhme, R., Hui, K.L.: The challenges of personal data markets and privacy. Electron. Markets 25(2), 161–167 (2015)

The Interrelation of Game Elements and Privacy Requirements for the Design of a System: A Metamodel

Aikaterini-Georgia Mavroeidi[(⊠)], Angeliki Kitsiou, and Christos Kalloniatis

Privacy Engineering and Social Informatics Laboratory, Department of Cultural Technology and Communication, University of the Aegean, 81100 Mytilene, Lesvos, Greece
{kmav,a.kitsiou,chkallon}@aegean.gr

Abstract. Due to the increased use of Information and Communication Technologies (ICTs), several methods have been developed in order to create more attractive interaction environments, so that users' interest on using services to be maintained. Gamification consists a method, aiming to increase users' engagement by implementing game design elements in services that are not games [1]. While using all these services, users' information is recorded and monitored. Except the importance of increasing the use of ICTs, it is crucial to ensure that users' personal information will be protected. To achieve it, privacy issues should be considered by software developers during the design phase of a service, in parallel with the game design elements. Based on our previous research [2], it was identified that the relation between gamification and privacy has not been examined sufficiently. As a result, a detailed analysis was conducted. In this work, in order to examine this relation in existent services, a detailed description of gamified services in several sectors has been conducted. Afterwards, based on the results of the conducted research and the examination of existent gamified services, a metamodel is presented, which describes how each game element conflicts with privacy requirements. By using this metamodel, software developers will be able to identify which mechanisms should be implemented in such services, so that users' privacy to be protected in parallel. The development of such services ensures the trust between users and them and consequently, users' engagements will be increased [3].

Keywords: Gamification · Game elements · Gamified services · Privacy · Privacy requirements

1 Introduction

The use of ICTs recorded in the literature [4, 5] has been increased during the last years [6]. Users' knowledge, habits and preferences differ, so the provision of services which will maintain users' interest is needed. After the second half of 2010, the method of gamification has been introduced in ICTs, aiming to increase users' engagement in using technologies [1, 7]. The core of this method is the implementation of game

© Springer Nature Switzerland AG 2019
S. Gritzalis et al. (Eds.): TrustBus 2019, LNCS 11711, pp. 110–125, 2019.
https://doi.org/10.1007/978-3-030-27813-7_8

design elements in applications that are not games [1, 8]. By using game elements, the applications have a more attractive environment and provide benefits, such as the increase of users' activities, sociability, quality and productivity of actions [8]. Although many examples of applications that use this method have been recorded in the literature, yet a standard definition has not been provided [1]. The most cited definition was published by Deterding et al. in 2011, who defined that "gamification is the use of game design elements in non-game contexts" [1].

Gamification has been implemented in several sectors, such as education, marketing, health, culture, tourism and security [9–23]. While interacting with all these applications, users' actions and personal information are recorded and monitored, e.g. in the case of gamified applications regarding health. Users have to be informed about the kind of stored data, the time and place that these data will be stored and the persons who have access [20, 21]. By ensuring this, the trust between users and services will be increased and consequently, they will use more the gamified applications [3]. Thus, it is also crucial to study this method in relation to privacy domain.

Especially, due to the implementation of the regulation "General Data Protection Regulation (GDPR)", it is mandatory to consider the protection of users' personal information, while developing services. This can be achieved by analysing and eliciting privacy requirements into systems [26–32]. According to the literature, several studies regarding privacy mention that the privacy requirements are the anonymity, pseudonimity, unlinkability, undetectability and unobservability [2, 26, 27, 30]. Several privacy requirements engineering methodologies have been recorded in the literature, which software developers can use for the development of systems which respects privacy [26–32]. Though, based on our previous work [2] the relation between privacy and gamification has not been examined sufficiently. Therefore, it was needed to conduct a detailed analysis of this relation [2]. On the one side, in order to gamify a service, game elements have to be implemented, while privacy requirements should be analysed. Both should be considered during the design of a system. Thus, the purpose was to examine if game elements respects privacy requirements. In order for this relationship to be more sufficient, in this work the findings, published in [2], were examined in existent examples of gamified services, by recording their game elements and identifying if they protect users' privacy. This approach results the development of the metamodel. It was noticed that many gamified services may harm users' privacy, as their personal information is stored and monitored for several reasons. As a result, during the development of gamified applications, techniques and mechanisms should be implemented by software developers, in order for users' personal information to be protected. In this work, by providing the metamodel, which presents how game elements impact with privacy requirements, developers will be able to manage which techniques have to be implemented, aiming to design services which respect users' privacy.

The rest of the paper is organised as follows. In Sect. 2 the amount of game elements, recorded in the literature are explained and presented. In Sect. 3 several examples of existent gamified applications are described, highlighting how their processes can violate users' privacy. In Sect. 4 the metamodel of this work is presented, describing how game elements conflict with privacy requirements. Finally, Sect. 5 concludes the paper and describes our future work.

2 Game Elements

The main principle of gamification is the game element, as by implementing game elements, the interaction environment of the ICTs is more attractive and interesting, promoting users' engagement [1]. To identify how and where these game elements can be applied, a number of studies, as following, were collected. It was identified that gamification has been studied in several sectors, such as education, marketing and health, while in some of these sectors there are examples of gamified applications. In Sect. 3, examples of such services are described. The use of these ICTs can be increased, providing benefits not only to users but also to developers, depending on the context of each gamified service. Specifically, the increased utilization of such services in marketing supports the products' promotion of each company [12]. In health sector, users can protect themselves by using services which remind them their daily pre-scriptions or exercise [33]. In addition, users can be educated through a more enter-taining way, having the illusion that they are playing a game. This makes the application/service more attractable, enhancing users engagement is increased in using thjs service [10].

In order to identify how gamification is implemented in several sectors, a number of studies were collected. In this research, it was noticed that there are different game elements which are used, depending on their concept. Some of them are mentioned in many studies, while others are not considerably described. The most cited elements in the literature are the "points" [8, 9, 11, 34–46], "badges" [8, 9, 12, 35, 36, 38–40, 43–47], "levels" [8, 9, 11, 12, 35–39, 44] and "leaderboards" [8, 11, 12, 36–40, 43, 44, 48]. It was noticed that, in most gamified services, users are required to collect points in order to pass several levels and win badges. In some cases, the results of users' actions are recorded in leaderboards, where they can see their position in relation to others. The elements "profiles" [11, 34–37], "rewards" [8, 11, 12, 34, 37, 39, 41, 42], "challenges" [8, 12, 34, 36–38, 40–42], "competition" [11, 12, 35, 37–39, 43] and "feedback and progressive information" [8, 9, 11, 35–38, 40] have been implemented in several gamified services, as well. Especially, the creation of a profile is required in most services, while in some of them, users can be connected with their social accounts, e.g. Facebook account. Except the badges, users can be rewarded with gifts, after, for instance, a challenge or a competition with other users. In addition, it is important to provide feedback to users regarding their progress in order to become aware of their actions.

According to the results of the research, the elements "quiz" [11, 34, 35, 39], "communication with other players" [9, 12, 35, 36], "notifications" [34–37] and "team tournaments, group tasks and collaboration" [11, 34–39] are not as popular as the aforementioned elements. Certainly, it does not mean that they are not preferable, since each one offers benefits to gamified applications. The collaboration or the communi-cation between users may enhance users' sociability, while users may be motivated to interact with such services. Adding on this, if users are notified for a task or their current status, there is a little chance of forgetting using the service [36]. Such a task could be the completion of a quiz. While users give correct answers, they collect points, pass levels and win rewards or badges. In that way, many elements are interdependent.

Although all gamified applications offer activities to users, according the literature, "alternative activities" [34, 36, 39] are not mentioned a lot, as most of the services have a specific scenario which users have to follow in order to manage the accomplishment of services purpose. Other elements that are not considerably described are the use of "time constraints" [12, 36, 39] during the completion of tasks, the "rules" [35, 39] of a service, e.g. the "content unlocking" [38] in order to pass levels, the "achievements" [9, 38, 39] and the "scoring systems" [12, 36]. Additionally, some services require the connection with users' "location" [35, 36] in order to complete tasks or they offer the creation of an "avatar" [35, 38], based on users' face and expressions. In Fig. 1, the variety of these elements is presented with the number of studies in which they are mentioned.

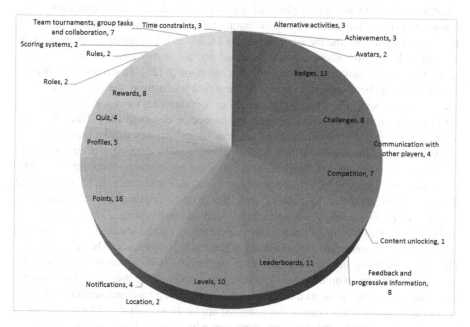

Fig. 1. The number of studies that elements are mentioned

3 Examples of Gamified Applications

Based on some game elements concepts, the use of gamified services requires the record of users' information and operations without providing information regarding this action. Thus, as most of the users' information is digitalised, privacy consists an important aspect to be considered during the development of ICTs in order for users' personal information to be protected [20]. By developing services which do not only engage users, but also protect their personal information, the trust between services and users can be strengthened [2].

Even though this fact is crucial, few researches, to our best knowledge, pay attention to the relation between gamification and privacy. Thus, in our previous work [1], a research was conducted in which this relation was examined. The game elements are the key concepts for the design of gamified services [7, 8] and in parallel, the privacy requirements should be considered for the development of systems [27]. As a result, the examination was between the game elements and the privacy requirements [1]. The elements differ on their concept and use. Some of them, such as badges, points, levels, do not violate privacy. For instance, the collection of points is not harmful by itself. In contrast, the number of these points can be recorded in leaderboards, which provide users' status connected to their names. Therefore, users' identity can be recognised and linked to their actions.

According to the literature, privacy can be protected by analysing privacy requirements during the design phase of a system [24, 25, 28]. In several studies, the mentioned privacy requirements are the anonymity, the pseudonimity, the unlinkability, the undetectability and the unobservability [1, 24, 26]. The ability of a subject to be unidentifiable among others can be protected by the anonymity, while by using a pseudonymous, a subject can protect his/her anonymity [25]. In parallel, the actions and the relations between users cannot be identified by ensuring the unlinkability in a system [25]. In addition, when the existence of a component cannot be detected by a third party, then the actions among subjects cannot be observed [25]. Thus, by satisfying all these privacy requirements in services, users' privacy can be protected.

According to the results of this identification, a more detailed analysis was conducted in this work, by selecting existent gamified applications, recording their elements and examining which requirements are violated. For instance, in [2] the element "location" was identified to conflict with the privacy requirements of anonymity, pseudonimity, unlinkability, undetectability and unobservability. Thus, in case an application uses this element the privacy requirements can be violated. The following examples of services were examined according to this approach. This examination, afterwards, supports the development of a metamodel, which consists a pattern for software developers in order to consider how privacy should be protected, based on the disadvantages of the elements during the design phase of a gamified service (Table 1).

In *education* sector, in one of the gamified applications, called "TEDEd" [6], users have to create a profile and they can choose an educational video, add its description and quiz and share it with other users. This application can be used by all ages and it consists an entertaining way of education by selecting a preferable topic. The privacy issue in this example concerns the creation of the profile and the quiz, since users' information and answers are recorded and consequently their identity can be compromised. Additionally, users' answers can be linked to their identity through the observation of their actions. The creation of a profile is required for the application "Khan Academy" [6] as well, where users can be educated on several topics and languages, such as science. The results of each user are recorded and assigned to his/her profile, so that the anonymity of the user and the connection with his/her actions can be harmed. "Yousician" [6], an application by which users learn an instrument, can be used by creating a profile, selecting an instrument, choosing a song and passing levels. The privacy issue in this application is that users' identity can be linked to their actions, preferences and progress, so as users can be detected and observed.

Table 1. Examples of gamified services and their impact on privacy requirements

Sector	Gamified service	Benefits of service to users	Game elements	Privacy requirements
Education	TEDEd	- Offer of preferable topics	1. Profiles, 2. Quiz	Anonimity, Pseudonimity, Unlinkability (1, 2) Undetectability, Unobservability (1)
Education	Khan Academy	- Provision of several languages - Education on several topics	Profiles	Anonimity, Pseudonimity, Unlinkability, Undetectability, Unobservability
Education	Yousician	- Can be educated on music through a more entertaining way	Profiles	Anonimity, Pseudonimity, Unlinkability, Undetectability, Unobservability
Education	Udemy	- Participation of teachers and students - Education on several topics	1. Profiles, 2. Quiz	Anonimity, Pseudonimity, Unlinkability (1, 2) Undetectability, Unobservability (1)
Education	Memrise	- provision of several languages - education on several topics	1. Profiles, 2. Communication, 3. Quiz	Anonimity, Pseudonimity, Unlinkability (1–3) Undetectability, Unobservability (1, 2)
Education	Duolingo	- Education on several languages - Provision of interesting graphics	1. Profiles, 2. Quiz	Anonimity, Pseudonimity, Unlinkability (1, 2) Undetectability, Unobservability (1)
Education	Coursera	- Participation and collaboration between teachers and students - Education on several topics - Earn online degree	1. Profiles, 2. Quiz, 3. Communication, 4. Collaboration	Anonimity, Pseudonimity, Unlinkability (1–4) Undetectability, Unobservability (1, 3, 4)

(continued)

Table 1. (*continued*)

Sector	Gamified service	Benefits of service to users	Game elements	Privacy requirements
Education	SoloLearn	- Education on programming - Sharing and getting feedback	1. Profiles, 2. Challenge, 3. Leaderboards, 4. Communication, 5. Quiz	Anonimity (1–5) Pseudonimity (1, 3–5) Unlinkability (1–5) Undetectability, Unobservability (1, 4)
Education	Byju'	- Education on several topics - Collaboration between users	1. Profiles, 2. Challenge, 3. Quiz, 4. Competitions	Anonimity(1–4) Pseudonimity (1, 3, 4) Unlinkability (1–4) Undetectability, Unobservability (1, 4)
Marketing	Nike+	- Monitoring of users' movements - Collaboration between users	1. Profiles, 2. Challenge, 3. Leaderboards, 4. Competition, 5. Notifications	Anonimity (1–5) Pseudonimity (1, 3–5) Unlinkability (1–5) Undetectability, Unobservability (1, 4, 5)
Marketing	4 Foods – Good 4 All	- Collaboration between users - Making food based on users' preferences	1. Profiles, 2. Competitions, 3. Leaderboards	Anonimity, Pseudonimity, Unlinkability (1–3) Undetectability, Unobservability (1, 2)
Marketing	My Starbucks Reward	- Rewards to users based on their orders	1.Profiles, 2. Notifications	Anonimity, Pseudonimity, Unlinkability, Undetectability, Unobservability (1, 2)
Health	Mango Health	- Protection of users' health - Rewards to users based on the completion of the tasks	1. Profiles, 2. Notifications	Anonimity, Pseudonimity, Unlinkability, Undetectability, Unobservability (1, 2)
Health	Asthma Hero	- protection of users' health - rewards to users based on the completion of the tasks - collaboration between patients and physicians	1. Profiles, 2. Notifications, 3. Roles	Anonimity, Pseudonimity, Unlinkability, Undetectability, Unobservability (1–3)

(*continued*)

Table 1. (*continued*)

Sector	Gamified service	Benefits of service to users	Game elements	Privacy requirements
Health	Respond Well	- protection of users' health - rewards to users based on the completion of the tasks - collaboration between users	1. Profiles, 2. Challenges, 3. Roles	Anonimity Pseudonimity Unlinkability Undetectability, Unobservability (1–3)
Personal Finance	Smartypig	- supports users to reach their financial goals	Profiles	Anonimity, Pseudonimity, Unlinkability, Undetectability, Unobservability

The application "Udemy" is an educational platform, where teachers can upload courses, in order for students to be connected and educated on different topics. As in the case of "TEDEd", the privacy issue concerns the connection of users' identity to their actions, progress, answers in quizzes, so that their actions can be detected and linked to them.

"Memrise" [6], is an educational application which teaches many languages and includes courses for art, history and maths. It provides several types of quizzes to students, where they have to collect points in order to pass levels. Users' progress is assigned to their profiles, which automatically means that their privacy can be violated, as in the previous examples. A similar example of application is the "Duolingo", which as "Memrise", provides quizzes to users and they have to give correct answers to pass levels. This application includes several colours and shapes, which make the interaction environment more attractive. As in the previous examples, the problem of this application is the connection of users' answers and progress to their profiles and therefore their actions can be detected and observed.

Except all these applications, there are some others, which include more game elements that may violate users' privacy. For instance, "Coursera" [6] is an online platform, where teachers have the opportunity to give lessons and students can earn their correspondent degree online. In this application, the identity of users or teachers is known to others, as they have to communicate or collaborate during the courses. Thus, their actions and information can be detected, while users are able to know the progress of the other ones. The case of communication concerns the application "SoloLearn" [6] as well, a gamified application that aims to learn users how to code. By completing challenges, users earn points and they have the opportunity to share their work to others and get feedback. The results are recorded in leaderboards, where users can compare their progress. For all these actions, the registration to this platform is required. All these opportunities of this platform show that users know the others' identity and their work can be linked to them. "Byju's" [42] is an application where users can be educated on chemistry, maths and physics topics by completing quizzes. They can challenge each other in competitions, which motivate them to work for better results. As users compete quizzes, their identities can be compromised, their actions can be linked to their accounts and their progress can be recorded, leading to a violation of their personal information.

In *marketing* sector, the concept or the aim of a gamified applications differs, while the developers and companies' purpose is to engage as more users as possible so as to raise their profits. For instance, Nike company launches a product in 2012, called "Nike + Fuelband" [43], which is a bracelet with a technique that can monitor users' movements. The purpose of this product is to engage customers to keep themselves fit. All participants have to download the Nike+ application and to connect it with the bracelet. When customers achieve their daily goals, an animated character is presented, celebrating this fact. The application provides feedback to users regarding their progress. Users have the opportunity to challenge their friends and the results are recorded in leaderboards. This opportunity means that users know the identities, the progress and the reaction of others, resulting in their privacy violation as well.

Another example where users can compete, is the gamified service "4 Foods – Good 4 All" [43]. The concept of this application is absolutely different to the previous example. The company "4 Food" launches this service in order to increase its selling. Users can create sandwiches based on their preferences and they can share them with other users. The most popular choices are recorded on the top of the leaderboard and their users win rewards. The privacy issue in this example concerns the recording of users' preferences and the recognition of their results regarding their actions resulting in their identities to be linked to their actions. One of the most used gamified services is the "My Starbucks Reward" [43]. The popular company, Starbucks, launches this gamified service, purposing on enhancing users experience and increasing its products. Users have to register on the application and by purchasing a product, they win stars which full in graphical cups and afterwards they win rewards, such as an extra cup of coffee. In addition, the company offers a Starbucks rewards credit card, which can be used for the payments of users' orders. Besides these benefits for customers, the provided processes are risky regarding their privacy. Their preferences, orders, payments, results of actions are directly linked to their identities, so as their privacy cannot be protected.

The benefits of gamified applications for users in health sector are crucial, since by them users can protect their health. For instance, "Mango Health" [44] is an application which sends notifications to users in order to remind them their daily prescription. Patients are rewarded with points when they take their medication and larger rewards are gift cards for specific companies. Similarly, "Asthma Hero" [44] is an application which reminds young patients who suffer from asthma for their medication. The application gives the opportunity to the patients to select their own hero character and to win rewards for their consistency, which is monitored by their physicians. The application "Respond Well" [44] tries to keep patients engaged in exercises, by providing virtual animated characters, music and three-dimensional (3D) graphics. Patients earn points and they can challenge their families and friends to exercise with them. The progress and repetition of patients is recorded and can be monitored by their doctors. In all these applications, patients have to create profiles, where their personal information is stored. In addition, they can interact with others, which means that other users can be informed about their progress and actions. Another privacy issue is that the progress of users is stored in order for doctors or physicians to be informed. Even though all these processes support users' health protection, they violate their privacy, since their identities are connected to their actions.

Another example of gamified applications is the "Smartypig" [42], aiming to help users reach their financial goals. Specifically, if users want to buy a product, then they have to save this goal and automatically, money from their bank account can be added to this goal. While users add money to their savings, a progress bar shows their progress. This application may help people saving money, but it can also be linked to their bank accounts, which is equally risky for their privacy. Specifically, in case of violation, a third party would be able to recognise the bank account of the user and since the application is connected to user's bank account, his/her credentials may be hacked in.

According to the above examination, most of the gamified services of several sectors use game elements, which violate plenty of privacy requirements and consequently users' privacy is not protected efficiently.

4 Metamodel

Based on the results of the aforementioned examination, many privacy issues arise. Even if the several benefits that the applications offer to customers or patients are important, depending on the context of each service, their personal information, progress and actions are recorded and monitored [9, 10].

Game elements provide advantages to users, while in parallel, some of them may harm users' privacy. As a consequence, it is needed to identify which are the benefits of the elements, which of their disadvantages could violate privacy and with which privacy requirements they conflict. In our previous work [2], the amount of the game elements that have been recorded in the literature, were presented, as it was identified that several elements are reported separately in each work. The examination of the requirements and the elements relation will support software developers to consider privacy issues during the implementation of game elements. Software developers should consider not only how users can be engaged to use gamified services in order to gain these benefits, but also to analyse the privacy requirements into these systems, so as to protect users' privacy. In that way, they will be able to implement techniques, which protect users' personal information and actions, without disturbing the aim of each game element. To be more clearly, a metamodel, presented in Fig. 2, has been developed, which illustrates this relation. The advantages and the disadvantages of each element have been recorded, while based on the disadvantages of each element, the violated privacy requirements have been assigned to each element. It's important to note that only the game elements which conflict with the privacy requirements are described, since these ones should be examined by the software developers. In this metamodel the relationship between users, game elements and privacy requirements is highlighted.

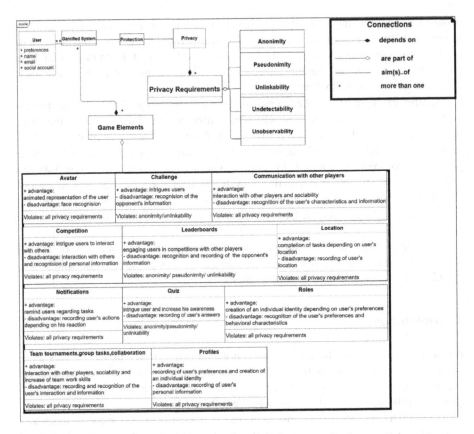

Fig. 2. Metamodel – the relation between game elements and privacy requirements

The user consists the beginning of the model, as without his/her participation a gamified service cannot be used. Thus, there are some required conditions before starting using a gamified service. These conditions are resulted by the examined applications and are assigned to the user. First of all, each user selects the gamified service based on his/her preferences. For instance, if a user prefers to be educated, the corresponding gamified applications will increase his/her interest. In case a user has health issues, there are services which support the protection of his/her health, by reminding a daily prescription. After selecting the preferable service, a user has to create a profile, where a name is needed, and to provide his/her email for the registration. Some applications provide also the ability of connecting by a social account, mostly a Facebook account.

The profile is one of the most used elements, since most of the gamified services require its creation. By the profile, users can create an individual identity in the service and their status and progress can be recorded. The elements avatar and role provide the creation of a specific identity, depending on users' face and users' preferences accordingly. The role of a user could be a teacher or a student in an educational gamified service. By creating an avatar, user can represent him/herself with an animated technique and based on his/her expressions and characteristics. These two elements provide a more entertaining representation of the user than a simple character in a service. There are also elements which support the increase of users' sociability, as by the *communication, collaboration* and *competition* users can interact with others. In addition, group tasks can enhance team work skills. In most of the gamified applications that there are competitions among users, the results are recorded in *leaderboards* and subsequently this element enforces users to compete each other by comparing their status, points and progress. *Challenges* is another element which intrigues users, as it supports users' interaction as well.

In some services mainly in these with educational concept, *quizzes* are used to increase users' knowledge by answering questions, collecting points and passing levels. The use of *notifications* is helpful for users as, for instance, they can be informed about their daily prescription in the case of health sector. Concluding, the connection with users' *location* consists a requirement in some services, in order for users to complete tasks and pass levels. Therefore, as many users can utilize many gamified services, increasing their engagement and therefore the aim of gamification is supported.

All these elements besides the benefits, have disadvantages which are harmful for users' privacy. All *privacy requirements* can be violated by the creation of a profile, as users' personal information, status, actions and progress can be recorded. The profile is connected to users' emails or social accounts and therefore their anonymity or pseudonimity cannot be protected. Users' actions can be linked to their identity and can be detected, so that their actions cannot be hidden and not observed.

The same violation concerns the use of an avatar or a role, as users' faces are recorded, and personal behavioural characteristics can be recognised, accordingly. The elements which support users' interaction and improve their sociability, are harmful for their privacy, as their personal information, actions and characteristics are recorded and consequently they can be recognised. These elements, as it was mentioned previously, are the competition, the communication and the collaboration between users. All privacy requirements can be violated, due to their concept. Another element which conflict with privacy requirements is the recognition of users' location. The recording of users' location automatically means that users' actions can be monitored, and their identity can be compromised. Similarly, users' actions can be linked to their identity by using notifications, their reactions are recorded. By recording users' progress and status in leaderboards, users' identity can be linked to their actions and except from the unlinkability, anonymity can be violated as well, while users' pseudonymous can be recognised by users' accounts. Similarly, by answering quizzes, whose context are based on users' information or habits, users' anonymity is at risk; their pseudonymous can be disclosed and the answers can be linked to each person. Concluding, in case of a challenge between users, the opponents' identity and information can be recognised and linked to their actions, so that their anonymity can be compromised.

The metamodel contributes towards this direction by presenting the relation between each element and the respective privacy requirement that may violated. On the one hand, game elements offer benefits to users and support the utilization of the gamified services, while on the other, their benefits are risky for users' privacy. According to the results, illustrated in the metamodel, most of the game elements may violate all privacy requirements and therefore privacy violation is inevitable.

By consulting this model, software developers will be able to understand how each element impacts on requirements, in order for them to think, during the design phase of a service, which mechanisms could prevent privacy violation. Thus, they will design gamified services which will engage users more and more on using ICTs, while reducing their privacy concerns by protecting their personal information.

5 Conclusions

As gamification is a growingly used method within ICTs, many users interact with gamified services. This interaction offers several benefits to users, respectively to the context of each service, such as their education through a more entertaining way or the improvement of their health. All these actions and personal information are stored and monitored by the services, raising privacy risks [41]. Thus, users' privacy protection is important while using gamified services. The aim of this study was to provide a metamodel which represents the relation between the two cores - *the game elements and the privacy requirements* - of these domains. The development of this metamodel, is based our previous work regarding the relation between gamification and privacy [2]. In order to provide a more sufficient description of the results, existent gamified services were analysed, highlighting the emerging privacy issues. In the correspondent section, based on the results, it is described how the offered benefits of each example could be at the same time a case of privacy violation. The goal of a gamified application should be the engagement of users, but not without taking into consideration the protection of users' privacy. As it was identified, the game elements conflict with the privacy requirements, so that a solution is needed. As far as gamification concerns, game elements are used to gamify a service [3], while, in order for privacy to be protected, the analysis of privacy requirements into systems is needed [22, 23]. Both these principles have to be considered during the design phase of a service. This metamodel gives the opportunity to software developers to check how each element may conflict to privacy requirements, so that then they will be able to apply appropriate techniques for privacy protection. By enhancing the trust between services and users, automatically, the use of gamified services can be increased, resulting in more profit regarding the marketing sector or in the empowerment of users' skills and knowledge by the use of educational services [3]. In our future work, the metamodel will be evaluated through a cooperation with software developers, in order for us to identify which parts have to be improved and which techniques/mechanisms have to be implemented. Afterwards, a more detailed version of the metamodel could be designed.

References

1. Deterding, S., Dixon, D., Khaled, R., Nacke, L.: From game design elements to gamefulness: defining 'gamification' (2011)
2. Mavroeidi, A.-G., Kitsiou, A., Kalloniatis, C., Gritzalis, S.: Gamification vs. privacy: identifying and analysing the major concerns. Future Internet **11**, 67 (2019). https://doi.org/10.3390/fi11030067

3. Stanculescu, L.C., Bozzon, A., Sips, R.-J., Houben, G.: Work and play: an experiment in enterprise gamification. In: Proceedings of the 19th ACM Conference on Computer-Supported Cooperative Work and Social Computing - CSCW 2016, pp. 345–357. ACM Press, San Francisco (2016)

4. Seth, A., Vance, J.M., Oliver, J.H.: Virtual reality for assembly methods prototyping: a review. Virtual Real. **15**, 5–20 (2011). https://doi.org/10.1007/s10055-009-0153-y

5. Azuma, R.: A survey of augmented reality. Presence: Teleoperators Virtual Environ. **6**(4), 355–385 (1997)

6. Conole, G., Dyke, M.: What are the affordances of information and communication technologies? ALT-J. **12**, 113–124 (2004). https://doi.org/10.1080/0968776042000216183

7. Mora, A., Riera, D., Gonzalez, C., Arnedo-Moreno, J.: A literature review of gamification design frameworks. In: 2015 7th International Conference on Games and Virtual Worlds for Serious Applications (VS-Games), pp. 1–8. IEEE, Skövde (2015)

8. Hamari, J., Koivisto, J., Sarsa, H.: Does gamification work? – a literature review of empirical studies on gamification. In: 2014 47th Hawaii International Conference on System Sciences, pp. 3025–3034. IEEE, Waikoloa (2014)

9. Gåsland, M.M.: Master: Game mechanic based e-learning- a case study. Norwegian University of Science and Technology, Norway, June 2011

10. Huang, W.H.-Y., Soman, D.: A practitioner's guide to gamification of education. University of Toronto, December 2013

11. The 10 Best Educational Apps that use Gamification for adults in 2018. https://yukaichou.com/gamification-examples/top-10-education-gamification-examples/

12. Lucassen, G., Jansen, S.: Gamification in consumer marketing - future or fallacy? Procedia - Soc. Behav. Sci. **148**, 194–202 (2014). https://doi.org/10.1016/j.sbspro.2014.07.034

13. Cafazzo, J.A., Casselman, M., Hamming, N., Katzman, D.K., Palmert, M.R.: Design of an mHealth app for the self-management of adolescent type 1 diabetes: a pilot study. J. Med. Internet Res. **14**, e70 (2012). https://doi.org/10.2196/jmir.2058

14. Huotari, K., Hamari, J.: Defining gamification: a service marketing perspective. In: Proceeding of the 16th International Academic MindTrek Conference on - MindTrek 2012, p. 17. ACM Press, Tampere (2012)

15. Xu, F., Weber, J., Buhalis, D.: Gamification in tourism. In: Xiang, Z., Tussyadiah, I. (eds.) Information and Communication Technologies in Tourism 2014, pp. 525–537. Springer International Publishing, Cham (2013). https://doi.org/10.1007/978-3-319-03973-2_38

16. Mehrbod, A., Mehrbod, N., Grilo, A., Vasconcelos, C., Silva, J.L.: Gamification in supported geocaching tours. In: 2017 International Conference on Engineering, Technology and Innovation (ICE/ITMC), pp. 1419–1423. IEEE, Funchal (2017)

17. Sever, N.S., Sever, G.N., Kuhzady, S.: The evaluation of potentials of gamification in tourism marketing communication. Int. J. Acad. Res. Bus. Soc. Sci. **5**, 188–202 (2015). https://doi.org/10.6007/ijarbss/v5-i10/1867

18. Almaliki, M., Jiang, N., Ali, R., Dalpiaz, F.: Gamified culture-aware feedback acquisition. In: 2014 IEEE/ACM 7th International Conference on Utility and Cloud Computing, pp. 624–625. IEEE, London (2014)

19. Döpker, A., Brockmann, T., Stieglitz, S.: Use cases for gamification in virtual museums (2013)

20. Heryadi, Y., Robbany, A.Z., Sudarma, H.: User experience evaluation of virtual reality-based cultural gamification using GameFlow approach. In: 2016 1st International Conference on Game, Game Art, and Gamification (ICGGAG), pp. 1–5. IEEE, Jakarta (2016)

21. Yonemura, K., Yajima, K., Komura, R., Sato, J., Takeichi, Y.: Practical security education on operational technology using gamification method. In: 2017 7th IEEE International Conference on Control System, Computing and Engineering (ICCSCE), pp. 284–288. IEEE (2017)

22. Yonemura, K., et al.: Effect of security education using KIPS and gamification theory at KOSEN. In: 2018 IEEE Symposium on Computer Applications and Industrial Electronics (ISCAIE), pp. 255–258. IEEE, Penang (2018)

23. Yonemura, K., Sato, J., Takeichi, Y., Komura, R., Yajima, K.: Security education using gamification theory. In: 2018 International Conference on Engineering, Applied Sciences, and Technology (ICEAST), pp. 1–4. IEEE, Phuket (2018)

24. Shahri, A., Hosseini, M., Phalp, K., Taylor, J., Ali, R.: Towards a code of ethics for gamification at enterprise. In: Frank, U., Loucopoulos, P., Pastor, Ó., Petrounias, I. (eds.) PoEM 2014. LNBIP, vol. 197, pp. 235–245. Springer, Heidelberg (2014). https://doi.org/10.1007/978-3-662-45501-2_17

25. Herzig, P., Ameling, M., Schill, A.: A generic platform for enterprise gamification. In: 2012 Joint Working IEEE/IFIP Conference on Software Architecture and European Conference on Software Architecture, pp. 219–223. IEEE, Helsinki (2012)

26. Pattakou, A., Mavroeidi, A.-G., Diamantopoulou, V., Kalloniatis, C., Gritzalis, S.: Towards the design of usable privacy by design methodologies. In: 2018 IEEE 5th International Workshop on Evolving Security and Privacy Requirements Engineering (ESPRE), pp. 1–8. IEEE, Banff (2018)

27. Pattakou, A., Kalloniatis, C., Gritzalis, S.: Security and privacy requirements engineering methods for traditional and cloud-based systems: a review. In: CLOUD Computing (2017)

28. Islam, S., Mouratidis, H., Kalloniatis, C., Hudic, A., Zechner, L.: Model based process to support security and privacy requirements engineering. Int. J. Secure Softw. Eng. 3, 1–22 (2012). https://doi.org/10.4018/jsse.2012070101

29. Liu, L., Yu, E., Mylopoulos, J.: Security and privacy requirements analysis within a social setting. J. Light. Technol. 151–161 (2003)

30. Kalloniatis, C., Belsis, P., Gritzalis, S.: A soft computing approach for privacy requirements engineering: the PriS framework. Appl. Soft Comput. 11, 4341–4348 (2011). https://doi.org/10.1016/j.asoc.2010.10.012

31. Deng, M., Wuyts, K., Scandariato, R., Preneel, B., Joosen, W.: A privacy threat analysis framework: supporting the elicitation and fulfillment of privacy requirements. Requir. Eng. 16, 3–32 (2011). https://doi.org/10.1007/s00766-010-0115-7

32. Jensen, C., Tullio, J., Potts, C., Mynatt, E.D.: STRAP: a structured analysis framework for privacy (2015)

33. King, D., Greaves, F., Exeter, C., Darzi, A.: 'Gamification': influencing health behaviours with games. J. R. Soc. Med. 106, 76–78 (2013). https://doi.org/10.1177/0141076813480996

34. Top Ten Gamified Healthcare Games that will extend your Life. https://yukaichou.com/gamification-examples/top-ten-gamification-healthcare-games/

35. de Paz, B.M.: Gamification: a tool to improve sustainability efforts. Ph.D. dissertation, University of Manchester, England (2013)

36. Seaborn, K., Fels, D.I.: Gamification in theory and action: a survey. Int. J. Hum.-Comput. Stud. 74, 14–31 (2015). https://doi.org/10.1016/j.ijhcs.2014.09.006

37. Top 10 Marketing Gamification Cases You Won't Forget. https://yukaichou.com/gamification-examples/top-10-marketing-gamification-cases-remember/

38. Werbach, K., Hunter, D.: For the Win: How Game Thinking Can Revolutionize Your Business. Wharton Digital Press, Philadelphia (2012)

39. Morford, Z.H., Witts, B.N., Killingsworth, K.J., Alavosius, M.P.: Gamification: the intersection between behavior analysis and game design technologies. Behav. Anal. **37**, 25–40 (2014). https://doi.org/10.1007/s40614-014-0006-1

40. Morschheuser, B., Hassan, L., Werder, K., Hamari, J.: How to design gamification? A method for engineering gamified software. Inf. Softw. Technol. **95**, 219–237 (2018). https://doi.org/10.1016/j.infsof.2017.10.015

41. Ahtinen, A., et al.: Mobile mental wellness training for stress management: feasibility and design implications based on a one-month field study. JMIR Mhealth Uhealth **1**, e11 (2013). https://doi.org/10.2196/mhealth.2596

42. Bista, S.K., Nepal, S., Paris, C.: Engagement and cooperation in social networks: do benefits and rewards help? In: 2012 IEEE 11th International Conference on Trust, Security and Privacy in Computing and Communications, pp. 1405–1410. IEEE, Liverpool (2012)

43. Chen, Y., Pu, P.: HealthyTogether: exploring social incentives for mobile fitness applications. In: Proceedings of the Second International Symposium of Chinese CHI on - Chinese CHI 2014, pp. 25–34. ACM Press, Toronto (2014)

44. Cheong, C., Cheong, F., Filippou, J.: Quick Quiz: a gamified approach for enhancing learning (2013)

45. Cramer, H., Rost, M., Holmquist, L.E.: Performing a check-in: emerging practices, norms and 'conflicts' in location-sharing using foursquare. In: Proceedings of the 13th International Conference on Human Computer Interaction with Mobile Devices and Services - MobileHCI 2011, p. 57. ACM Press, Stockholm (2011)

46. McDaniel, R., Lindgren, R., Friskics, J.: Using badges for shaping interactions in online learning environments. In: 2012 IEEE International Professional Communication Conference, pp. 1–4. IEEE, Orlando (2012)

47. Denny, P.: The effect of virtual achievements on student engagement. In: Proceedings of the SIGCHI Conference on Human Factors in Computing Systems - CHI 2013, p. 763. ACM Press, Paris (2013)

48. Amo, L.C., Liao, R., Rao, H.R., Walker, G.: Effects of leaderboards in games on consumer engagement. In: Proceedings of the 2018 ACM SIGMIS Conference on Computers and People Research - SIGMIS-CPR 2018, pp. 58–59. ACM Press, Buffalo-Niagara Falls (2018)

Audit, Compliance and Threat Intelligence

Decentralised and Collaborative Auditing of Workflows

Antonio Nehme[✉], Vitor Jesus, Khaled Mahbub, and Ali Abdallah

School of Computing and Digital Technology, Birmingham City University,
Birmingham, UK
{antonio.nehme,vitor.jesus,khaled.mahbub,ali.abdallah}@bcu.ac.uk

Abstract. Workflows involve actions and decision making at the level of each participant. Trusted generation, collection and storage of evidence is fundamental for these systems to assert accountability in case of disputes. Ensuring the security of audit systems requires reliable protection of evidence in order to cope with its confidentiality, its integrity at generation and storage phases, as well as its availability. Collusion with an audit authority is a threat that can affect all these security aspects, and there is room for improvement in existent approaches that target this problem.

This work presents an approach for workflow auditing which targets security challenges of collusion-related threats, covers different trust and confidentiality requirements, and offers flexible levels of scrutiny for reported events. It relies on participants verifying each other's reported audit data, and introduces a secure mechanism to share encrypted audit trails with participants while protecting their confidentiality. We discuss the adequacy of our audit approach to produce reliable evidence despite possible collusion to destroy, tamper with, or hide evidence.

Keywords: Audit trails · Confidentiality · Accountability · Collusion

1 Introduction

A virtual organisation, defined as a collaboration of independent organisations to fulfill a business requirement [13], requires tasks and decision making to be spread among the different administrative and security domains of participants. These collaborations necessitate a way to keep track of transactions between the involved parties, and evidence of actions needs to be available to assign accountability in case of a dispute. Evidence should be reliable, and its processing should not disclose confidential information to any party.

A number of studies shed light on the importance of audit trails in systems involving multiple participants. Examples of these systems include banking scenarios, logistics, supply chain, and e-government [12,24,26,27]. Werner et al. [25] highlight the importance of reliable audit trails in the financial accounting sector. Kuntze et al. [11] stress on the importance of data authenticity, integrity and

© Springer Nature Switzerland AG 2019
S. Gritzalis et al. (Eds.): TrustBus 2019, LNCS 11711, pp. 129–144, 2019.
https://doi.org/10.1007/978-3-030-27813-7_9

privacy for evidence stored in forensic databases; they state that maintaining the confidentiality of parties involved in a chain of evidence is challenging.

To illustrate the challenge, we present a hypothetical scenario: car insurance companies rely on data about the driver's behaviour and habits to calculate their annual fees. When an individual applies for renewal, the insurance company sends a request to assess the applicant to the Ministry of Transport. This ministry requests the car mileage from garages that perform vehicles annual checkups and any arrest warrant for the applicant from the police department, and checks the databases of traffic cameras for the neighbourhood in which the car is most frequently used. Insurance companies do not get all the details about the driver due to the confidentiality of this data; they receive a report with an assessment from the Ministry of Transport and use it to determine the insurance fees. Audit records for every request should be kept: each organisation maintains a log, and an audit service is used to build audit trails. A privileged insider at the Ministry of Transport, colluding with an insurance company, modifies the mileage received from the garages to increase insurance fees. This insider also modifies the local logs, and colludes with the audit service to modify the audit records. As seen in this scenario, a collusion with an entity managing a central audit service renders its data unreliable. Moreover, audit records in workflows include sensitive information for all participants. In this scenario, audit records stored at the Ministry of Transport or with a central audit system expose personal and confidential data.

For a workflow audit architecture to be trusted, one participant should not have the option of colluding with the authority that manages the audit system to breach the confidentiality of, tamper with, or destroy evidence [29]. A central approach in which a single system is trusted to collect, verify, and store logs is a single point of failure in this case. In practice, workflow engines, commonly used to coordinate interactions between workflow participants and to provide auditing services, are a representation of a central approach for audit [12,17]. Some approaches, [26] for example, propose holding each participating administration accountable to store its own audit logs. Although this practice protects the confidentiality of participants, it does not provide protection against tampering with and destroying evidence.

We, therefore, follow a trustless approach to produce reliable evidence. We define trustless audit by not giving an organisation the ability to generate evidence without a verification of its authenticity. Our architecture retrieves and verifies audit records in a distributed way immediately after generation by participants, while protecting the confidentiality, integrity, and availability of this data from malicious entities working individually or colluding with each other. Following our approach, malicious behaviour of tampering with, deleting, or false reporting of audit records is detected by honest participants. Our contribution is an architecture that offers mitigation from collusion-related threats to tamper with or destroy multi-party workflow audit data. This depends on the collaboration of participants to verify and obtain a copy of encrypted audit records reported to an audit server, as well as to ensure the authenticity of this server.

We use Shamir secret sharing mechanism [18] to minimise the risk of confidential data exposure.

In a multi-party workflow, our architecture:

- Offers a means to verify reported audit records.
- Supports distributed storage of audit data at any degree of details.
- Introduces a data structure for audit trails covering arbitrary topology.
- Offers audit capability to any K out of N participants.

This rest of this paper is organised as follows. Section 2 presents related work. Section 3 presents the problem statement and the threat model. A detailed explanation of our approach is presented in Sect. 4, and an analysis of its adequacy to fulfil our goals in Sect. 5. Implementation and evaluation are covered in Sect. 6, and we conclude the paper in Sect. 7.

2   Related Work

Many audit frameworks proposed in the literature log events as evidence to verify abiding to security policies and regulatory requirements. Rudolph et al. [17] designed an audit trail with a summary of participation exchanged between participants to show fulfilment of tasks and enforce behavioural policies during workflow execution; they extended their work in [22] to cover the anonymity of participating entities, but did not discuss the security of audit trails at storage and their protection from destruction. Hale et al. [10] present a design and verification framework for services interactions across different clouds to verify abiding to information sharing policies. Other solutions [5–8,12,19,27] cover a variety of audit data including signatures, users' consents for access control, data provenance, service level agreements related logs, and records of database access. However, a trusted central system is used to process logs in [19] and to store audit records in the other frameworks. This raises trust and confidentiality problems since collusion with the central point in any of these cases makes tampering with or destroying evidence possible, as well as breaching the secrecy of audit data.

To protect the confidentiality of audit data, especially when relying on a third party service as proposed in [15] and [16], a common practice is to encrypt audit data prior to its submission to the outsourced storage. [1,2,23] are proposals that require a trusted party to protect encryption keys for audits, and Wouters et al. [26] rely on the user to protect the key in their approach. Entities with encryption keys can breach the confidentiality and in some cases the integrity of audit data; also, refusing to share these keys when an audit is required leads to withholding evidence. The framework proposed by Ray et al. [16] uses a secret sharing scheme to split encryption keys to multiple logging hosts; however, their approach covers logging for single applications, and does not consider multi-party interactions.

For forensic investigations, a high degree of assurance for the integrity of digital evidence is required at the collection, generation, and storage phases [29]. A variety of hash based approaches, relying on hash chains and hash trees, are proposed in [4, 21, 28, 29] to assure the integrity of audit records collected by a cloud service provider. Zawoard et al. [28] mitigate possible tampering with evidence that can result from collusion between users, investigators, and cloud service providers. They encrypt the log files with a public key belonging to a law enforcement agency to protect users' privacy, and adopt a hash-chain scheme referred to as 'Proof of Past Log (PPL)', covering the entire log history for every user on a daily basis. However, these approaches trust the logging entity, being the cloud provider, to report correct audit data and to assure its availability. A proposal by Ahsan et al. [3] is an extension that covers some of the limitations of [28]. In their work, log records generated by cloud service providers are not trusted, and users are required, within a specific timing, to verify their logged activity with their cloud provider and to file a complaint in case of any activity that needs to be denied. Logs attributed to a user are then stored on the cloud service provider servers and encrypted with this user's private key. To mitigate withholding evidence by users, a secret sharing mechanism is proposed to distribute shares of every user's keys to different cloud providers that are assumed not to collude. This approach covers auditing users' activities in a single cloud only, and does not consider multi-party workflows; it also assumes continuous human cooperation for its verification phase, and does not consider destruction of evidence by a cloud provider.

Blockchain is another approach that uses hash chains and the consensus of a large network of nodes to protect data at storage [24]. Some approaches, [20, 24] for example, use blockchains to produce audit trails for processes involving multiple parties; however, this technology does not scale to store large transactions, and therefore only hashes of these transactions are stored on the blockchain [20]. While similar approaches verify the integrity of audit records, they do not protect against destruction of evidence.

To the best of our knowledge, our approach improves the availability, confidentiality, and integrity of audit records in distributed systems. We combine practices in the literature for collective building of audit trails with forensic approaches to protect digital evidence, and introduce verification mechanisms in our architecture to assert accountability of participants in multi-party workflows.

3   Problem Statement and Threat Model

This work argues the need for improvement in audit approaches used for workflows covering multiple administrative domains. Every participant should be accountable for a contribution reflecting an action or a decision in a workflow. Existent audit approaches, discussed in the previous section, depend on trusted parties to record or store audit records; this renders the integrity and availability of these records questionable. Also, trusting a single entity with encryption keys leaves room for withholding evidence. When following approaches discussed in the literature, the problems below can be faced:

- Destroying or withholding evidence

- Tampering with audit data at storage
- Reporting incorrect audit data

3.1 Threat Model

This model excludes compromised elements being under the control of an attacker. Actions are considered to reflect the intentions of the administration managing an element, rather than a fault in the system. Certificate authorities and key issuers are honest; they distribute correct cryptographic keys and do not expose participants' secrets.

The adversary vector includes participants that aim to rig an audit reporting process to avoid non-repudiation. Adversary's goal can be achieved by destroying or tampering with audit records, or by using incorrect cryptographic keys for encryption or signatures to jeopardise the records' usability. The entity managing the audit server can also be malicious, and may attempt to tamper with, destroy, or hide audit records from some participants. A number of malicious entities (including workflow participants and the audit server) can collude to falsify the audit process; this includes skipping the verification of reported audits, hiding audit data from honest participants, cooperating to distribute different versions of records, and delaying the workflow with false alerts. Breaking the confidentiality of workflow transactions using audit records is another malicious goal for an adversary.

Under this model, we aim to verify the authenticity of reported audit records as they are generated as well as their integrity during storage or distribution, and to protect their confidentiality at every stage of the audit process. We also achieve the availability of evidence when a definable number of participants are honest. We consider audit data reported by colluding entities to be unreliable, but prove any malicious behaviour resulting from collusion by using reliable audit records reported by honest participants.

4 Proposed Approach

We propose a confidentiality friendly and decentralised approach for workflow audit. Encrypted audit trails, covering arbitrary workflows, are checked for authenticity as they are built, and are distributed to participants to protect from tampering with or destroying evidence. To safeguard the confidentiality of this data, a threshold of key shares is required to reconstruct the decryption key. This also minimises the chance of witholding evidence by an entity that is holding the key. Audit trails can be constructed with any degree of details ranging from a summary of interactions to full transactions.

4.1 Notation

We use a graph to represent workflows, in which nodes(vertices) represent an organisation in the workflow, and edges with weights represent the order of their

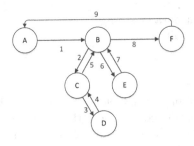

Fig. 1. Our representation of workflows.

interactions. In this regard, edge (A, B) in Fig. 1 is the first interaction in the workflow manifested by a message sent from organisation A to B. Workflows covered in this work are pre-established, meaning that the participating entities and their order of interaction are known by participants at the beginning of the workflow execution and do not change until it finishes.

For ease of representation, we introduce the notation below used to describe cryptography operations:

- An encrypted message sent from A to B, containing $Payload_{A \to B}$ and the signature of the sender over the payload, is represented by

$$Payload_{A \to B}(Sign_A, Enc_B) = Enc_B[(Payload_{A \to B}) + Sign_A(Payload_{A \to B})].$$

- An additional signature over the encrypted message, $Sign'_{sender}$, can be sent alongside the cipher text. The message in this case is represented by:

$$Payload_{A \to B}(Sign_A, Enc_B, Sign'_A) =$$
$$Payload_{A \to B}(Sign_A, Enc_B) + Sign_A[Payload_{A \to B}(Sign_A, Enc_B)]$$

- $Hash$ is a one-way hash function with a strong collision resistance.
- Shares of a workflow private key wfl_Pri, split with Shamir secret sharing to N shares, are referred to as $K_1...K_N$. The equivalent public key is wfl_Pub.
- String X concatenation with Y is represented by: $X||Y$.
  When presenting this architecture, the terms *node* and *participant* are used interchangeably to indicate a participants in a workflow.

4.2   System Overview

Our architecture uses a special node, referred to as the 'Audit Server'. This audit server can be hosted by any node or managed by a separate entity as a central or distributed system, but is not trusted by participants. It is only used to display audit records to participants during the workflow, and not to permanently store any data. For every action, an audit record is published on the audit server by a participant, and verified by another. Every participant in the workflow is given credentials to publish encrypted data on this server. Participants check the authenticity of the information on the server, and update their local storage of audit data continuously. Every participant has a certificate, and every workflow has a key pair which public part is known by all participants, but the private part is shared between them following Shamir secret sharing mechanism [18].

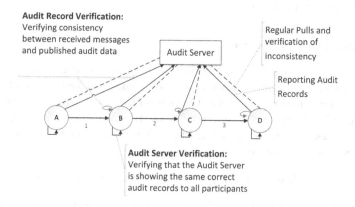

Fig. 2. Overview of the proposed architecture.

As shown in Fig. 2, the proposed approach includes two types of security verifications.

- The *Audit Record Verification* requires every node that receives a message to check it against its equivalent audit record published on the audit server.
- The *Audit Server Verification* requires every node to check for any inconsistency suggesting malicious behaviour from the audit server.

Before going through the details of these verification mechanisms, we present our key management scheme, and the data structure we use for our audit trails.

4.3 Key Management

We assume that certificates for every participant are managed with public key infrastructure (PKI). While certificates can be used in multiple workflows, workflow keys are only used in a single workflow topology.

Workflow key management is handled by an entity that generates a key pair (wfl_Pub, wfl_Pri), splits (wfl_Pri) following Shamir secret sharing mechanism [18], and securely distributes (wfl_Pub, K_i) to participants; a threshold K of shares (K_i) can reconstruct wfl_Pri. Workflow key distribution can either be done through direct messages to each participant over a secure channel, or by encrypting each share of the key with the corresponding participant's private key and posting them to the audit server.

This critical role should be given to the participant that has the least incentive to be dishonest with the key distribution and to expose wfl_Pri. This is

generally the first or last participant depending on the workflow: a first participant in one workflow can be a travel agency required to keep track of bookings
for its customers, and the last participant in another workflow can be a car
manufacturing industry that needs to keep track of where parts of customised
vehicles, ordered by customers, are from. Alternatively, this role can be assigned
to a dedicated key manager.

4.4   Audit Data Structure

This work covers logging for every interaction between participants in a workflow.
A message, sent from a participant to another, contains a payload which includes
the data for the intended recipient. Cryptographic operations are performed to
assure the authenticity and confidentiality of the transaction. For simplicity, we
assume the linear topology shown in Fig. 2. A message sent from C to D in the
workflow would be of the form

$$Msg_{C \to D} = Payload_{C \to D}(Sign_C, Enc_D)$$

In turn, audit data published by C on the audit server should have the exact
same payload, but is encrypted with the workflow public key, and signed after
encryption:

$$Audit_{C \to D} = Payload_{C \to D}(Sign_C, Enc_{wfl-Pub}, Sign'_C).$$

The second signature verifies that the audit server has not tampered with the
audit record. Each payload includes data to the receiver and audit records of the
previous transactions of the workflow when applicable. In this case

$$Payload_{C \to D} = Data_{C \to D} + Audit_{B \to C}.$$

Recursively, a decryption of an audit record with wfl_Pri, recovered from a
threshold K out of N parts (K_i) of wfl_Pri, leads to another encrypted one
which in its turn gets decrypted with the same key.

4.5   Audit Record Verification

Throughout the workflow, participants are required to verify the correctness of
the audit records equivalent to the messages that they receive.

As shown in Fig. 3, an audit record is published by every participant after
sending a message as well as the last participant after receiving the final message.
We only show the content of the $Payload$ in the exchanged messages for the
clarity of the figure.

A recipient decrypts the Msg with its private key, and verifies the sender's
signature. It then performs $Audit\ Record\ Verification$: the recipient updates its
storage of audit records from the audit server, then checks if the audit records of
previous transactions in the message are identical to what is shown on the audit
server. It also verifies that the sender of the message did not omit any audit

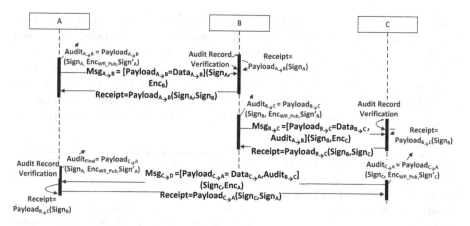

Fig. 3. Sequence diagram for our approach on a workflow that starts and ends with participant A. Upwards arrows represent reporting to the Audit Server.

records that should be included, and that these audit records are for the right previous transactions; this is feasible since every participant knows the topology of the pre-established workflow, and can therefore verify the signatures on the audit records. The recipient then re-encrypts the payload and sender's signature with wfl_Pub, and checks if the cipher version of it is on the audit server.

Back to Fig. 3, after a successful *Audit Record Verification* the recipient of a message keeps the payload with the sender's signature as a receipt. The recipient then sends this receipt back after adding its signature to the sender; this is a proof of delivery. In case any of these steps goes wrong, protocol is to raise concern for malicious behaviour.

Another test to verify the authenticity of the audit server is *Audit Server Verification*. Details about this mechanism is covered in the next section.

4.6   Audit Server Verification

Audit Server Verification algorithm is executed by every participant right after sending or receiving a message, and at a recurrent basis during the workflow. The frequency of execution is configured depending on the average execution time of a workflow. The aim is to ensure that the audit server is displaying the same authentic workflow audit records to every participant, and to distribute these records to participants. Tailoring responses to participants is possible if the Audit Server is malicious. We present the following mechanisms to target this challenge:

Digest on the Fly: when publishing audit records, each participant is required to add a digest of its local audit records storage, including the one that is being published, signed with its private key. Back to Fig. 2, $Audit_{B \to C}$ in this case would be published alongside

$$Hash(Audit_{A \to B} || Audit_{B \to C}) + Sign_C[Hash(Audit_{A \to B} || Audit_{B \to C})].$$

Referring to Algorithm 1, participants verify that the audit records that they published on and pulled from the audit server are still displayed; they then update their storage of audit records. After that, they compare the hash value of their stored audit records with the signed digest reported by the last publisher. Different digest values suggest that the audit server is showing different records to participants. Detecting a malicious activity from the audit server requires an honest participant to publish an audit record after this activity was committed.

Algorithm 1. Audit Server Verification Algorithm.

Requirement: Verify the authenticity of the Audit Server
Update local storage of audit records for participants
Input: $Reported\_Recs[]$ ▷ Audit records reported by a participant
$Stored\_Recs[]$ ▷ Audit records stored Locally with a participant
Output: Boolean indicating if Audit Server is honest

1: $Server\_Recs[] \leftarrow Pull\_Recs()$ ▷ Pull audit records from the server
2: **if** $Reported\_Recs \mathrel{!=} \varnothing$ **then**
3:     **for each** R∈Reported_Recs[] **do**
4:        **if** R does not exist in $Server\_Recs[]$ **then**
5:           return **False**
6: **if** $Stored\_Recs \mathrel{!=} \varnothing$ **then**
7:     **for each** R∈Reported_Recs[] **do**
8:        **if** R does not exist in $Server\_Recs[]$ **then**
9:           Return **False**
10: $Local\_Recs[] \leftarrow Server\_Recs[]$ ▷ Updating Stored Records
11: H← $Hash$(Local_Recs[])   ▷ Comparing Digests
12: **if** H==Last Published Digest **then**
13:    Return **True**
14: **else**
15:    Return **False**

Verify at the End: alternatively, the same steps of the Algorithm are followed, except that the hash comparison is only done at the end of the workflow. The final node publishes a signed digest of the records it has, and other participants follow and do the same. Not having identical digest values suggests a malicious behaviour from the audit server.

Combo: This combines both of the previous two approaches.

4.7 Protocol

This section lists the actions required to reach our security goals:

- Participants keep their receipts, and are required to alert others if a signed receipt of delivery is not received after sending a message.

- *Audit Record Verification* is always performed by recipients on message delivery. Failure of verification alerts all participants.
- *Audit Server Verification* is performed by a sender after publishing a record, a receiver when getting a message, and by every participant on a recurrent basis during the workflow. Failure of verification alerts all participants.

Following this protocol is essential to reveal any malicious activity by entities working on their own or colluding. We discuss potential attack scenarios in the next section.

5   Analysis

In this section, we discuss attack scenarios caused by a malicious node or a malicious audit server working individually, collusion among participants, and collusion between the malicious participants and the audit server. We analyse how each scenario is handled following our approach.

5.1   Malicious Participant

Working individually, a malicious participant can attempt to **truncate audit trails**: such participant attempts to publish incorrect audit data for the message it sent, or to send incorrect audit records of previous transactions in a message. This is caught by the *Audit Record Verification* performed by the honest recipient of the message.

5.2   Malicious Audit Server

A malicious audit server may attempt to hide audit records from all or some participants, or to tamper with these records.

Hiding Audit Records: a malicious audit server can attempt to hide audit records from some participants to limit the distribution of audit data and facilitate destruction of evidence. This is detected by digest verification of any adopted mechanism.

Tampering with Audit Records: this is detected as soon as an honest node reports and audit record with **Digest on the Fly** or **Combo** mechanisms, or at the end of the workflow when **Digest at the End** is followed.

Fig. 4. Collusion between participants with coloured background. (Colour figure online)

5.3   Collusion Between Nodes

What colluding participants can achieve and the impact of their collusion vary according to their positioning in a workflow. We discuss possible malicious behaviour of consecutive and non-consecutive colluders.

Non-consecutive Colluders: one malicious node in Fig. 4.1 can report an audit record for the other to use as part of their message. This is detected by the honest participant performing *Audit Record Verification*.

Consecutive Colluders: one node can cover for the other by skipping the *Audit Record Verification* phase. This leads to one of the cases below:

- Truncating the audit trail if C in Fig. 4.2 publishes a corrupted audit record, or a record not including previous audit data
- Having audit trail with a false record, if C reports different data for audit than what it sent to D.

Audit records posted or verified by nodes not following protocol are unreliable. Audit data published by B is reliable, since B has a receipt of delivery signed by C to prove its honesty. Honest node E also has a receipt, and it makes sure D publishes the equivalent audit record of the message it sent on the audit server. If there are more than two consecutive colluding nodes, the nodes that have followed the protocol and that surround the colluding participants will have credible audit data.

5.4   Collusion Between Participants and the Audit Server

In this section, we illustrate cases of collusion between participants and the audit server and discuss the adequacy of each verification mechanism. In Fig. 5.1, malicious node C can sign two different versions of an audit record; it relies on the audit server to display the correct record for only D and E, since they require it for the *Audit Record Verification*, and to display the faulty one to A and B. This is detected with any *Audit Server Verification* mechanism that is used:

1. If we publish signed digests with audit records (**Digest On the Fly**), this malicious activity is caught when node D, the first honest node following the malicious activity, publishes its audit data.

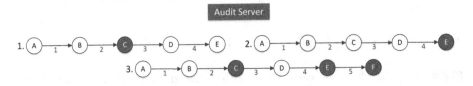

Fig. 5. Malicious audit server colluding with participants.

2. With **Verify at the End**, the malicious behaviour gets detected when comparing hash values at the end. When comparing audit records, two versions of a record incriminate both the audit server and the publishing node.
3. The combination of methods (**Combo**) also detects this malicious behaviour.

In Fig. 5.2, **Digest on the Fly** does not detect the collusion with the Audit Server since there is not an honest node that follows the malicious one. However, it does not lead to any data loss since all transactions have been covered in the record before it.

The combination of methods (**Combo**) combines the advantages of the two verification mechanisms; Fig. 5.3 is a scenario where **Combo** method is a good option:

- Attempts from C and the audit server to show A and B different versions of $Audit_{C \rightarrow D}$ than the one sent to D is detected on the fly.
- E and F cannot collude with the audit server to show honest participants different audit data.

6   Preliminary Evaluation

The implementation of the proposal is available on our Github repository[1]. In this section, we simulate a number of workflows relying on the same audit server. For this evaluation, we use a linear topology of nodes following our protocol, and consider the traffic of requests to the Audit Server to be log-normally distributed [9,14]. To simulate server load, we introduce a log-normally distributed delay of the form $e^{\mu+\sigma Z}$ to the Audit Server's response time. The figure below shows the

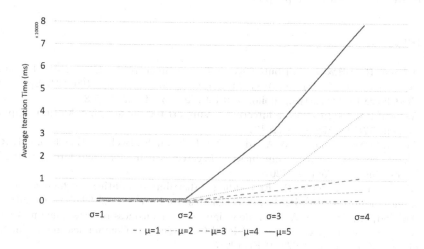

Fig. 6. Average processing time for different log-normally distributed delays.

---

[1] https://github.com/antonionehme/audit-repository-simulations/tree/master/AuditProject/AuditProject.

average processing time for each case. While the audit server processing power is inversely proportional to μ, σ reflects the multitude of workflows running simultaneously.

Following this evaluation method, changing the number of nodes and the size of the exchanged *Payload* resulted in graphs with different scales for the Average Iteration Time, but with similar slopes for the lines. Comparing the slope of curves in Fig. 6, servers with high computational power show stability and reliability at scale. Less powerful servers can still be used for systems that can afford latency at busy times.

7   Conclusion and Future Work

In this work, we presented an approach to enhance the availability, integrity and confidentiality of audit trails of workflows throughout the collection and storage of evidence. Collusion to hide or tamper with audit data is detectable, and the chance of withholding evidence is reduced due to the audit capability of K out of N participants.

This is part of a larger project to develop solutions for digital government workflows in which reliable audit is a key requirement. Decision making involving multiple government departments requires a collusion-proof audit system to assure the accountability while protecting the confidentiality of participants. This approach meets these requirements by providing a high level of assurance on the availability, integrity and confidentiality of digital evidence. We proposed this approach as part of a government digital transformation strategy, and we are working on integrating government-tailored scenarios and on evaluating our audit architecture for this purpose.

References

1. Accorsi, R.: BBox: a distributed secure log architecture. In: Camenisch, J., Lambrinoudakis, C. (eds.) EuroPKI 2010. LNCS, vol. 6711, pp. 109–124. Springer, Heidelberg (2011). https://doi.org/10.1007/978-3-642-22633-5_8
2. Accorsi, R.: A secure log architecture to support remote auditing. Math. Comput. Modell. **57**(7), 1578–1591 (2013)
3. Ahsan, M.M., Wahab, A.W.A., Idris, M.Y.I., Khan, S., Bachura, E., Choo, K.K.R.: Class: cloud log assuring soundness and secrecy scheme for cloud forensics. IEEE Trans. Sustain. Comput. (2018)
4. Alqahtani, S., Gamble, R.: Embedding a distributed auditing mechanism in the service cloud. In: 2014 IEEE World Congress on Services, pp. 69–76, June 2014
5. Aravind, A., Sandeep, A.: Workflow signature for business process domain: a new solution using IBMKD. In: 2015 Global Conference on Communication Technologies (GCCT), pp. 619–622. IEEE (2015)
6. Bates, A., et al.: Transparent web service auditing via network provenance functions. In: Proceedings of the 26th International Conference on World Wide Web, pp. 887–895. International World Wide Web Conferences Steering Committee (2017)

7. Flores, D.A.: An authentication and auditing architecture for enhancing security on egovernment services. In: 2014 First International Conference on eDemocracy eGovernment (ICEDEG), pp. 73–76 April 2014)

8. Gajanayake, R., Iannella, R., Sahama, T.: Sharing with care: an information accountability perspective. IEEE Internet Comput. **15**(4), 31–38 (2011)

9. Goseva-Popstojanova, K., Li, F., Wang, X., Sangle, A.: A contribution towards solving the web workload puzzle. In: International Conference on Dependable Systems and Networks (DSN 2006), pp. 505–516. IEEE (2006)

10. Hale, M.L., Gamble, M.T., Gamble, R.F.: A design and verification framework for service composition in the cloud. In: 2013 IEEE Ninth World Congress on Services, pp. 317–324, June 2013

11. Kuntze, N., Rudolph, C.: Secure digital chains of evidence. In: 2011 IEEE Sixth International Workshop on Systematic Approaches to Digital Forensic Engineering (SADFE), pp. 1–8. IEEE (2011)

12. Lim, H.W., Kerschbaum, F., Wang, H.: Workflow signatures for business process compliance. IEEE Trans. Dependable Secur. Comput. **9**(5), 756–769 (2012)

13. Nami, M.R., Malekpour, A.: Application of self-managing properties in virtual organizations. In: 2008 International Symposium on Computer Science and its Applications, CSA 2008, pp. 13–16. IEEE (2008)

14. Paxson, V.: Empirically-derived analytic models of wide-area TCP connections (1993)

15. Rajalakshmi, J.R., Rathinraj, M., Braveen, M.: Anonymizing log management process for secure logging in the cloud. In: 2014 International Conference on Circuits, Power and Computing Technologies [ICCPCT-2014], pp. 1559–1564, March 2014

16. Ray, I., Belyaev, K., Strizhov, M., Mulamba, D., Rajaram, M.: Secure logging as a service-delegating log management to the cloud. IEEE Syst. J. **7**(2), 323–334 (2013)

17. Rudolph, C., Kuntze, N., Velikova, Z.: Secure web service workflow execution. Electron. Notes Theor. Comput. Sci. **236**, 33–46 (2009)

18. Shamir, A.: How to share a secret. Commun. ACM **22**(11), 612–613 (1979)

19. Sundareswaran, S., Squicciarini, A.C., Lin, D.: Ensuring distributed accountability for data sharing in the cloud. IEEE Trans. Dependable Secur. Comput. **9**(4), 556–568 (2012)

20. Tian, F.: A supply chain traceability system for food safety based on HACCP, blockchain & internet of things. In: 2017 International Conference on Service Systems and Service Management (ICSSSM), pp. 1–6. IEEE (2017)

21. Tian, H., et al.: Enabling public auditability for operation behaviors in cloud storage. Soft. Comput. **21**(8), 2175–2187 (2017)

22. Velikova, Z., Schütte, J., Kuntze, N.: Towards security in decentralized workflows. In: 2009 International Conference on Ultra Modern Telecommunications & Workshops, ICUMT 2009, pp. 1–6. IEEE (2009)

23. Waters, B.R., Balfanz, D., Durfee, G., Smetters, D.K.: Building an encrypted and searchable audit log. In: NDSS, vol. 4, pp. 5–6 (2004)

24. Weber, I., Xu, X., Riveret, R., Governatori, G., Ponomarev, A., Mendling, J.: Untrusted business process monitoring and execution using blockchain. In: La Rosa, M., Loos, P., Pastor, O. (eds.) BPM 2016. LNCS, vol. 9850, pp. 329–347. Springer, Cham (2016). https://doi.org/10.1007/978-3-319-45348-4_19

25. Werner, M., Gehrke, N.: Multilevel process mining for financial audits. IEEE Trans. Serv. Comput. **8**(6), 820–832 (2015)

26. Wouters, K., Simoens, K., Lathouwers, D., Preneel, B.: Secure and privacy-friendly logging for egovernment services. In: 2008 Third International Conference on Availability, Reliability and Security, pp. 1091–1096, March 2008
27. Yao, J., Chen, S., Wang, C., Levy, D., Zic, J.: Accountability as a service for the cloud: from concept to implementation with BPEL. In: 2010 6th World Congress on Services (SERVICES-1), pp. 91–98. IEEE (2010)
28. Zawoad, S., Dutta, A., Hasan, R.: Towards building forensics enabled cloud through secure logging-as-a-service. IEEE Trans. Dependable Secur. Comput. 13(2), 148–162 (2016)
29. Zawoad, S., Dutta, A.K., Hasan, R.: SecLaaS: secure logging-as-a-service for cloud forensics. In: Proceedings of the 8th ACM SIGSAC Symposium on Information, Computer and Communications Security, pp. 219–230. ACM (2013)

Gender Inference for Facebook Picture Owners

Bizhan Alipour$^{(\boxtimes)}$, Abdessamad Imine$^{(\boxtimes)}$, and Michaël Rusinowitch$^{(\boxtimes)}$

Lorraine University, CNRS, Inria, 54506 Vandœuvre-lès-Nancy, France
{bizhan.alipour,abdessamad.imine,michael.rusinowitch}@loria.fr

Abstract. Social media such as Facebook provides a new way to connect, interact and learn. Facebook allows users to share photos and express their feelings by using comments. However, its users are vulnerable to attribute inference attacks where an attacker intends to guess private attributes (e.g., gender, age, political view) of target users through their online profiles and/or their vicinity (e.g., what their friends reveal). Given user-generated pictures on Facebook, we explore in this paper how to launch gender inference attacks on their owners from pictures meta-data composed of: (i) alt-texts generated by Facebook to describe the content of pictures, and (ii) comments posted by friends, friends of friends or regular users. We assume these two meta-data are the only available information to the attacker. Evaluation results demonstrate that our attack technique can infer the gender with an accuracy of 84% by leveraging only alt-texts, 96% by using only comments, and 98% by combining alt-texts and comments. We compute a set of sensitive words that enable attackers to perform effective gender inference attacks. We show the adversary prediction accuracy is decreased by hiding these sensitive words. To the best of our knowledge, this is the first inference attack on Facebook that exploits comments and alt-texts solely.

Keywords: Social network · Privacy · Inference attack · Gender inference · pictures

1 Introduction

In attribute inference attacks, the attacker aims to guess user's private attributes (such as gender, age, political view, or sexual orientation) from user's publicly available data. The attacker can train machine learning classifiers based on the collected data in order to infer private attributes. Recent works have investigated friend-based [9] and behavior-based [21] inference attacks on Facebook users.

Friend-based attacks are based on the intuition that friends share similar attributes. Indeed, the attacker proceeds in two steps: (i) drawing up the friend list of the target user; (ii) computing correlations from the public data of the

This work is supported by DIGITRUST (http://lue.univ-lorraine.fr/fr/article/digitrust/).

S. Gritzalis et al. (Eds.): TrustBus 2019, LNCS 11711, pp. 145–160, 2019.
https://doi.org/10.1007/978-3-030-27813-7_10

target user and his/her friends in order to identify hidden attributes of the target user [8]. As for Facebook behavior-based attacks, they are based on the intuition that *you are how you behave*. Thus, the attacker examines user behavior from liked pages and joined groups to infer his/her private attributes [2]. However, in a real scenario, the amount of available information to an attacker is rather small. In this work, we focus on Facebook as it is the largest social network in the world. More precisely, we consider the gender inference problem as gender can be considered as a sensitive information. Indeed, users wish to hide their gender for a variety of reasons: (1) They want to strengthen protection against discrimination. For instance, setting the gender to female results in getting fewer instances of an ad related to high paying jobs than setting it to male [5]. Targeting by sex is just one way Facebook and other tech companies let advertisers focus on certain users and exclude others. Facebook lets advertisers spend only on those they want to reach [17]; (2) They use the protection of anonymity to reduce the social risks of discussing unpopular and taboo topics [1,22]; (3) users want to prevent any form of sexual harassment and stalking as reported by the survey participants in [10].

Picture Alt-Text and Comments. Unlike previous works, we attempt to learn the target user gender based on his/her online pictures. Note that publishing pictures enable their owners to increase connectivity and activity on social networks. Nevertheless, they lose privacy control on their pictures because of some information (*meta-data*) added during online publication, such as: (i) Automatic Alt-Text (AAT) included by Facebook platform to describe the content of pictures, and (ii) comments posted by the closest friends as well as by strangers. Facebook launches AAT, a system that applied computer vision technology to identify faces, objects, and themes from pictures displayed by Facebook users to generate descriptive alt-text that can be used by the screen reader. This system allows blind people to feel more connected and involved in Facebook. The alt-text always starts by *Image may contain* and is followed by a list of recognized objects. Facebook provides a list of 97 objects and themes that provides different sets of information about the image, including people *(e.g., people count, smiling, child, baby)*, objects *(e.g., car, building, tree, cloud, food)*, settings *(e.g. inside restaurant, outdoor, nature)*, and themes *(e.g., close-up, selfie, drawing)* [20]. On the plus side, AAT provides free additional information about photos, and makes blind people feel more included and engaged in photos. On the negative side, this technology also provides the social network with yet another entry point in user private life, namely pictures. Furthermore, when observing a picture on Facebook, people write instinctively comments to express their feeling about the picture. These comments contain potentially sensitive information and are often available to the attacker.

Contributions. To raise awareness of social network users about their privacy, we propose to show the possibility of gender inference attack based on seemingly innocent data: *alt-text* which is generated by Facebook and picture *comments* which are written by target friends, friends of friends or ordinary users. Using machine learning techniques, we have developed a framework to determine how these pieces of information lead to design feature sets that can be exploited by an attacker to infer gender of picture owners.

Unlike existing inference attacks that require an exhaustive search in the target user networks, groups, and liked pages, our attack only needs target user public pictures. Additionally, unlike twitter gender inference attack that is based on target user writing sample [13], we intend to launch gender inference attack even when the user's writing style is unavailable. For instance in Fig. 1(a), the user has hidden most of his/her attributes on the profile, and *location* is the only attribute available to the attacker. Figure 1(b) shows the possibility of gender inference attacks based on alt-text and comments. In this example, Facebook generates the alt-text by detecting *one person* in the picture which has a *beard* and takes the picture in a *close-up* theme. The detection of *one person* guarantees that the alt-text and comments linked to the picture are pointing to one person. Hence, the presence of *beard* in alt-text, *son of epic, beard man* in comments can lead to gender inference attack. This attack target users who concern about their privacy (users who hide any types of available information such as friend list, liked pages, groups, and attributes on the profile) but they do not consider pictures meta-data (which are coming from Facebook and friends, friends of friends and ordinary person) as a harmful information.

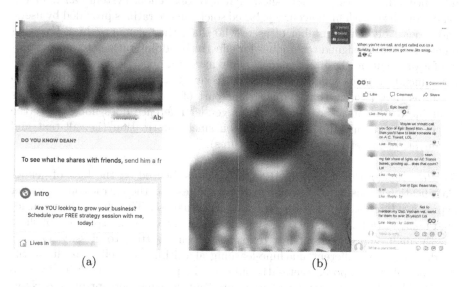

(a)   (b)

Fig. 1. User profile: (a) hiding attributes (b) alt-texts and comments in picture.

We notify two observations. Firstly, the alt-text is useful to filter/select the most informative image for the gender inference attack (see Subsect. 4.2). Secondly, sensitive information can be extracted from comments.

Outline. The paper is organized as follows: we review related work in Sect. 2. In Sect. 3 we describe our gender inference problem and overview our framework to analyze pictures. Section 4 presents in detail our methodology. Section 5 discusses our experimental results. We conclude the paper in Sect. 6.

2   Related Work

In this section, we review a number of recent studies that demonstrated attribute inference attacks on Facebook and Twitter.

Hidden Attribute Inference Attacks on Facebook. In [2], the authors inferred user private attributes using the public attributes of other users sharing similar interests and an ontologized version of Wikipedia. The authors of [7] proposed a new privacy attacks to infer attributes (e.g., locations, occupations, and interests) of online social network users by integrating social friends and behavioral records. They showed by increasing the availability of target users online information their results have serious implications in Internet privacy. In [8], the authors extended the Social-Attribute Network (SAN) framework with several leading supervised and unsupervised link prediction algorithms for link and attribute inferences. In [19], the authors show that a recommender system can infer the gender of a user with high accuracy, based solely on the ratings provided by users, and a relatively small number of users who share their demographics. Focusing on gender, they designed techniques for effectively adding ratings to a users profile for obfuscating the users gender, while having a nonsignificant effect on the recommendations provided to that user. To sum up, these inference attacks are costly as they assume that the entire or part of social network information is available to the attacker. Our work for gender inference does not explore the target user network and it relies only on small information (i.e. alt-text and comments of target user published pictures).

Twitter Gender Prediction. In [12], the authors focused on the task of gender classification by using 60 textual meta-attributes, for the extraction of gender expression linguistic in tweets written in Portuguese. Therefore, they considered many data (e.g., characters, syntax, words, structure, morphology of short length, multi-genre, content-free texts posted on Twitter) to classify author's gender via three different machine-learning algorithms as well as evaluate the influence of the proposed meta-attributes in the process. The work in [15] consists in identifying the gender of users on Twitter using perceptron and Naive Bayes from tweet texts. These works try to infer gender of tweet authors by syntactically or semantically analyzing the tweets. Unlike Twitter-based works, we discard the target user comments as they are irrelevant. Indeed, the target user is often careful to not disclose gender. More precisely, we try to infer gender indirectly by using comments underneath his/her pictures. These comments may be posted by friends, friends of friends or strangers.

3   Model Overview

In this section, we give the problem description and then present a brief overview of our framework.

Problem Description. In this study we consider three different scenarios according to the data availability: In the first scenario, we only consider alt-texts dataset as input data to infer the target user gender. This scenario happens when the pictures do not receive any comment, or when the comments have been hidden by their owners. In the second scenario, we have only access to comments dataset. We assume pictures are publicly visibile and Facebook is unable to generate alt-texts for them. In the last scenario, we use both extracted comments and alt-texts dataset. We also introduce some working hypothesis:

(1) We have no access to the gender of commenters who wrote the comments underneath pictures.
(2) We ignore the comments written by the target, since we assume the target is clever enough to hide gender information in his/her own texts.
(3) We do not know whether the commenters are target user friends, friends of friends, or ordinary persons.
(4) We do not perform any computer image processing on the target pictures.
(5) We do not consider user profile name as an input to our attack process. Although some names only used for a specific gender, the cultural, and geographic origin of names is known to have a great effect on the reliability of gender inference methods [14]. Moreover, the Facebook user may use the shortened name as a chosen name. It is due to privacy concerns, and it is a popular tactic to be identifiable only to friends, but not so easily to a stranger.

Let us now discuss the difficulty that arises when we try to solve the problem. In some situations, comments and alt-text seem to convey contradictory information. Below, we represent two examples where the comments alone orient gender inference towards one value but checking alt-text reveal that the conclusion is wrong.

Image 1:
Generated alt-text: 1 person, smiling, child and closeup
Comment: He looks so damn happy
Image 2:
Generated alt-text: dog, outdoor and nature
Comment: Who got u that handsome

The first image comment contains masculine pronoun HE, orienting the labeling towards male gender. The presence of *child* in alt-text suggests that the comment is pointing to a baby which is boy. In the second image, the comment orients also the labeling towards male as *handsome* is more often used for men. However checking the alt-text suggests that there is only a dog inside the picture. In order to avoid these misleading situations we pre-process the collected datasets and filter the pictures according to some rules defined in Subsect. 4.2.

Our Framework. Figure 2 depicts the five components (detailed in Sect. 4) of our framework for gender inference:

1. Data crawling: To perform attribute inference attack, we need to collect pictures meta-data such as alt-texts generated by Facebook and comments generated by friends, or friends of friends or ordinary users.
2. Data pre-processing: We prune the extracted data by applying two preprocessing steps. In the first step, we filter the pictures based on their generated alt-texts, and in the second step we prune the comments.
3. Features extraction: This process converts the input data into a set of features.
4. Feature selection: It is the process of selecting a subset of features which contribute most to the output.
5. Gender classification: We build a model to classify the target user gender.

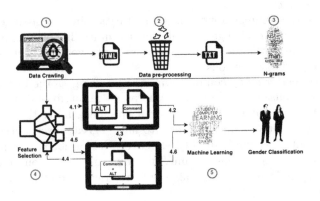

Fig. 2. Our framework.

4   Methodology

In this section, we describe in detail our methodology for gender inference attack. Basically, we discuss the way of extracting the raw data from the internet, finding useful information from the extracted data and prune the extracted data in such a way that present better prediction accuracy.

4.1   Data Crawling

Our objective is to infer the gender by collecting pictures meta-data. For each picture that we encounter, our crawler extracts the alt-text, and comments from the HTML file related to the picture. The gender of the user who posted the picture is collected (when available) in order to create labeled datasets to be exploited by our supervised machine learning algorithms. Our data is labeled with two genders *female* and *male*, corresponding to biological sex. The data is derived from random Facebook users. Let U be the set of target user pictures $U = \{u_1, u_2, u_3, .., u_m\}$. For every picture we extract $u_i = <a_i, c_i>$ where a_i is an alt-text generated by Facebook and c_i is the set of comments for that picture. We denote (i) $A = \bigcup_{0 < i \le m} a_i$ the set of all extracted alt-texts, and (ii) $C = \bigcup_{0 < i \le m} c_i$ the set of all extracted comments[1].

After constructing the comments and alt-texts dataset C and A respectively, we exploit these two datasets to launch gender inference attacks. The possibility of an attack depends on how informative are alt-texts and comments.

4.2 Data Pre-processing

Initially, we perform two pre-processing steps to clean collected data. We define a *singular form* to be a form that points only to one person. For example, *Handsome man* is a singular form that point to one man. A *plural form* is a form that pointing to more than one person. For instance, *beautiful women* is a plural form. Now we discuss about pre-processing which consists of:

A: Filtering the Picture w.r.t the Following Alt-Texts Rules. Facebook provides various types of information about the image through alt-text, and they categorize this information into four tags including *people, objects, settings,* and *themes* (as explained in Sect. 1). In this works [3], for example, they showed emotional words such as *cute* are selected by their methods for images containing *dog* and *kid*. As we discussed in Sect. 3, it was problematic to select picture containing useful meta-data. To solve the problem, we used *people* and *objects* tags inside picture generated alt-text.

Below, we describe the rules that we set to keep the pictures meta-data in our inference analysis.

Rule 0. As a default rule, we keep the picture meta-data if there is no *person* in *people tag*, no *animals* in *objects tag*, and no *child* inside the alt-text.

Rule 1. We keep the picture meta-data if the generated alt-text contains *1 person*. Note there might be other tags such as *objects, setting,* and *themes*. This rule is satisfied when there is only *1 person* in *people tag* and no *animals* in *objects tag* no *child* in the generated alt-text.

Example 1. In the following example, we keep the picture meta-data as there is *1 person* in *people tag* and there is no other tags.
Generated alt-text: 1 person
Comments$_1$: Hot mom!
Comments$_2$: Thats a really good picture!

---

[1] $\bigcup$ is the disjoint union.

Rule 2. If the number of people mentioned by alt-text is more than *1* in *people tag*, then we analyze the comments without considering *animals* and *child* tags. We keep the picture meta-data if comments point only to one gender and contain at least one singular form. By having all male or female words in the comments, we can be certain that people with the same gender are inside the picture and we can assume that one of those people might be the owner. In another hand, if there are mixed genders in the picture, then we are not sure (for that picture) the owner is male or female.

Example 2. In the following example, according to alt-text, there are four people inside the picture. In this case, we consider the plural and singular form of words. Hence, the presence of a HANDSOME MAN which is pointing to one person leads us to keep the picture meta-data for further analysis. Note that in this example there is no word pointing to different gender *female* and *male*.
Generated alt-text: 4 people, people smiling
Comments₁: Handsome man, And a yummy sunday
Comments₂: Wow! I never thought this day would happen

Rule 3. If alt-text contains *1 person* in *people tag* and some *animals* in *objects tag*, then we further analyze the comments. We keep the picture meta-data if comments orient to only one gender. An example of such a situation is given below:

Example 3. Generated alt-text: 1 person, dog and indoor
Comments₁: Sorry for your loss
Owner reply: Thank you
Comments₂: aw, i'm so sorry
Comments₃: RIP sweet Lady

B: Cleansing Comments: In this work, we focus on English writing. So, in the second step we clean the comments as follow: (i) discarding non English comments by using python libraries such as *TextBlob, Guess_language*, and (ii) removing animated and graphic symbols such as *GIF*.

4.3   Features Extraction

N-grams. Feature extraction is the process of converting the original data to a dataset that contains a reduced number of features. The extracted features comprise information related to the desired properties of the original data. Difficulty in analyzing data from social media raises from the presence of different kinds of textual errors, such as misspellings and grammatical errors. Traditional Natural Language Processing (NLP) techniques cannot always deal with texts that often do not follow even the simplest and most basic syntactic rules [16]. In order to capture syntactic similarities, we employ n-grams. Basically, n-grams are a set of co-occurring words within a given window n. The basic point of n-grams is that they capture the language structure from the statistical point of view, like which words are likely to appear together in *male/female comments/alt-text* dataset.

Facebook users use the shortened form of a word (abbreviation) more often to save time on typing and expressing their feelings and thought in shortcuts inside comments. N-grams finds normal and deformed words that might be used more often by Facebook users. As a result, we received a feature *love u*, which contains a deformation letter *u* that refer to pronoun *you*. Note, the *u* in *love u* can be considered as a misspelled letter such as *a* by NLP techniques.

Optimum Window Size. Optimum n-grams length depends on the data type. For example, if the size of n in n-grams is too short, it may fail to capture important block of words. On the other hand, if it is too long, it may fail to capture the general knowledge [4]. For terminology extraction, Kenneth Church proposes a window size of 5 ($n \leq 5$). This size is a good compromise: on one hand, it is large enough to show some semantic relationships between words, and on the other hand, it is not too large to lose the relationships that demand strict adjacency between words [6]. With that in mind, we employ n-grams on *alt-texts* and *comment* dataset separately to generate distinct feature set. Our experiments showed that introducing *5-grams* on *comments dataset* and *6-grams* on *alt-texts dataset* degraded the performance, so we kept the lengths up to *4-grams* and *5-grams* in *comments* and *alt-texts dataset* respectively.

Let F_c be the comments feature set containing (f, v) where f is the feature and v is the occurrence of the feature. In this work, F_c is the sequence of n words, where $n \in \{1, 2, 3, 4\}$, generated by target user friends, friends of friends or ordinary users to express their feelings about the target user pictures. Let F_a be the alt-texts feature set: F_a is the sequence of n words, where $n \in \{1, 2, 3, 4, 5\}$, generated by Facebook. After extracting features from each dataset, we applied four feature selection algorithms to reduce the feature space and noise in the represented data.

4.4   Feature Selection Techniques

Feature Selection is the process of selecting features which contribute more to the prediction output (in our case, *male* and *female*). The choice of feature selection methods differs according to the problem and available data. Below, we discuss four feature selection methods that we have employed: *Chi-Square*[2] is used to test if the relationship of a dependent variable is significant to an independent variable. *Information Gain*[3] indicates the amount of information the independent variable presents with respect to the classification target attribute. It measures the difference in information was available before knowing the attribute value and after knowing the attribute value. *Feature importance*[4] provides a score

---

[2] https://scikit-learn.org/stable/modules/generated/sklearn.feature_selection.chi2.html.

[3] https://www.bogotobogo.com/python/scikit-learn/scikt_machine_learning_Decision _Tree_Learning_Informatioin_Gain_IG_Impurity_Entropy_Gini_Classification_Error. php.

[4] https://www.scikit-yb.org/en/latest/api/features/importances.html.

for each feature, the higher the score more important or relevant is the feature towards the output variable. Feature importance is an inbuilt class that proceeds with Tree Based Classifiers. *Univariate feature selection*[5] examines each feature individually to determine the strength of the relationship of the feature with the response variable. Algorithm 1 describes our feature selection process. We introduce the following notations:

1. LS is a document that associates to each occurrence of a feature the corresponding label (in our case *female, male*) of the profile from which this occurrence comes.
2. FSA_i where $i \in \{1, 2, 3, 4\}$ are feature selection algorithms used in this study.
3. $Score(i, f, LS)$ is the score of feature f with algorithm FSA_i.
4. T is a threshold. We keep the features that contribute more than T to the final result. We generally set the threshold to 0.5.
5. Res_i $i \in \{1, 2, 3, 4\}$ is the set of features with a score above the threshold.
6. MLA_m where $m \in \{1, 2, 3, 4, 5, 6\}$ are machine learning algorithms.
7. $Accuracy(m, F, L)$ measures the accuracy of MLA_m when applied to a set of features F and a labelling L of profiles. Accuracy is obtained as the ratio of correct predictions to the total of predictions.
8. $PS(J)$ is the intersection of feature sets obtained by selection algorithms with index in J.
9. $V(m, J)$ is the accuracy of machine learning algorithm MLA_m applied to PS_J and LS.
10. $(\bar{m}, \bar{J})$ is the combination of a feature set and a machine learning algorithm that gives the highest accuracy.

Note that FSA_i takes LS corresponding to F_c and F_a separately as input and generate score for each feature according to their predictive significance. Res_i contains features that are above the threshold. Using different feature selection methods lead to different selected features that might generate different prediction performance. In order to identify more representative features for better prediction, we evaluate all the possible individual and combined feature selection methods [11, 18]. Later we run machine learning algorithms in order to find the accuracy of each individual and combined feature selection algorithms. Finally, we select the feature set and machine learning algorithm that give the highest accuracy. We used six machine learning algorithms such as *Logistic Regression, Random Forest, K-Nearest Neighbors, Support Vector Machine, Naive Bayes,* and *Decision Tree* to compare the performance of each individual and combined feature selection algorithms.

5   Experimental Results

We first describe the datasets that we used for the evaluation, followed by the representation of machine learning results in different scenarios.

---

[5] https://scikit-learn.org/stable/auto_examples/feature_selection/plot_feature_selectio n.html.

input : LS, T, FSA_i, $(1 \leq i \leq 4)$, MLA_m, $(1 \leq m \leq 6)$
output: Best Features Set BFS

Step1:
for *all i* **do**
 | $Res_i \leftarrow \{f \mid score(i,f,LS) \geq T\}$
end
Step 2:
for *all* $J \subseteq \{1,2,3,4\}$ **do**
 | $PS(J) \leftarrow \bigcap_{i \in J} Res_i$
 | **for** *all m* **do**
 | | $V(m,J) \leftarrow Accuracy(m, PS(J), LS)$
 | **end**
end
$(\bar{m}, \bar{J}) \leftarrow Argmax \ \{V(m,J)\}$
$BFS \leftarrow PS(\bar{J})$

Algorithm 1. Best feature selection algorithm

5.1 Experimental Setup

Datasets. Using a python crawler, we collected a set of 3,500 pictures. We note that among those pictures, Facebook was unable to generate alt-text for 200 pictures. Moreover, we collected 16,935 comments from 3,500 single pictures, among which 400 pictures did not receive any comment.

Evaluation Metrics. We evaluate our attack using the standard *Accuracy, Precision, Recall,* and *F1_score* metrics. Below, we describe each one briefly.

Accuracy: The attacker's output has two classes *Male* and *Female*. Accuracy is the fraction of the correct predictions (predicting male as male and female as female) for unknown data points.

Recall: It refers to the percentage of total relevant results that correctly classified. Recall is defined as the number of true positives divided by the number of true positives plus the number of false negative.

Precision: Precision means the percentage of results which are relevant. Precision is defined as the number of true positives divided by the number of true positives plus the number of false positives.

F1_score: It takes precision and recall into account to evaluate the model.

Experiments. We considered the gender inference attack as a binary classification problem. To that end, we have applied well-known supervised classification algorithms in our work. To select the suitable classifier for our work, we tested several supervised machine learning algorithms such as *Logistic Regression, Random Forest, K-Nearest Neighbors, Support Vector Machine, Naive Bayes* and

Decision Tree. Experiments carried out for *alt-texts feature set, comments feature set,* and *combined feature set.* To evaluate the classifier, we selected the same number of male and female to prevent biased classification. The evaluation was conducted by splitting the dataset into train/test size. Train-test splitting was preferable in this study as it runs k-times faster than k-fold. We vary the size of the training set to measure the difference in the attack accuracy. Finally, we choose the train-test size of *70-30* which gives the best accuracy. The following experimental results we obtained by using classifiers implemented in Python library *scikit-learn*. Below, we present our results for each scenario.

5.2   Alt-Texts Feature Set

Here, we discuss the scenario where we have only access to the alt-texts dataset. In this scenario, the input of Algorithm 1 is the corresponding LS to alt-texts feature set. Figure 3 displays our inference results on alt-texts dataset. In addition to accuracy, we also show the result of *Precision, Recall,* and *F1-Score.* According to Algorithm 1, the intersection of *Feature importance,* and *Univariate feature selection* performs the best and generate 68 features. The effectiveness of the selected features was measured by creating a classifier which only used these features *(red bars).* According to Fig. 3, *Logistic Regression* performs slightly better than *Decision Tree* classifier in *Accuracy.* Based on the result, an attacker can infer the target user gender with accuracy of 84%. Finding important metrics depends entirely on the problem. As the target variable classes *(female, male)* in our dataset are balanced, then we can use *Accuracy* as an important metric in our work. Note *F1-Score* takes the harmonic mean between *Precision* and *Recall.* So, we can observe that *Logistic Regression* performs better than other

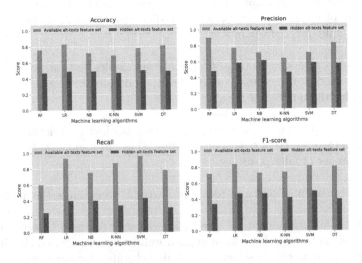

Fig. 3. Accuracy, Precision, Recall, and F-Score evaluation of alt-texts dataset (Color figure online)

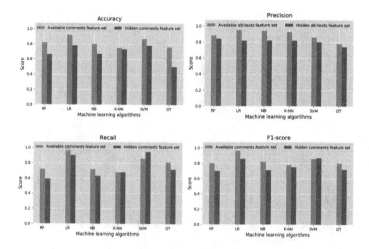

Fig. 4. Accuracy, Precision, Recall, and F-Score evaluation of comments dataset (Color figure online)

supervised classifiers in the alt-texts dataset. Based on *Accuracy* and *F1-Score* sub-graphs. *Logistic Regression* also perform slightly worse than *Support Vector Machine* in *Recal* sub-graph. In the other hand, Fig. 3 *(blue bars)* represents a significant deterioration in *Accuracy, Recal* and *F1-Score*

5.3 Comments Feature Sets

In this subsection, we demonstrate the interest of comments for performing inference attacks. In this scenario, we have only access to the comments dataset, and the input of the Algorithm 1 is the corresponding *LS* to comments feature set. According to Algorithm 1, the intersection of *Chi-Square, Feature importance*, and *Univariate feature selection* performs the best and create 66 features. Figure 4 displays our inference attack results on comments dataset. We draw the *Accuracy, Precision, Recall*, and *F1-Score* to compare the effectiveness of selected features. Figure 4 *(red bars)* shows the performance of each classifier by using selected features. According to Fig. 4 *(red bars)*, *Logistic Regression* performs better than other classifiers in all evaluation metrics. In the other hand, Fig. 4 *(blue bars)* represents the reduction on *Accuracy, Precision* and *F1-Score* after hiding these 68 features from the comments feature set. As a result, we can infer the target user gender by using only comments dataset with the accuracy of 96%.

5.4 Combined Feature Sets

In the last scenario, we train the machine learning classifiers by alt-texts and comments datasets. We use in Algorithm 1 the union set of generated alt-texts and comments feature sets. We refer to this set as a *combined feature set* which

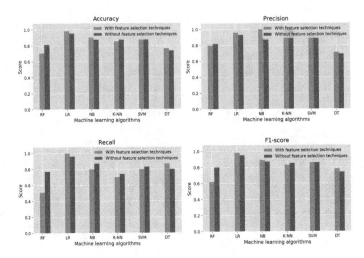

Fig. 5. Accuracy, Precision, Recall, and F-Score evaluation of combined dataset (Color figure online)

contain 134 features. We run Algorithm 1 on top of the combined feature set to check if there is a feature set that presents higher accuracy. With that, we create a new combined feature set by 97 features. *Univariate feature selection* performs the best on the combined feature set. Figure 5 *(red bars)* outlines the performance of each classifier by using the new combined feature set (97 features). Figure 5 *(red bars)* shows that the *Logistic Regression* perform better than other classifiers in *Accuracy, Recall,* and *F1-Score* by using these 97 features. In the other hand, Fig. 5 *(blue bars)* shows the performance of classifiers by using those 134 features. It is observable that the classifiers metrics vary slightly. By this result, we understand that *Logistic Regression* performs best in our study. *Logistic Regression* is a discriminative model which is appropriate to conduct when the dependent variable is binary. So, it learns better between the dependent and independent variable in our dataset. Accordingly, the combination of alt-texts and comments dataset gives the highest accuracy. That means, we can infer the gender of the target user by a high probability of 98% if both alt-texts and comments are available.

6   Conclusion

In this work, we have presented a gender inference attack on Facebook by leveraging some easily collected datasets. Unlike other works, we have used *comments* that are written by target user friends, friends of friends or regular users and *alt-text* generated by Facebook to infer the target user gender. This type of attack can be categorized as an indirect attack. In a nutshell, our results demonstrate that anyone can find hidden attributes of Facebook users by just considering simple available information. As future work, we plan to propose counter-measures to picture owners, considering a trade-off between privacy risks and comments-based social benefits.

References

1. Bargh, J.A., McKenna, K.Y., Fitzsimons, G.M.: Can you see the real me? Activation and expression of the "true self" on the internet. J. Soc. Issues **58**(1), 33–48 (2002)
2. Chaabane, A., Acs, G., Kaafar, M.A., et al.: You are what you like! information leakage through users' interests. In: Proceedings of the 19th Annual Network & Distributed System Security Symposium (NDSS) (2012)
3. Chen, Y.-Y., Chen, T., Hsu, W.H., Liao, H.-Y.M., Chang, S.-F.: Predicting viewer affective comments based on image content in social media. In: Proceedings of International Conference on Multimedia Retrieval, p. 233. ACM (2014)
4. Church, K.W., Hanks, P.: Word association norms, mutual information, and lexicography. Comput. Linguist. **16**(1), 22–29 (1990)
5. Datta, A., Tschantz, M.C., Datta, A.: Automated experiments on ad privacy settings. Proc. Privacy Enhancing Technol. **2015**(1), 92–112 (2015)
6. Fkih, F., Omri, M.N.: Learning the size of the sliding window for the collocations extraction: a ROC-based approach. In: Proceedings of the 2012 International Conference on Artificial Intelligence (ICAI 2012), pp. 1071–1077 (2012)
7. Gong, N.Z., Liu, B.: Attribute inference attacks in online social networks. ACM Trans. Privacy Secur. (TOPS) **21**(1), 3 (2018)
8. Gong, N.Z., et al.: Joint link prediction and attribute inference using a social-attribute network. ACM Trans. Intell. Syst. Technol. (TIST) **5**(2), 27 (2014)
9. He, J., Chu, W.W., Liu, Z.V.: Inferring privacy information from social networks. In: Mehrotra, S., Zeng, D.D., Chen, H., Thuraisingham, B., Wang, F.-Y. (eds.) ISI 2006. LNCS, vol. 3975, pp. 154–165. Springer, Heidelberg (2006). https://doi.org/10.1007/11760146_14
10. Kang, R., Brown, S., Kiesler, S.: Why do people seek anonymity on the internet? Informing policy and design. In: Proceedings of the SIGCHI Conference on Human Factors in Computing Systems, pp. 2657–2666. ACM (2013)
11. Lee, K.: Combining multiple feature selection methods. In: Mid-Atlantic Student Workshop on Programming Languages and Systems (MASPLAS 2002), p. 12. Citeseer (2002)
12. Filho, J.A.B.L., Pasti, R., de Castro, L.N.: Gender classification of twitter data based on textual meta-attributes extraction. New Advances in Information Systems and Technologies. AISC, vol. 444, pp. 1025–1034. Springer, Cham (2016). https://doi.org/10.1007/978-3-319-31232-3_97
13. Merler, M., Cao, L., Smith, J.R.: You are what you tweet... pic! gender prediction based on semantic analysis of social media images. In: 2015 IEEE International Conference on Multimedia and Expo (ICME), pp. 1–6. IEEE (2015)
14. Mihaljević, H., Santamaría, L.: Telling the gender from a name (2018)
15. Miller, Z., Dickinson, B., Hu, W.: Gender prediction on Twitter using stream algorithms with n-gram character features. Int. J. Intell. Sci. **2**(04), 143 (2012)
16. Stavrianou, A., Brun, C., Silander, T., Roux, C.: NLP-based feature extraction for automated tweet classification. Interact. Data Mining Nat. Lang. Process. **145** (2014)
17. Tobin, A., Merrill, J.B.: Facebook is letting job advertisers target only men (2018)

18. Tsai, C.-F., Hsiao, Y.-C.: Combining multiple feature selection methods for stock prediction: union, intersection, and multi-intersection approaches. Decis. Support Syst. **50**(1), 258–269 (2010)
19. Weinsberg, U., Bhagat, S., Ioannidis, S., Taft, N.: BlurMe: inferring and obfuscating user gender based on ratings. In: Proceedings of the sixth ACM Conference on Recommender Systems, pp. 195–202. ACM (2012)
20. Wu, S., Wieland, J., Farivar, O., Schiller, J.: Automatic alt-text: computer-generated image descriptions for blind users on a social network service. In: Proceedings of the 2017 ACM Conference on Computer Supported Cooperative Work and Social Computing, pp. 1180–1192. ACM (2017)
21. Xu, W., Zhou, X., Li, L.: Inferring privacy information via social relations. In: 2008 IEEE 24th International Conference on Data Engineering Workshop, pp. 525–530. IEEE (2008)
22. Yurchisin, J., Watchravesringkan, K., McCabe, D.B.: An exploration of identity re-creation in the context of Internet dating. Soc. Beh. Pers.: Int. J. **33**(8), 735–750 (2005)

Unifying Cyber Threat Intelligence

Florian Menges$^{(\boxtimes)}$, Christine Sperl, and Günther Pernul

University of Regensburg, Universitätsstraße 31, 93053 Regensburg, Germany
florian.menges@ur.de

Abstract. The threat landscape and the associated number of IT security incidents are constantly increasing. In order to address this problem, a trend towards cooperative approaches and the exchange of information on security incidents has been developing over recent years. Today, several different data formats with varying properties are available that allow to structure and describe incidents as well as cyber threat intelligence (CTI) information. Observed differences in data formats implicate problems in regard to consistent understanding and compatibility. This ultimately builds a barrier for efficient information exchange. Moreover, a common definition for the components of CTI formats is missing. In order to improve this situation, this work presents an approach for the description and unification of these formats. Therefore, we propose a model that describes the elementary properties as well as a common notation for entities within CTI formats. In addition, we develop a unified model to show the results of our work, to improve the understanding of CTI data formats and to discuss possible future research directions.

Keywords: Incident reporting · Incident management ·
Incident response · Reporting formats · STIX · IODEF · VERIS

1 Motivation

In the age of digitization, information systems play a more integrated and important role in modern society than ever before. This also applies to critical infrastructures that are essential for the functioning of society today. At the same time, however, these systems are becoming increasingly complex and vulnerable to attacks. It can be observed that today's systems are mostly defended by traditional security measures that only provide basic protection against common threats. In contrast, reliable protection of systems against sophisticated and targeted attacks remains a problem and continues to intensify the arms race between threat actors on the one side and security experts on the other. To be ahead in this game, a trend towards the exchange of Cyber Threat Intelligence (CTI) information has emerged to be aware of threats at an early stage. This can either strengthen threat prevention or contribute to the mitigation of already occurred incidents and improve the overall system security.

The benefits of CTI exchanges are recognized and promoted by various governments, industry and research. This has already led to legal reporting obligations for industries that are relevant to the functioning of the society in different

© Springer Nature Switzerland AG 2019
S. Gritzalis et al. (Eds.): TrustBus 2019, LNCS 11711, pp. 161–175, 2019.
https://doi.org/10.1007/978-3-030-27813-7_11

economic areas such as the United States[1], the European Union[2] and Germany[3]. At the same time, the industry has started to introduce a wide range of threat intelligence platforms such as the Collective Intelligence Framework (CIF)[4] and community solutions like Open Threat Exchange (OTX)[5].

But while sharing CTI undoubtedly can create benefits, there are issues on how to conduct the exchange of threat intelligence. The structure as well as the content of threat intelligence reports are essential aspects for a mutual understanding of the shared information and, therefore, for the success of the exchange itself. To support the exchange process, several organizations have developed competing formats and standards to represent CTI, which are already used by companies to some extent. The formats differ in their focus on certain CTI areas, notations and presentation concepts while actually serving similar purposes. This can lead to several issues, such as incompatibilities or comprehension problems, which may even question the whole exchange process. Uniform definitions and notations and a common understanding of the data structures is therefore an important success factor for the exchange CTI information. With this work, we make the following contributions as a step towards unification of CTI data structures:

- We introduce a meta model that describes the key elements of threat intelligence formats
- We propose a common notation for CTI base elements to support the mutual understanding for available components
- We apply our findings to a unified model, which serves as a basis for the understanding and discussion of future opportunities in the area of threat intelligence sharing

The remainder of this paper is organized as follows: In Sect. 2 we cover the Related Work. Section 3 introduces a meta model and unified notation for CTI data structures. Section 4 introduces a unified CTI model based on the meta model and the unified notation as well as a discussion about possible starting points for improving the current situation based on this model. The paper is concluded in Sect. 5.

2   Related Work

In the field of threat intelligence and cybersecurity, a lot of research has been conducted in the last years. However, the number of publications covering approaches for modelling and unifying CTI is limited. This stands in a contrast to the fact that exchanging CTI has become more urgent to face security

---

[1] https://www.congress.gov/bill/113th-congress/house-bill/3696.
[2] https://eur-lex.europa.eu/legal-content/EN/TXT/PDF/?uri=CELEX: 32016L1148.
[3] http://tinyurl.com/y44jmaz4.
[4] https://csirtgadgets.com/collective-intelligence-framework.
[5] https://otx.alienvault.com/.

incidents [19]. It can be observed that especially research work that considers available CTI data formats and the underlying data structures is rare. Most common in the area of modelling and unifying CTI are ontology proposals that clarify terms and their relations to each other in a defined area. Ontologies that can be found in literature can be distinguished in specialized and generic approaches.

Specialized approaches describe specific aspects or elements of threat intelligence as shown in the following. Falk and Way present an ontology that focuses on threat actors [6] and Grégio et al. propose an ontology that describes suspicious behavior of malware [9]. These works focus on particular threat intelligence aspects, while the big picture of CTI is not covered.

Generic approaches on the contrary have a broader scope. Fenz et al. perform valuable fundamental work prior to the establishment of most of the CTI sharing formats. They define syntax relations of different security concepts based on existing guidelines like the German IT Grundschutz Manual [7]. Falk proposes a threat intelligence ontology utilizing the Lockheed Martin Cyber Kill Chain in combination with events and threat actors. Although providing a broader scope, this work also does not fully cover the aspects of CTI or its data structures [5]. Iannacone et al. create a graph-based ontology for representing threat intelligence information, which provides a broader view on different aspects of threat intelligence. However, it shows a clear focus on specific attacks and lacks important CTI concepts such as attacker techniques and campaigns and does not consider underlying data formats other than STIX[6] [11]. Oltramari et al. focus on combining human and machine elements to create a cyber security ontology offering a detailed description of the included elements. Nevertheless, the research lacks a specific relation to CTI as well as the consideration of relevant data formats [18].

Other research work focuses on common specifications in the field of threat intelligence. First Howard and Longstaff establish a widely known and accepted language for computer security incidents where basic terms of an incident are defined [10]. Burger et al. create a taxonomy model for cyber threat intelligence sharing which organizes the different formats like IODEF[7] and STIX in the categories Transport, Session, Indicators, Intelligence and Attributes [4]. Mavroeidis and Bromander develop a model to compare the different taxonomies, ontologies and sharing formats to enable the finding of further research areas [14]. However, these approaches neither cover the basic properties of CTI formats nor their specific notation elements, as we provide in this paper.

A further research direction focuses on approaches that incorporate specific data formats for representing CTI information. Obrst et al. utilize different standards such as MAEC[8], CEE[9], Cybox[10] and STIX, to create a comprehensive

---

[6] https://stixproject.github.io/about/STIX_Whitepaper_v1.1.pdf.
[7] https://tools.ietf.org/html/rfc5070.
[8] https://maecproject.github.io/.
[9] https://cee.mitre.org.
[10] https://cyboxproject.github.io/.

cyber ontology. Although, this research gives a broad overview on CTI data structures, it is limited to formats related to STIX. Moreover, data types, attributes and notation issues are not covered [17]. Zhao et al. propose a unified representation of CTI using an ontology based model for threat intelligence built on the study of security incidents and on elements of STIX2[11]. This model allows a more specific representation of threat intelligence data. However, as it only incorporates STIX2, it does not cover differences between CTI data formats [23].

Summarizing, it can be stated that the literature for CTI models is limited. Predominant are ontologies, which can be categorized in specialized and holistic. Other approaches focus on structuring and comparing different concepts. Some works cover data formats but a comprehensive view on CTI data structures from different sources is lacking. Moreover, attempts in finding a common notation and creating a unified models don not incorporate all the relevant incident sharing data formats. Even though all these approaches contribute their part to generate insight to threat intelligence information, a comprehensive view on CTI data structures from different sources has not been conducted yet. A meta model considering the syntax from different threat intelligence sharing formats and a holistic view with integrated data formats both are currently missing. Moreover, there is no academic work covering key elements of CTI sharing formats or unifying their notations to the best of our knowledge.

3 A Standardized Representation for Threat Intelligence Information

A successful exchange of cyber threat intelligence strongly depends on a mutual understanding of contents shared by the parties involved. The heterogeneous nature of sharing formats is one of the main barriers in sharing this data. Therefore, it is important to find an agreement on basic terms as well as unified definitions for shared elements. To build a foundation for such an agreement, we propose a meta model as a guidance for the modelling, classification and comparison of CTI formats in this section. We also propose a standardization of threat intelligence elements. This includes a unified nomenclature and classification for CTI elements as a step towards the homogenization of CTI data formats.

3.1 Meta Model for Threat Intelligence Information

As a first step we aim to create a common understanding of relevant concepts for the representation of CTI. Therefore, we introduce a meta model that provides a comprehensive specification, covering both the basic structuring elements and coherences that can be used to express intelligence information. The model is intended to support the verification and extension of existing models as well as the creation of further model instances. It also serves as a basis for understanding elements and relationships within existing formats.

---

[11] https://oasis-open.github.io/cti-documentation/.

From a methodical perspective, the developed model is following the archety-pal abstraction concepts for meta modeling by Sprinkle et al. [20]. Accord-ing to this concept, the elements Class, Association, Specialization and Con-straint are used to compose the model. To realize a more accurate represen-tation for CTI concepts, Association elements are further detailed into the elements Composition and Aggregation. This allows an additional differentia-tion between mandatory and optional relationships and therefore increases the model's expressiveness.

The meta model (see Fig. 1) is developed based upon the characteristics of state-of-the-art formats for structured CTI representation STIX1/2, IODEF and IODEF2[12], VERIS[13] and X-ARF[14] as outlined in Menges and Pernul [16]. Fur-ther formats that can be found in literature, such as MISP[15], openIoC [16] are excluded from the development process. This is mainly due to their limited data model and focus on threat intelligence events and indicators as outlined by Burger et al. [4]. The model development process is realized in two consecutive steps. First, the relevant literature in the areas of CTI in general and state-of-the-art formats is reviewed. Within this review, important concepts for representing CTI are identified. In the second step, the structures and characteristics of these formats are analyzed to validate and supplement the insights gained from the literature review. This process results in the identification of fundamental con-cepts such as elements, properties and relationships of CTI. These concepts are then translated into appropriate meta-types that are finally combined to build the CTI meta model.

First, we discuss the different aspects important for representing CTI that are derived from the literature. These aspects are translated into the first meta model building blocks. All of the examined formats define a set of base entities, each of which represents one of its core components in an object oriented way as shown by Bourgue et al. [2]. The resulting Object entities enable the fundamental representation of CTI data and attributes. The formats also define capabilities to introduce Relationships between these objects. In addition, the examined formats define one distinct root element that collects all base entities into a reportable collection, which we define as Report in the proposed model. Burger et al. show that basic CTI objects can be assigned to the three different categories Indicator, Intelligence and Attribution [4]. For the development of our model, we translate these assignments into three kinds of classes that inherit from the base class Object that are defined in the following.

Indicator objects describe patterns or behaviors that show the likelihood that an incident is occurring, has already occurred or will probably occur in the future. This includes representations for genuine system observations as well as

---

[12] https://tools.ietf.org/html/rfc7970.
[13] http://veriscommunity.net.
[14] http://xarf.org/.
[15] https://www.misp-project.org/.
[16] https://github.com/mandiant/OpenIOC_1.1.

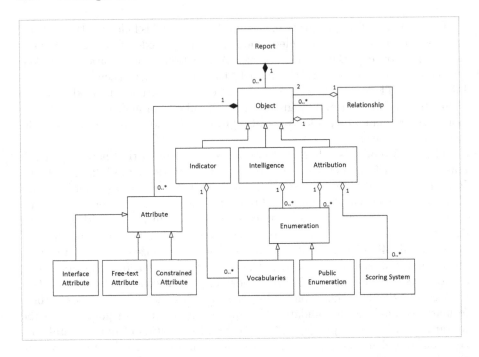

Fig. 1. CTI meta model

indication objects for structuring observations and assessing the probability of them being part of an incident.

Intelligence objects are used to represent specific knowledge about threats or incidents. This includes the combination of findings from indicators or past occurrences to derive a specific threat behavior or attack pattern. Moreover, the intelligence objects also define specific actions and countermeasures for known threats that can be performed for the prevention of incidents or impact mitigation.

Attribution objects describe the source, the target as well as the circumstances of an incident. More precisely, the source defines both information about entities involved in an incident and their possible location, objectives or interests. The target includes entities affected by an incident including vulnerabilities that are used to compromise the entity. Moreover, Attribution also describes the circumstances of an incident, including information such as the effects of an incident or the start and end of an attack.

The described objects serve as a structural foundation for describing CTI information. To cover all aspects of representing CTI information, the defined object attribute definitions also have to be examined and differentiated in detail. As shown by Burger et al. [4], Steinberger et al. [21] as well as Menges and Pernul [16], the specification and usage of object attributes is decisive for the interoperability of CTI formats. More precisely, there are two main types of attribute definitions: Constrained Attributes and Free-text Attributes. Constrained Attributes usually lead to structured and comprehensible information due to their underlying guidelines. Free-text Attributes without guidelines, however, lead to unpredictable and non-structured information that reduces the format interoperability and automation capability. Besides these attributes, the model also includes an Interface Attribute, which is derived from the format specifications and, therefore, introduced with the specification analysis of this section.

Another vital aspect for CTI formats is the integration of interoperability frameworks to ensure a mutual understanding of the represented contents. Syed et al. [22] consider interoperability frameworks as integral elements within their proposed threat intelligence ontology. Mavroeidis and Jøsang [15] also underline the central role of these frameworks for structuring threat information. The frameworks include Vocabularies, Public Enumerations and Scoring Systems, which are tied to CTI objects. In the following, we provide a short description of these frameworks underlining their contribution for CTI interoperability and automation capabilities.

Vocabularies (also internal Enumerations) represent lists of predefined content for object attributes that are supplied with CTI formats. An example for a vocabulary is SecurityCompromiseVocab provided by STIX. It defines the possible values *Yes, Suspected, No* and *Unknown* as allowed attribute contents for the attribute SecurityCompromise within an incident object. It therefore provides a clear field definition based on predefined values, preventing ambiguities. This enables a common understanding for contents that are expressed using vocabularies. A more detailed introduction to the application of vocabularies within the exchange of CTI is given by Fransen et al. [8], while emphasizing their contribution to the automation capabilities of CTI.

Public Enumerations provide publicly available registers that can be used to clearly specify particular CTI aspects such as configurations, platforms, weaknesses or vulnerabilities. An exemplary enumeration is Common Vulnerabilities and Exposures (CVE)[17], which provides a broad collection of uniquely identifiable vulnerability definitions and descriptions for different systems. CVE is publicly administered and therefore available for any participant in an intelligence exchange process. Using this enumeration, vulnerabilities can be clearly described within a CTI format using a reference to its unique identifier provided by the enumeration. The importance of integrating enumerations into CTI formats and the accompanying benefits of interoperability and automation capabilities are described by Brown et al. [3].

Scoring Systems provide a consistent method to capture the characteristics of particular threat intelligence aspects, mapping them into quantitative descriptions. More precisely, numerical values are generated from the underlying information, enabling the assessment and comparability of the information. An exemplary system is the Common Vulnerability Scoring System (CVSS)[18]. It

---

[17] https://cve.mitre.org/.
[18] https://www.first.org/cvss/.

allows to capture and assess the characteristics of a vulnerability. CVSS provides different calculation rules that quantify the gathered vulnerability information and translates it into a numerical score reflecting the severity of the vulnerability. Integrated into threat intelligence standards, Scoring Systems provide a structured way to express ratings and assessments in a common understandable and interoperable form. The importance of these systems is also shown by Brown et al. [3] and Kampanakis [12] underlining their contribution to the interoperability of CTI. The literature based elements of the meta model, are now validated, supplemented and relationships are established using the specifications of the considered CTI formats.

When comparing the defined objects with the format specification, the central role of the Report element is confirmed. It serves as the base component to reference the core CTI objects. Since the specifications basically allow to create empty reports, the relationship between Report and the core objects is defined as an aggregation. Although, all formats allow to build relationships between objects, there are particular differences between them. Comparing the formats, there are two different types of possible relationships. On the one hand, relationships can be expressed as single objects that provide attributes for defining the objects to be connected, which is for example the case for STIX2. Their relationship is defined as a composition, since relationship objects cannot exist without their referenced entities. On the other hand, references can also be defined using attributes within the objects to be connected, which is for example the case for IODEF. This relationship on the contrary is defined as aggregation, due to the optional nature of their references.

The specifications also confirm that the base elements of the formats considered can be categorized into Indicator, Intelligence and Attribution, while inheriting from the base Object. Vocabularies and Public Enumerations both of which inherit from the enumeration entity, show different usages within CTI formats. While Vocabularies find usage within any CTI object in different manifestations, Public Enumerations are restricted to the layers Intelligence and Attribution. The Intelligence layer can for example be provided with CAPEC[19], an enumeration for defining particular attack patterns, whereas the attribution layer can be provided with the previously described enumeration CVE for defining particular vulnerabilities within targeted entities. The Scoring Systems implemented within the examined formats are restricted to the attribution layer. More precisely, applied Scoring Systems such as CVSS and CWSS[20] describe the severity of vulnerabilities, whereas systems such as CCSS[21] describe the severity of configurations issues on specific targets. Since both targets and vulnerabilities are allocated to the Attribution layer, this also applies to Scoring Systems that describe their severities.

Finally, the CTI attribute definitions will be examined more closely. As stated above, a clear distinction between constrained and free-text attributes

---

[19] https://capec.mitre.org/.

[20] https://cwe.mitre.org/cwss/cwss_v1.0.1.html.

[21] https://nvlpubs.nist.gov/nistpubs/Legacy/IR/nistir7502.pdf.

has to be made for a description of CTI formats. Considering the specifications, a great deal of both types of attribute can be identified. The considered formats define numerous free-text attributes such as "description" or "notes" allowing to insert arbitrary contents. Similarly, the formats also provide various constrained attributes such as *DateTime* enforcing a specific format. In addition to these types, the analysis of the specifications reveal another important CTI attribute enabling the attachment of structured external information to an incident description. An example for this is the *AdditionalData* element within the IODEF specification. It enables the encapsulation of entire XML documents that confirm with another schema. This type of attribute is also included into the meta model and called Interface Attribute due to its capabilities of interfacing other formats. Putting all this together, the developed model defines the elements and relationships of threat intelligence formats beginning with its core object types and definitions of possible attribute types to integration capabilities for interoperability frameworks.

3.2   A Unified Notation for Threat Intelligence Elements

After developing the meta model for describing the fundamental elements within CTI formats, we aim to create a common understanding for their core components in this section. When looking at CTI formats, one obstacle towards the interoperability between them is the usage of different notations. As a consequence, comparable or identical threat situations are often expressed in different terms. This leads to misunderstandings and hampers the comparability and compatibility of threat information. To counteract possible misunderstandings, we propose a unified notation for threat intelligence information in this section. Therefore, we first identify the component types for representing threat intelligence information and classify them in accordance to the meta model definitions. Following this, we match the component types to the corresponding components of the CTI formats considered. In the last step, we propose a rule set to create a unified notation for threat intelligence components and apply it to the identified components. Table 1 gives an overview on the results of this unification process, which is described in the following.

Central CTI Components and Classifications: The first step of this process is the identification and classification of the component types that are essential for describing threat intelligence information from the literature. The basis for this is the incident taxonomy provided by Howard and Longstaff [10]. It defines the Attackers, their Targets, used Vulnerabilities as well as the Result of an incident, all of which can be classified as Attribution components. This work also defines the term Action, representing activities within an attack that can be classified as an Indication element. Alongside this fundamental incident description, additional terms for describing threat intelligence information can be derived from the work of Mavroeidis and Bromander [14]. This includes the element Indicator also classified as indicator element and the terms Method, Course of Action and Incident classified as intelligence components.

Table 1. A unified notation for threat intelligence

Component type	Classification	STIX	STIX2	IODEF 1&2	VERIS	X-ARF		Rule	Mapping
Indicator	Indicator	Indicator	Indicator	Indicator	Indicator	-		2	Indicator
Action	Indicator	Observable	Observed data	Record	Threat action	Attachment		3	Action
Attacker	Attribution	Threat actor	Threat actor	Threat actor	Actor	Source		1	Actor
Target	Attribution	Exploit target	Exploit target	System	Asset	Destination		1	Asset
Vulnerability	Attribution	Vulnerability	Vulnerability	Vulnerability	Vulnerability	Attachment		2	Vulnerability
Result	Attribution	Impact assessment	Impact assessment	Assessment	Impact assessment	-		1	Assessment
Campaign	Attribution	Campaign	Campaign	Campaign	Related incidents	-		2	Campaign
Method	Intelligence	TTP	Attack pattern	Attack pattern	Vector	Category		1	Attack pattern
Course of action	Intelligence	Course of action	Course of action	Defined COA	Corrective actions	-		2	Course of action
Incident	Intelligence	Incident	Report	Incident	Incident	Incident		2	Incident

Matching with CTI Formats: In the second step of the process, each of the state-of-the-art CTI formats is analyzed to identify the components corresponding to the previously defined component types. Table 1 provides columns for each formats showing its component assignments to the corresponding component types. The formats IODEF and IODEF2 were combined into one column IODEF 12, since both formats use identical notations for the base component types. The assignment is done by semantically matching the component type definitions from the literature with the component specifications of the respective formats and is shortly described in the following. All assignments relate to components that allow clear allocations to the respective component types. Wherever no component type is available or the comparison results in incomplete or ambiguous matchings, the respective field is left blank.

A Ruleset for Creating a Common CTI Notation: In the last step, we propose a common notation for each of the components. To achieve this, we firstly propose a ruleset that defines how to derive notation elements from the previously matched components. The ruleset enables the reproducibility of notation elements as well as the derivation of notation elements for possible future extensions of the notation. The most important factor for this notation is full coverage for all characteristics of the CTI base components. According to this, the first rule defines that the component representing the according component type in the most general manner is mapped to the notation. This ensures a high degree of expressibility for the notation elements. Another important factor is the practicability of the notation, since the success of intelligence sharing formats depends on a widespread usage and therefore user acceptance. As a result, the second rule defines that, if a component notation is already used by different formats, it is mapped to the notation. Finally, the third rule defines that if none of these rules apply, the component type definition from the literature will be mapped to the notation. The defined rules are applied for the mapping of all CTI components in ascending order provided that the first matching rule determines which component will be mapped. An example for the mapping according to the first rule is the component type Target. Its mapping candidates are Exploit Target, System, Asset and Destination. Asset matches the first rule, since it is the most general representation of these candidates. It enables the description of systems, services etc. regardless of their role within the incident. In contrast to this, Exploit Target implies an asset's role within an attack, whereas System and Destination only allow a limited view on affected entities. An example for the second rule is the attribute Campaign, which provides the mapping candidates Campaign and Related Incidents, both of which are equally general representations for the component type. As a result the second rule applies and Campaign is mapped as the attribute that is already used by multiple formats. Finally, Action is an example for the third rule. None of the candidates for Action provides a more general representation and none of them is used in multiple formats. Therefore, the component definition Action is mapped to the notation.

4 Towards Unified Threat Intelligence Data Structures

In the previous Sect. 3 we developed a meta model and a unified notation for the description of essential CTI elements. These findings are applied to develop a unified base model for the representation of CTI data formats in this section. The model illustrates the results of this work, contributes to the understanding of CTI data structures and serves as a basis for a discussion of future possibilities and challenges for CTI data formats. The unified CTI model is shown in Fig. 2 and described in the following. The essential components of CTI data formats defined in Chap. 3 are the model's foundation and have been translated into entity types for the development of this model. As a next step, the relationships between the entities are defined. In doing so, we refrain from consolidating redundant relationships, since the formats do not only represent data structures for the storage of information, but they may also be used as a tool for the expression incident information as for example shown in Böhm et al. [1]. A reduction of relationships also leads to reduced expression capabilities. Therefore, the integration of the relationships within the data model is achieved by obtaining existing relationships between entities from underlying formats and transferring them into the unified model. As a result, the relationships within the unified model are a superset of the relationships obtained from the underlying formats. The identified CTI entity categories Attribution, Intelligence and Indicator, as shown in Chap. 3.1, are mapped as classification swimlanes to illustrate the entity classification assignments. In addition to the integration of entities, relationships and classifications, the entities are populated with structured properties according to the meta model. Therefore, vocabularies, enumerations and scoring systems are assigned to the entities according to their occurrence within the CTI formats under consideration. Based on these properties, several entry points for possible improvements of CTI data formats are identified in the following and presented according to their classification lane.

Within the **Attribution Layer**, entity types *Actor* and *Campaign* only provide internal vocabularies for their structured description. External resources and scoring systems are not available for these types. As a result, properties and information about actors need to be collected and specified each time an incident is detected. An online resource, like an enumeration that collects information about attackers and allows to map it to an incident would be conceivable as a possible extension. *Asset* entities are described by vocabularies as well as by enumerations. One possible extension would be an additional scoring system to evaluate the criticality of the assets, as for example pointed out by Kim and Kang [13]. Moreover, the asset itself can be specified using the CPE[22] and CCE[23] enumerations, defining the software platform configuration and even allow the mapping of CVE vulnerabilities. However, since assets allow the relationship to single enumeration items, more complex systems with different components, such as cyber-physical systems, can hardly be described. *Impact Assessment*

---

[22] https://nvd.nist.gov/products/cpe.
[23] https://nvd.nist.gov/config/cce/index.

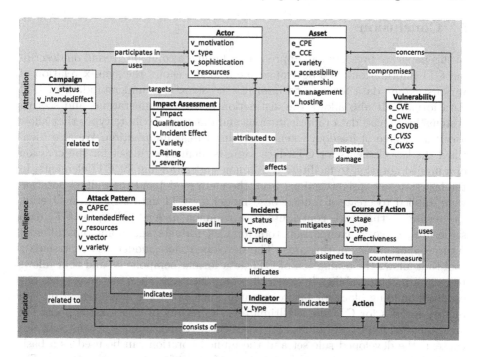

Fig. 2. Unified CTI data model

entities provide different internal vocabularies for the structured description of an assessment, as for example values for a subjective impact qualification rating from "low" to "high". Although, results of impact assessments may vary widely across different companies, a common calculation base for a more informative exchange would be conceivable. This could for example be achieved using an impact assessment scoring system that allows the integration of environmental variables like the industry sector of a company and thus may provide a common calculation basis for the gravity of incidents. Within the **Intelligence Layer**, the entity *Course of Action* offers different possibilities for extensions. On the one hand, there are no metrics or scorings available, that would allow a transparent evaluation of the countermeasures conducted. Moreover, an external enumeration that for example provides known procedures for the treatment of specific incidents could contribute to the expressiveness of the course of action objects. Beyond that, the association of vulnerabilities with course of action entities could provide additional value. Similar to this, *Incident* and *Attack Pattern* entities, also do not allow the integration of scoring systems. The **Indicator Layer** lastly represents system observations without the use of contextual data. Therefore, enumerations or scoring systems are not available for these entity types, which the meta model has shown already.

5   Conclusion

In this paper we presented an approach for finding a common ground on describing CTI information. The developed meta model shows the syntax relation of various extant data formats to improve the structural understanding of CTI data formats. It also allows the distinction between enumerations and scoring systems for precise data representations and different attribute types that allow a certain degree of freedom when describing threat information. We also identified the key elements for CTI data formats, defined a ruleset for the creation of a unified notation to facilitate a common understanding for CTI elements. In the last step, the insights gained from the meta model and the unified notation were applied to create a unified base model for CTI data structures. Overall, the results of this work contribute to a common understanding for CTI data structures, serve as comparison tool for CTI formats and point out different future opportunities in this area. The developed meta model also represents a tool that allows the evaluation of CTI data format components and that allows to establish comparability between the components. It therefore represents one essential building block for future research, such as for the development of data quality metrics for CTI data. Ultimately, the results of this work support the creation of an industry standard for representing threat intelligence data. In this context, the developed rule set and the unified notation can be used as a basis for the integration of component definitions from different formats into one. The unified model serves as an initial model for the creation of a standardization for CTI data formats as well as for data format optimization within the integration process.

Acknowledgments. This research was supported by the Federal Ministry of Education and Research, Germany, as part of the BMBF DINGfest project (https://dingfest.ur.de).

References

1. Böhm, F., Menges, F., Pernul, G.: Graph-based visual analytics for cyber threat intelligence. Cybersecurity 1(1), 16 (2018)
2. Bourgue, R., Budd, J., Homola, J., Wlasenko, M., Kulawik, D.: Detect, share, protect. Technical report, ENISA, November 2013
3. Brown, S., Gommers, J., Serrano, O.: From cyber security information sharing to threat management. In: Proceedings of the 2nd ACM Workshop on Information Sharing and Collaborative Security, pp. 43–49 (2015)
4. Burger, E.W., Goodman, M.D., Kampanakis, P., Zhu, K.A.: Taxonomy model for cyber threat intelligence information exchange technologies. In: WISCS 2014 Proceedings of the 2014 ACM Workshop on Information Sharing & Collaborative Security, WISCS 14, pp. 51–60 (2014)
5. Falk, C.: An ontology for threat intelligence. In: 15th European Conference on Cyber Warfare and Security, ECCWS 2016, pp. 111–116 (2016)
6. Falk, C., Way, C.: Using an ontology to classify cyber threat actors using an ontology to classify cyber threat actors (2018)

7. Fenz, S., Ekelhart, A.: Formalizing information security knowledge. In: Proceedings of the 4th International Symposium on Information, Computer, and Communications Security - ASIACCS 2009, p. 183 (2009)
8. Fransen, F., Smulders, A., Kerkdijk, R.: Cyber security information exchange to gain insight into the effects of cyber threats and incidents. e & i Elektrotechnik und Informationstechnik **132**(2), 106–112 (2015)
9. Grecio, A., Bonacin, R., Nabuco, O., Afonso, V.M., De Geus, P.L., Jino, M.: Ontology for malware behavior: a core model proposal. In: Proceedings of the Workshop on Enabling Technologies: Infrastructure for Collaborative Enterprises, WETICE, pp. 453–458 (2014)
10. Howard, J., Longstaff, T.: A common language for computer security incidents (1998)
11. Iannacone, M., et al.: Developing an ontology for cyber security knowledge graphs. In: Proceedings of the 10th Annual Cyber and Information Security Research Conference on - CISR 2015, March 2017, pp. 1–4 (2015)
12. Kampanakis, P.: Security automation and threat information-sharing options. IEEE Secur. Priv. **12**(5), 42–51 (2014)
13. Kim, A., Kang, M.H.: Determining asset criticality for cyber defense. Technical report, Naval Research Lab Washington DC (2011)
14. Mavroeidis, V., Bromander, S.: Cyber threat intelligence model: An evaluation of taxonomies, sharing standards, and ontologies within cyber threat intelligence. In: Proceedings - EISIC 2017, pp. 91–98 (2017)
15. Mavroeidis, V., Jøsang, A.: Data-driven threat hunting using Sysmon. In: Proceedings of the 2nd International Conference on Cryptography, Security and Privacy, pp. 82–88. ACM (2018)
16. Menges, F., Pernul, G.: A comparative analysis of incident reporting formats. Comput. Secur. **73**, 87–101 (2018)
17. Obrst, L., Chase, P., Markeloff, R.: Developing an ontology of the cyber security domain. In: CEUR Workshop Proceedings, vol. 966, pp. 49–56 (2014)
18. Oltramari, A., Cranor, L.F., Walls, R.J., McDaniel, P.: Building an ontology of cyber security. In: CEUR Workshop Proceedings, vol. 1304, pp. 54–61 (2014)
19. Sillaber, C., Sauerwein, C., Mussmann, A., Breu, R.: Data quality challenges and future research directions in threat intelligence sharing practice. In: Proceedings of the 2016 ACM on Workshop on Information Sharing and Collaborative Security, pp. 65–70 (2016)
20. Sprinkle, J., Rumpe, B., Vangheluwe, H., Karsai, G.: 3 metamodelling. In: Giese, H., Karsai, G., Lee, E., Rumpe, B., Schätz, B. (eds.) MBEERTS 2007. LNCS, vol. 6100, pp. 57–76. Springer, Heidelberg (2010). https://doi.org/10.1007/978-3-642-16277-0_3
21. Steinberger, J., Sperotto, A., Golling, M., Baier, H.: How to exchange security events? Overview and evaluation of formats and protocols. In: IEEE International Symposium on Integrated Network Management (IM), pp. 261–269 (2015)
22. Syed, Z., Padia, A., Finin, T., Mathews, L., Joshi, A.: UCO: a unified cybersecurity ontology. In: Proceedings of the AAAI Workshop on Artificial Intelligence for Cyber Security, pp. 14–21 (2015)
23. Zhao, Y., Lang, B., Liu, M.: Ontology-based unified model for heterogeneous threat intelligence integration and sharing. In: 2017 11th IEEE International Conference on Anti-Counterfeiting, Security, and Identification (ASID), pp. 11–15, October 2017

Author Index